The Servant's Hand

The Servant's Hand

English Fiction from Below

Bruce Robbins

Duke University Press   *Durham and London 1993*

The author gratefully thanks the Rutgers University Research
Council, which aided in the preparation of this volume.

First paperback edition Duke University Press, 1993
© 1986 Columbia University Press
Printed in the United States of America on
acid-free paper ∞
Library of Congress Cataloging-in-Publication Data appear
on the last printed page of this book.

Contents

Even the negation of our present political situation is a dusty fact in the historical junk room of modern nations. If I negate powdered wigs, I am still left with unpowdered wigs. If I negate the situation in Germany in 1843, then according to the French calendar I have barely reached 1789, much less the vital center of our present age.

KARL MARX, *Early Writings*

He is no longer a menial, but my equal or superior, so that I have felt, when entertaining doctors of divinity and law, and discoursing about divine mysteries, that a living epistle was circulating behind our backs, and quietly ministering to our wants, far more apocalyptic to an enlightened age than any yet contained in books.

HENRY JAMES, SR.
(Quoted in Richard Poirier, *A World Elsewhere*)

Preface

For it seemed vain and arrogant in the extreme to try to better that anonymous work of creation; the labours of those vanished hands.

VIRGINIA WOOLF, *Orlando*

And time for all the works and days of hands
That lift and drop a question on your plate

T. S. ELIOT, "The Love Song of J. Alfred Prufrock"

There is a paradox in these quotations. On the one hand, they indicate that something is missing. Where are the vanished bodies to which these hands belong? Who does the lifting and dropping? As Brecht asks in "Questions of a Worker who Reads," "Caesar beat the Gauls. / Didn't he even have a cook with him?" These passages remind us of the exclusion of the people from literary representation. On the other hand, they also suggest a less familiar point. In the last decades of the twentieth century, the reasons for the long lack of popular representation can be said to fall within the realm of common knowledge. We are aware of how society was structured in past times, of who wrote and read and who didn't, of the cultural consequences of unequal power. Knowing all this, we are likely to assume that the dominators have monopolized the power to represent, while the dominated have had no option but to endure passively through centuries of abusive synecdoche. But if this is so, if ordinary people were invisible because they were powerless, then why do they, or their hands, actively exercise so much power? In these two passages, what gives them the competence of "creation" and permits them to raise an overwhelming question in the simple act of serving at table? Amputated, the hands above are the mark of an absence, an area of non-representation. They are agents without a principal, parts without a whole. But the energies that these *disjecta membra* exert are in-congruous. And this incongruity throws some doubt on assumptions about the social history of Western literature, and about the theory of history in general.

This book began as an attempt to make historical sense of three unpleasant and related facts. First, the fact that in most of Western literature, ordinary people have been figured, or defigured, like the hands above. Instead of full representations of the life of the people, literary tradition has typically offered only servants, mere appendages of their masters. Moreover, all that has been represented of these prefabricated tropes is their effects, their momentary performance of useful functions. It is as expository prologues, oracular messengers, and authorial mouthpieces, rhetorical "doublings" of the protagonist, accessories used to complicate or resolve the action, that servants fill the margins of texts devoted to their superiors. For the most part it is in this oblique way, if at all, that Western literature has acknowledged and incorporated the divisions of class.

Second, there is the surprising and (to one trained as a historical critic) annoying sameness of these formal manifestations of literary service. Much has changed between Homer and Virginia Woolf, but the literary servant has not undergone proportional changes; servants are the commonplaces of many times and places. Thus a critic like Northrop Frye can claim, using this figure as a prime exhibit, that the essential forms of literature are independent of their social context. At the outset of my research, my aim was to salvage the servant from Frye's fetishizing of recurrence, reasserting the principle that social being determines social consciousness by displaying the historical variables that this apparent constancy concealed. But this tactic had to be abandoned. The jokes, character types, parallelisms, and plot devices that made up the literary servant were of course not entirely identical from Terence to Thackeray, but the differences, I found, were not particularly illuminating—were less illuminating, at any rate, than an analysis of the disturbing fact of continuity. To take that continuity as my given, while refusing the independence of literature from social determination that appears to result from it, is the major theoretical challenge of this book.

Third and perhaps most disturbing was the major presence of these commonplaces in the novel of the nineteenth century, the very bastion of realism and the most cooperative witness to literature's engagement with social change. Rather than grapple with the new and exotic industrial worker, no longer ruled by custom and deference but by the cash nexus, novelists turned to those vestigial, unrepresentative members of the same class who lived in their homes, whose hands opened their doors, cooked and served their meals, brought up their children, initiated them into sexuality and closed their eyes when they died. Domestic servants were not hard to find; the Industrial Revolution had multiplied their numbers enormously, making this anachronism the largest single occupational group in nineteenth-century England. But to find them was not to see them as they were. Rather than take up the life of the domestic as a subject in its own right, the novel turned back to literary tradition: to Roman, Elizabethan, and Restoration comedy, to the much-repeated master-servant tropes and devices that earlier novelists had already borrowed from Shakespeare and Molière. The novels of Richardson and Fielding, Forster and Woolf, Austen and Scott, even Dickens and Gaskell, reinscribe and rejuvenate the conventions of the literary servant. At the very heart of realism is the scandal of a figure which both stands for the confrontation of the Two Nations and refuses to represent historical and social difference at all, which is merely instrumental, and yet which seems to enjoy an uncanny life of its own, producing effects incongruous with its social position and moments of vision incongruous with literary functionality.

For the purpose of investigating this scandal, some of the techniques and assumptions of historical criticism had to be bypassed or themselves investigated. Historical information about actual servants, for example, could not offer an organizing principle. To collate what the novels say with what the history books say about this unlikely and unlovable group would simply not be pertinent to the larger issue of how literary functionality is linked to society itself, or to the great majority of humankind who were not domestic servants. Considering the scale of the phenomenon, the "background" or "context" of a single period was also incapable of providing the required focus:

matters usually assumed to be local to nineteenth-century England had to be observed from a global or world-historical perspective. Finally, neither the originality of authors nor the organic wholeness of individual texts could be respected. As the common property of any novelist willing, *en bon bricoleur,* to make use of available materials, the literary servant is too repetitive for treatment by author, just as it is too minor, fragmentary, and marginal to any given text to be treated by work. Getting it on the map at all means foregoing the completeness of the "reading" and forcing the literary canon off-center. Yet it also means revaluing the canon. In breaking off the "history" in whose name I had begun working from the "politics" for which it is so often synonymous, my argument makes room for the sort of political effect I have called "utopian." And in dissociating political effect from the topicality of literary realism, this argument reassesses the political impact and import of commonplaces, that is, of what is most traditional about literary tradition.

Portions of this book have appeared in somewhat different form in *Raritan, A Quarterly Review,* (Spring 1985), vol. 4, no. 4. Copyright ©1985 by Bruce Robbins; *Representations,* (Spring 1984), no. 6; and *The Henry James Review,* (Spring 1984), vol. 5, no. 3. I am grateful to the editors of these journals for permission to reprint.

My work on this subject began with a kind invitation by John Clive to address the Harvard Victorians. Over a forbidding distance, Robert Kiely and Harry Levin saw it through the dissertation stage with exemplary perceptiveness and patience. Among the others who have helped along the way, I would like to thank Terpsi Argyrou-Birchler, Dan Brudney, Jim Clifford, Ivor Indyk, Carol Kay, Jim Rodgers, Kiernan Ryan, and Richard Waswo. I owe a special debt to the insight and generosity of Jonathan Arac. Without Elsa, who did not type, proofread, or show undue enthusiasm, this book would not have been written. It is dedicated to Bessie Peters, who left her family and came to America because she did not want to be a servant, and to my parents.

The Servant's Hand

Introduction:
The Secret Pressure of
a Working Hand

The history of subaltern social groups is necessarily fragmented and episodic.

ANTONIO GRAMSCI, *Prison Notebooks*

When she held her hands out, she took her eyes from Mr. Jaggers, and turned them watchfully on every one of the rest of us in succession. "There's power here," said Mr. Jaggers.

CHARLES DICKENS, *Great Expectations*

A. J. Munby (1828–1910), Victorian barrister and man of letters, also led what a contemporary was to call a "secret life." His passion was female manual laborers, especially servants. He carried this torch into the secrecy of *their* lives, warming the process of enlightenment with a libidinal glow. With respectful ardor he accosted servants in the street and interrogated them over tea, played Kiss in the Ring with them at the Crystal Palace and visited them at the hospital, took photographs and offered philanthropy, jotted down his gleanings in a monumental diary. The diary, bequeathed to Trinity College, Cambridge, at his death in 1910 on condition that it not be opened before 1950, also records another clandestine adventure. For thirty-six years Munby was married to a maid-of-all-work, never publicly acknowledged as his wife, who addressed him as "Massa" and continued her secret service in his household.

The unequal power and erotic hunger that underlie Munby's observation of servants make his diary a revealing illustration of what usually seems to have been involved in the literary representation of the people. The authority that defined his marriage also defined his relations with the servants he encountered more casually. Even when the diary gives a generous transcription of a servant's actual words, it is Munby who is not only transcribing but establishing the framework, limits, tone, and center of the reported conversation. Even his extraordinary openness and sensitivity cannot abolish the structural exclusions built into the dominance of the speaker and into the dominant discourse itself. And yet it is also clear that through Munby's mediation, the dominant discourse—which could not have allowed his experiences to be published—is exposed to an alien, powerful, and apparently unprecedented pressure. Consider for example the following extract from the diary for November 23, 1860:

Dressed in Litchfield's room, and went to Clapham to dine with the Ellises. Georgie as usual intelligent and charming, and Alice piquante and laughingly sarcastic. I look on Georgie with interest and affection, because *they say* she would marry me if I asked her. . . . All these young ladies, white bosomed, fairylike with muslin and flowers, found a foil for their elegance in a pretty but coarsemade rustic and redhanded waiting maid. Gentle, and beautiful in face as they—and her name *Laura* too—why should she have a life so different? Why should she wear a cotton frock and a cap and hand me dishes—why should these imperious misses order her about so? . . . This girl's large eyes have glanced at me furtively before: and tonight, as the young ladies crowd the hall door and I am helping grandmamma to her carriage, Laura, waiting in the background, says low "Let me carry your bag, Sir"—and I give it to her; and in the dusk outside she holds the carriage door open for me—and as she closes it and gives me the bag, somehow her thick broad hand comes more than once in contact with mine, and does not retreat. Oh ho! Here we have a scene for a novel: the hero from his chariot bows farewell to the elegant imperial creature who thinks she has him captive, but meanwhile his real adieus are given, in secret pressure of her working hand, to the humble serving maid who hands him to the door![1]

Who presses whom? It is the maid's hand that "comes . . . in contact" with Munby's "and does not retreat." But in the "secret pressure of her working hand," the "of" remains ambiguous. If it is he who makes his adieus, it is she who "hands him to the door." The subject of the action is lost in a sudden tingling close-up of hands touching, a short circuit that throws the rest of the scene into unfocused dimness and performs a social reversal akin to those perceptual reversals of figure and ground popularized by Gestalt psychology. Does this gesture belong to the revolutionary initiative of a servant woman who does not know her place and demands a sort of equal representation? Or is it the product of Munby's sexually acquisitive projections, an Other fashioned out of his desires and anxieties? One cannot say whether the pressure is given or taken, the master's or the servant's.

This indeterminacy at the point where master and servant touch is all the more surprising in that the literary sensibility that informs the passage is otherwise rather old-fashioned. The sort of novel into which Munby wryly imagines his experience translated is the sort that calls its carriages chariots, one that shares its stylized tableaux of "elegant imperial creature" and "humble serving maid" with the repetitive idiom of romance and melodrama. Behind the whole passage lies the model of innumerable theatrical subplots and episodes of comic relief. Laura is still very much a *literary* servant. The maid parallels the mistress as the "foil" that brings out the "elegance" of the jewel, as the indistinct "background" that sets the upper-class foreground in sharper relief. It is true that for once the maid steps forward out of her conventional obscurity, but the structural inequality of this conventional parallelism remains intact. Since the setting is still the drawing room, and not the kitchen, more can be revealed about the mistress than the maid; Munby may prefer to flirt with the latter, but he cannot describe her as "intelligent and charming" or "piquante and laughingly sarcastic." He can hardly write "about" her at all. As in centuries of literary tradition, she appears by the grace of a hierarchical parallelism that brings her out of invisibility only within a frame that excludes most of her subjectivity, routine, plans, destiny.

This literary marginality is not especially worth noting in its own right. For some time now, literary critics have seen no reason to contest the received opinion that even in the novel there has never been a satisfactory representation of the common people. It was George Orwell, in his chosen role as naive observer of that which is empirically evident but morally unsayable, who first pointed out this nakedness of our imperial genre. The working class, he writes in his essay on Dickens, is simply not represented in the novel. Dickens himself "does not write about the proletariat," and in this "he merely resembles the overwhelming majority of novelists, past and present. If you look for the working classes in fiction, especially English fiction, all you find is a hole." There are of course exceptions, Orwell acknowledges, such as agricultural laborers, "criminals, derelicts, and, more recently, the working-class intelligentsia. But the ordinary town proletariat, the people who make the wheels go round, have always been ignored by novelists. When they do find their way between the covers of a book, it is nearly always as objects of pity or as comic relief." The proof that Dickens, like his fellow novelists, "does not in reality know very much about them" is that "they come into his novels chiefly as servants, and comic servants at that."[2]

These sentences no longer seem as provocative as they must have been in 1939. In the half century since the Red Thirties, Orwell's indignation has not disappeared, but it has moved into the academy, where sympathetic literary critics would perhaps only be surprised that, with all he knew of class domination, Orwell still expected from the novel anything different. Today educated common sense is less likely to dispute Orwell's judgment than to take it for granted, while wondering perhaps whether the issue is really of much significance one way or the other. After all, these days novelists routinely avail themselves of the liberty to write about more or less anything they please, including the working class, and this inclusiveness of subject matter does not seem to have shaken the foundation of things or to have given anyone much reason for self-congratulation. If the consummation is inconsequential, then there is little merit in arguing over, say, the extent of those antecedents to it that Orwell may have missed. A triumphant chronicle of the climb toward literary democracy would thus seem uncontroversial, complacent, and misled. Like universal suffrage, the literary representation of the people seems one of those questions which no longer excite either hope or anxiety.

A further reason for choosing not to respond to Orwell's provocation, even if (or because) one embraces his political ideals, is provided by another figure of the thirties, Kenneth Burke. In *Criticism and Social Change,* Frank Lentricchia retrieves for the 1980s a question that the Left did not want to hear from Burke in 1936: what in fact are the political effects of that realistic depiction of the sufferings of the working class that has always been assumed to be a major goal of literature? Burke "asks the intellectual left to consider the worker at the symbolic—not the existential—level, as the embodiment of an ideal, and then to weigh the rhetorical value of that symbol in its American setting, and to measure the extent to which that symbol is persuasively forceful, whether it disseminates revolution or perhaps something else, perhaps reaction. . . . you can't expect, he says in effect to his progressive friends, on the one hand, to keep painting these riveting portraits of workers under capitalism, of degradation and alienation—you can't expect people to accept these portraits as the truth, which is your rhetorical desire, after all, and then, on the other hand, at the same time, expect people to want to identify with workers, or become workers, or even enlist their energies of intellect and feeling on behalf of workers. . . . You must therefore . . . rethink your representations of workers. 'You must somehow bring them within, make sure their fate and ours are bound up with each other.' "[3] Burke is afraid that "a discourse weighted with symbols of proletarian life and exploitation might succeed only in isolating . . . workers' agony" (p. 32), dissociated as that discourse is from the "utopian yearning" (p. 29) and "images of 'the good life' " (p. 32) that effectively mobilize allegiance and action. In order to mobilize those whom the image of the alienated worker leaves unmoved, what is needed is to replace the usual realism of the present with a rhetoric " 'looking both forwards and back' " (p. 37), projecting images of the desirable while it also reaches back to engage with the compromised values of the unconverted. "Burke is here urging that the rigors of the worker be inserted within a rhetorically more encompassing ('representative') symbol so that the fate of the working class will be organically integrated with the fate of society as a whole. . . . The role of such rhetoric is not the persuasion of doubters that 'there is' totality but the creation and insemination of a vision—we may say a heuristic fiction—whose promised child is a consenting consciousness for radical social change" (p. 32).

Burke's insistence that questions about the politics of literature be shifted from the level of realism to the level of rhetoric, thus making room in political discourse for "unrealistic" visions or fictions of shared social fate, helps to circumvent Orwell's complaint about the omission of the working class from the novel. But it also has the further, paradoxical effect of renewing interest in such figures as Munby's Laura, the "servants, and comic servants at that" whom Orwell, along with most other leftist critics, dismisses. Looking back at the novel from Burke's perspective, that is, without assuming that it *should* have provided a portrait of the working class that somehow always fails to materialize, one can look at what it does provide in a different and more positive light.

In occupying itself with servants rather than with proletarians, the novel cast its lot with rhetoric rather than with realism. As part of the novel's comic inheritance, the literary servant, like Munby's maid, is surrounded by what Lukács calls "the rarified atmosphere of dramatic generalization."[4] She or he enjoys little or no existence apart from her or his effect upon the destiny of the masters; as on the stage, the servant's presence is taken up with the performance of peremptory aesthetic duties. Serving as architect of the plot, the Plautine slave has no time to transmit much of the lived experience of Roman slavery. A soubrette or confidant in Molière is no great reflector of seventeenth-century domestic service. If either happens to reveal matters of interest to the social historian, this momentary mimesis remains incidental to their comic instrumentality. And the same holds for the novel. Its servants may be identified as butlers, tweenies, and slavies, but the considerable textual space allotted to them is filled with much the same repertory of comic gestures and devices: expository prologues, flashbacks, oracular messages, and asides; the verbal entertainment of conscious punning or unconscious bumbling; a pointed "doubling" of the protagonist, for example as foil or parody; an instrumental role in complicating and resolving the action. In this thin and functional figure, there is very little of either the heroism or the sufferings of the working class. And yet by Burke's criteria, neither its almost complete submission to rhetorical effect nor its notorious ideological impurity disqualifies the literary servant from the domain of significant political representation. Indeed, rhetorical effect and ideological impurity are his two major desiderata for political discourse; they are precisely what would be required for a successful representation of what Burke calls "the people."

In order even to entertain the notion that the literary servant might serve as representative of the people, neither the term "the people" nor the term "representation" can be left as they stand in Orwell's argument. For Orwell, representation means realism. What socialists (like himself) demand from the novel is a serious, central, accurate account of working-class life for its own sake—as opposed, that is, to the marginality, the "literariness," and the rhetorical manipulations of "pity" and "comic relief." If this demand has had so little impact on literary criticism (in spite of unabating enthusiasm for the dystopian Orwell), it is in part because the discipline as a whole has rightly found Orwell's notion of literary representation naive. Unfortunately, that naivete has permitted the discipline to ignore the call for greater *political* representation that Orwell confuses with it. But contemporary Marxist and post-structuralist theory, while echoing the critique of naive representation, has also renewed Orwell's specifically political challenge. Foucault argues, for example, that realism's concealment of the medium of language in which ideas and things are brought together also conceals the action or event of bringing them together, and thus the powers and interests by which this signifying practice is traversed.[5] If representation is not to be conceived as a mirror held up to nature but as a signifying practice, then it and not nature is responsible for its statements, and political questions can be addressed to it. Indeed, they must be addressed to it, for when the sense of representation as "making present to the mind" is discarded, as Raymond Williams notes in *Keywords,* the more visible difficulties of the political sense of the word become unavoidable, difficulties of "standing for something that is *not* present" (my italics).

Given the absence of the object represented, it is not absurd to ask of literary representations, as of political representatives, whether there are limits to their mandates and whether they are subject to recall.[6] Orwell seems to assume that writing about the working class could and should be as faithful and intimate to its experience as if it were speaking for itself. But it does not speak for itself, and that is why it is represented by others. Edward W. Said puts this point forcefully in *Orientalism:* "if the Orient could represent itself, it would; since it cannot, the representation does the job. . . . there is no such thing as a delivered presence, but a *re-presence,* or a representation. The value, efficacy, strength, apparent veracity of a written statement about the Orient therefore relies very little, and cannot instrumentally depend, on the Orient as such. On the contrary, the written statement is a presence to the reader by virtue of its having excluded, displaced, made superogatory any such *real thing* as 'the Orient.'"[7]

It would appear to follow that literature's social exclusions are even more absolute and unrelieved than Orwell suggests. But leaving open for the moment the question of differences between Arabs in Orientalist discourse and the domestic working class in the novel—above all, the possibility that for the latter the "secret pressure" can work in both directions, that representation can register a pushing back from below—there is one extenuating factor that holds in both cases. To insist that exclusion is built into the brute linguistic and institutional fact of who is and is not speaking is to cast doubt on the political credentials of realism, but it is also to reassert the materiality of language, which is denied when realism claims transparency. And to make language material again is to rediscover in it powers and interests that realism had ascribed only to what it called reality. Even more important, it is to recognize between those powers and interests a certain room for maneuver guaranteed by the play of language, which is not free play but which is no more reducible to the extra-linguistic hegemony of the powers that be than it is reducible to the authentic voice of the working class. In other words, once literary representations are no longer judged by the criterion of an impossible immediacy, as Orwell judges them, and it is acknowledged for better or worse that they enjoy a relative autonomy, then their inescapable "literariness" is no longer simply the sign of a monotonous exclusion, as Orwell perceives it, but becomes a medium or arena of political skirmishing, alive with the turbulent significance of moves and countermoves. Turning away from inquiries into "the correctness of the representation" and "its fidelity to some great original"—in this case, the working class—as Said concludes, we can find a great deal more in its language: "style, figures of speech, setting, narrative devices."[8] Even the narrative and rhetorical devices, modes and functions whose shamelessly nonrepresentational artifice constitutes the comic servant are thus not to be dismissed out of hand, but can be investigated as the site of unknown and perhaps surprising confrontations.

Orwell also uses the concept of representation in another sense. "If you ask any ordinary reader which of Dickens' proletarian characters he can remember, the three he is certain to mention are Bill Sykes, Sam Weller, and Mrs. Gamp. A burglar, a valet and a drunken mid-wife—not exactly a representative cross-section of the English work-ing class" (pp. 82–83). "Representative" here suggests both the typical and the ethically normative. It rules out the lurid abnor-malities of drunkenness and crime together with the servility of servants, who cannot stand for the working class (though in Dickens' time they were more numerous than miners and textile workers combined) because they are mere "hangers-on" (p. 82).[9] In represent-ing the working class it is not enough, in other words, to represent either a large statistical plurality or a widely shared experience like subordination and material want. Presumably even valets have experi-enced those, or at least the former. Judging from Orwell's repeated emphasis on the unsuitability of servants for the task of representa-tion, it seems that what must be represented is the unique, indepen-dent essence of the working class, the ethical ground of its being that at once makes it an antonomous unity and distinguishes it from those to whom it is subordinated.

This demand leads Orwell into a double articulation. Having ar-gued at the beginning of the essay, as we saw, that "the people who make the wheels go round" are not represented in Dickens' novels, he concludes by resting Dickens' final message and achievement on his representation of "the native decency of the common man" (p. 140). The argument asks "the people" to serve simultaneously as a missing social particularity and a commanding moral universal, as absence and presence, as nothing and everything.

The problem here goes deeper than a nominalist distrust of the collective noun "the people." As the embarrassed quotation marks around it suggest, the continuity or identity between the oppressed in one period and another has seemed questionable for some time. Uncertainty as to whether "people" is singular or plural, a unity or not, has existed since the word was introduced into English. Before reaching the higher indefiniteness of its quasi-pronomial use (people say), it had already accumulated as many perplexities as the diverse collectivities of class, occupation, stratum, status, ethnicity, region, and religion to which it has referred. Contemporary cultural criticism is less troubled by the empirical heterogeneity of the groups lumped together, or rather mobilized, by this term than by the leading role composed for and attributed to "the people" by the world-historical narratives (democratic, populist, nationalist, socialist) of modern politics. The dangers of such narrativization emerge from the critique of "humanism" elaborated by figures like Foucault, Derrida, and Althusser. To assign "the people" the protagonist's part in a universal drama, they suggest, is to allow and require it to stand in for a universal Man, an absolute origin and standard of human value that, alienated from itself by historical injustice, is little by little struggling to emancipate and realize itself in history. But any protagonist defined in such a way that it can claim all of history to be its own story is in effect claiming to be a humanist essence, outside the contingency of historical existence. In order to open history up to change that comes from unpredictable groups and unprecedented directions, it is necessary to expose, as Althusser does in his polemical characterization of history as "a process without a subject," the sleight-of-hand that uses history to preserve a "Generic Essence of Man."[10] In Stuart Hall's words, "just as there is no fixed content to the category of 'popular culture,' so there is no fixed subject to attach to it—'the people.' 'The people' are not always back there, their culture untouched, their liberties and their instincts intact, still struggling on against the Norman yoke or whatever: as if, if only we can 'discover' them and bring them back on stage, they will always stand up in the right, appointed place and be counted."[11]

Among contemporary anti-humanists, this set of assumptions—which Orwell shares with a great deal of Marxist literary criticism and historiography—has been replaced by a general emphasis on the historical variability of "the people" and a specific and more marked emphasis on the extent to which, far from serving as an absolute origin of alternative values and aspirations, it has been constituted by the ideology of its rulers. "The people" has not made its own history but has been made by history: in its resistances as well as in its submission, at the very core of its being, it does not define itself but is defined by shifting modes of production and configurations of power. Like the critique of realism, this anti-humanism would seem to discourage anyone from reviving Orwell's realist-humanist questions about the people's literary representation. And yet here too the effect is the reverse. Indeed, once again we are led to reexamine with new interest the familiar "servants, and comic servants at that" who, in the absence of more genuine representatives of the people, in fact populate the English novel.

By the most frequent definitions, the servant not only "occupied himself with the personal needs of an employer" but did so "in such a way that this occupation established a relationship of personal dependence on the employer."[12] Dependence is also Orwell's keynote. He is reluctantly fascinated by Dickens' treatment of these "hangers-on" who, like the Bath footmen, give "dinner parties in imitation of their 'betters'" and who, like Sam Weller and other faithful family retainers, "identify themselves with their master's family" (pp. 113–114). But if "the people" has no independent essence and is largely fashioned by its rulers, then the humorously or repulsively essence-less servant is no longer an anomaly. Just as the revision of representation makes the comic, functional, rhetorical mode of the servant's literary existence into a significant political variable, and thus suggests a new political perspective on literary tradition, so the revision of "the people" revitalizes all those centuries of spare, marginal supernumeraries who are defined mainly by their indefiniteness. In this sense at least, they are "representative" after all.

The question is, representative of what? Is the effect of these representations solely to insist on the vulnerability of the people to the definitions of its rulers? The enterprise of studying the novel's servants has the advantage of taking up material that is actually there (the object riddled with error, as Benjamin said) instead of lamenting over what is missing. But what is there is only worth studying if what it represents is not self-evident. From what has been said already it should be clear at any rate that the literary servant does not represent actual servants, or at most does so only tangentially. On the whole, novelists were no more interested than playwrights in conveying anything historically precise about domestic service. This disparity between art and life is observable from the very beginnings of the novel. Both Defoe and Fielding, for example, took an active part in the politics of their time, in the course of which each made statements and proposals concerning "the poor" that manifestly contradict the evidence of their fiction. In several pamphlets devoted to the reform of domestic service, Defoe complained of "the Pride, Insolence, and exorbitant Wages of our *Women Servants, Footmen,* &c." His "Proposal for Amendment of the same" comprised a series of measures to put them back in their place: the limiting of wages, the regulation of dress, putting service on a contractual basis so as to discourage sudden departures and refusing to hire servants without certificates of good character.[13] But this policy accords ill with his better-known writings. "Of the bad servants whom Defoe attacked in his didactic works," one critic justly remarks, "almost none appear in his fiction."[14] Servants like Friday, the young Moll, and Roxana's Amy compose a far different picture—and one that has as little to do with the lives of contemporary servants as the Restoration comedies Defoe saw in London.

In a study of Fielding's *Enquiry into the Causes of the Late Increase of Robbers* and *Proposal for Making an Effectual Provision for the Poor,* Malvin Zirker notes a similar difficulty in reconciling the "social criticism of fashionable life and the apparent exaltation of the unfashionable hero characteristic of the novels with the thoroughgoing aristocratic, institutionalized, conventional social attitudes expressed in Fielding's pamphlets on the poor.[15] Fielding proposed, among other things, giant workhouses—some decades before Bentham's Panopticon— that would allow no family life for their inmates, as well as strict controls over working-class leisure (e.g., drinking and gambling). There was of course to be no corresponding control over the same activities when practiced by the fashionable. Yet there is hardly anything Fielding mocks with greater regularity in his comic works than a double moral standard for master and man. For example, in *True Patriot* No. 28 (May 6–13, 1746), which owes something to the impersonation of a footman in Swift's *Direction to Servants,* he makes the servant's "place" much less determinate by the irony of its parallels:

If we lose our Characters, we shall lose our Places, and never after be received into any other Family. Herein our Situation differs from that of our Betters; against whom no Profligacy is any Objection. And if by Treachery they happen to be discarded in one Place, (for that is the only Crime they can be guilty of), they are nevertheless received with open Arms in another. How many Men of Fashion do we know, whose Characters would prevent any Person from taking them into his Family as Footmen, who are well received, caressed and promoted by the Great as Gentlemen.[16]

This discrepancy between the class-bound harshness of actual proposals and the stylizations of fiction would seem less dependent on genre than on the local, transgeneric workings of comic rhetoric. There are moments of comic transcendence even within the didactic pamphlets themselves. If one judged it from the conclusion, the *True Patriot* number (which was occasioned by a servant's sensational murder of his mistress) would seem to leave no doubts about the servant's proper place. "Let us content ourselves," the footman counsels his brethren, "with the low State of Life to which it hath pleased God to call us." However, the "like master like man" similitude—one of comic rhetoric's more frequent tropes—forces a "turn" away from this conventional class position as soon as it appears. Whatever the specific reason for which Fielding brings master and man into parallel, their proximity generates an excess of potential points of contact. This excess is registered in the compressed multi-directionality that Freud observed in comic language; its effect, he suggested, was to slip censored or contradictory ideas past the reason's defenses.[17] The sentence above continues:" . . . and not conclude when we see our Masters grow great, high and honorable by their Rogueries, that it would succeed with us in the same Manner." The sudden swerve in the direction of high and honorable rogues (and away from the servants themselves) carries an implicit denunciation of an inequality that is certainly effective (they, not we, will get away with it) but no less certainly illegitimate. By speaking of servants only indirectly, as one term of a comparison, the comic *topos* jars them slightly but distinctly from their designated social place.

My object here will be to describe how, in the absence of any realistic depiction of "the people," rhetoric like this functions as political representation. But before getting on with this effort, it may be useful to clear up one possible source of confusion. I am not arguing, like Orwell, that novelists did not discuss domestic servants directly, and instead fell back on ready-made rhetorical devices, because they could not see the institution for what it was. Given the level of Victorian technology, Orwell suggests, even Dickens simply could not imagine life without household help:

He was writing at a time when domestic service must have seemed a completely inevitable evil. There were no labor-saving devices, and there was huge inequality of wealth. It was an age of enormous families, pretentious meals and inconvenient houses, when the slavey drudging fourteen hours a day in the basement kitchen was something too normal to be noticed. And given the *fact* of servitude, the feudal relationship is the only tolerable one. . . . If there have got to be masters and servants, how much better that the master should be Mr. Pickwick and the servant should be Sam Weller. Better still, of course, if servants did not exist at all—but this Dickens is probably unable to imagine. Without a high level of mechanical development, human equality is not practically possible; Dickens goes to show that it is not imaginable either.[18]

The implication of Orwell's technological determinism is that since the evil was felt to be necessary, no one could afford to recognize that it was an evil. But this recognition did not wait upon the advent of better plumbing, smaller families, and unpretentious meals. Nineteenth-century novelists who were not in practice obliged to forego domestic service could and did refuse the institution in theory. Consider for example this statement by Dickens' friend and collaborator Wilkie Collins:

Life means dirty work, small wages, hard words, no holidays, no social station, no future, according to her experience of it. No human being ever was created for this. No state of society which composedly accepts this, in the case of thousands, as one of the necessary conditions of its selfish comforts, can pass itself off as civilized, except under the most audacious of false pretenses.[19]

On the other end of the political spectrum, Rudyard Kipling agrees that the institution of domestic service is representative of English civilization, or the lack of it: "a country where for twelve or fourteen pounds a year sixteen-year-old girls were obliged to carry thirty or forty pounds of water at a time to the fourth floor," he says, has no right to accuse other countries of barbarism.[20] Far from taking service for granted, both writers present it as definitive of their societies, as a sort of national shame. The ideas that Elizabeth Gaskell puts in the mouth of John Barton are equally far-reaching: "he considered domestic servitude as a species of slavery; a pampering of artificial wants on the one side, a giving-up of every right of leisure by day and quiet rest by night on the other. How far his strong exaggerated feelings had any foundation in truth, it is for you to judge."[21] If novelists like Gaskell and Collins continued to rely on comic, feudal retainers (think of Gabriel Betteredge in *The Moonstone,* Dixon in *North and South,* or Sally in *Ruth*), it is not because they naively accepted an idealized, feudal view of domestic service. The reasons for the persistence of these feudal vestiges into modern texts will have to be sought elsewhere.

Having dismissed the hypothesis of a direct correspondence between the servants of art and those of life, we can begin the analysis of these representations by remembering, as everyone in Dickens' time knew, that the servants of life are themselves signs—signs of their masters' status. It is appropriate that modern social historians, following Rowntree, have defined the Victorian middle class as the "servant-keeping" class, for the desire to be defined as middle class was a major reason for keeping servants. As Eric Hobsbawm puts it, "the safest way of distinguishing oneself from the laborers was to employ labor oneself."[22] In describing servants, most authorities agree that nonfunctional symbolism prevails over functional necessity. For Marx, the servant is a textbook case of luxurious, unproductive labor (and technically, therefore, not even an instance of exploitation): "the extraordinary increase in the productivity of large-scale industry . . . permits a larger and larger part of the working class to be employed unproductively. Hence it is possible to reproduce the ancient domestic slaves, under the name of a servant class." "The capitalist who hires servants," a commentator writes, "is not making profits, but spending them."[23] Economically gratuitous, servants are mere signs of money, itself a sign.

The dizzying irony of human beings disappearing into the exigencies of sign production is the distinctive emphasis that Thorstein Veblen gives to his account of domestic service in *The Theory of the*

Leisure Class (1899). For Veblen, "the chief use of servants is the evidence they afford of the master's ability to pay." The existence of "a class of servants, the more numerous the better, whose sole office is fatuously to wait upon the person of their owner" is not merely unproductive but a means of demonstrating the master's "ability to sustain large pecuniary damage without impairing his superior opulence."[24] No rational calculation of self-interest or pleasure could possibly explain the human monstrosity of domestic service, but only the need to be seen "in a performance of conspicuous leisure."

> Personal contact with the hired persons whose aid is called in to fulfil the routine of decency is commonly distasteful to the occupants of the house, but their presence is endured and paid for, in order to delegate to them a share in this onerous consumption of household goods. The presence of domestic servants, and of the special class of body servants in an eminent degree, is a concession of physical comfort to the moral need of pecuniary decency.[25]

Veblen's almost inhuman dryness is very much to the point. By their nature, or their lack of it, servants invite a post-humanist perspective on society and meaning. If all representations stand at a distance from the objects they represent, servants call attention to that distance. They are signs of the arbitrariness of signs. And in insisting on their status as signs, their distance from any natural dispensation, their subjection to human will or whim, servants inescapably extend the awareness of these things to the social hierarchy itself, of which they are of course also signs. "At the superior nudist camps," Robert Graves and Alan Hodge write in *The Long Week End*, "a nice class distinction was made: the butlers and maids who brought along the refreshments were forced to admit their lower social standing by wearing loin-cloths and aprons respectively." From Marivaux's *L'Ile des esclaves* to Barrie's *The Admirable Crichton*, this is one surprise hidden in the lack of autonomous essence that enables and constrains servants to stand for others. Since their place is so artificial, they suggest that the society that places them is also artificial. The vein of whimsical humor that tends to surround them is in part perhaps a tribute to the notion that here is one category of prosperous, undeserving poor for whom it is unnecessary to feel sorry. But it also carries with it a certain playfulness about society as a whole, a perspective that encourages whims of social rearrangement and re-distribution.

The latent social bearing of these signs that advertise their ar-bitrariness can be illustrated briefly by William Hazlitt's essay "Footmen" (*New Monthly Magazine,* September 1830). When Hazlitt too suggests that the menservants of the rich are nothing but other people's signs, his intention is clearly to satirize the other people:

It is the very insignificance, the non-entity as it were of the gentlemen of the cloth, that constitutes their importance, by setting off the pretentions of their superiors to the best advantage. What would be the good of having a will of our own, if we had not others about us who are deprived of all will of their own, and who wear a badge to say "I serve"? How can we show that we are the lords of creation but by reducing others to the condition of machines, who never move but at the beck of our caprices?[26]

It is curious that Hazlitt makes no effort to remedy the injustice he exposes by filling in these human blanks, imagining the detail of lives led in "the condition of machines." He does not much sympathize with the "others" who are "deprived of all will of their own." Their masters offer them as metaphors, and Hazlitt seems content to take them as such. But what is even more curious is the way the essay digresses from its satire of the aristocracy into a confused but poi-gnant fantasy of "the world turned upside-down," a sort of double vision in which the servants of the aristocracy themselves come to signify the power to remake society. There is a peculiar logic in this trajectory. Intended as a metaphor of his master's lordly will, the footman radiates that will. Like all metaphors, he is an embodiment of the possibility of drastic transformation. In fact, his "non-entity" seems to make the same appeal to the imagination that Hazlitt had attributed three years earlier to the insipid heroes of Scott. The hero of a romance, he said, "is not so properly the chief object in it, as a sort of blank left open to the imagination."[27] The blank, as on an ancient map, beckons the reader into an unknown of fulfilled wishes. And this is where Hazlitt's essay proceeds to follow its footmen. When he includes himself among the "lords of creation," it is not merely for purposes of satire but because, gazing at these inhuman signs of omnipotence, he suddenly finds himself ready to participate in the creation of a new social world.

Deliver me from the filth and cellars of St. Giles's, from the shops of Holborn and the Strand, from all that appertains to middle and to low life; and commend me to the streets . . . with groups of footmen lounging on the steps and insulting the passengers—it is then I feel the true dignity and imaginary pretensions of human nature realized! There is here none of the squalidness of poverty, none of the petty artifices of trade; life's business is changed into a romance. The true ends and benefits of society are here enjoyed and bountifully lavished, and all the trouble and misery banished, and not even allowed so much as to exist in thought. Those who would find the real Utopia, should look for it somewhere about Park-Lane or May-Fair.[28]

For all its initial and continuing sarcasm, this flight of romantic fancy is ambivalent enough to sustain a genuine anticipation of utopian reversal. By the time Hazlitt declares that the "pampered" footmen "have no earthly business but to enjoy themselves," he has almost surrendered himself to a wishful enjoyment of carnivalesque social fluidity.

Without referring back to "the people" as its ground or origin, utopianism (even of this negative and incipient sort) can claim to be a popular political representation. Judging from this illustration, a minimal description of its formal effects might begin as follows: the servant functions as a sign that carries awareness of the unnaturalness and arbitrariness of signs into a social hierarchy that would like to present itself as natural, rooted, and fixed. But this is not to suggest that literature enjoys the playful privilege of squirming free from historical and ideological determinations. To do so would be no more and no less meaningful than to affirm that in representing the people's ideological dependence, the literary servant simply repeats ruling class ideology. What is misleading in both the blanket assertion and the blanket denial of freedom can perhaps be cleared up by paying attention to the term "ideology." Adding considerations of power and interest to the term "language" used above, "ideology" need not be taken as reducing all linguistic playfulness to the sobrieties of the dominant discourse. It should be understood not as a synonym for false consciousness but as a necessary mediator between people and the real conditions of their existence, a body of symbols that must exist in some form under any social system. This revision in turn entails a revisionary understanding of power. A term that permits the necessary discrimination—that is, the sense of language transmitting power, yet not unidirectionally—is Gramsci's "hegemony." Gramsci argues that "there can, and indeed must, be hegemonic activity even before the rise to power." Hegemony is only achieved in fact by "the gradual but continuous absorption . . . of the active elements produced by allied groups—and even of those which came from antagonistic groups and seem irreconcilably hostile."[29] The need to obtain consent requires a hegemonic class or group to concede something to those it governs—not to meet them halfway, but to recognize, include, respond to the oppositional or alternative tendencies that threaten it. Thus hegemony is not absolute domination but a continually fluctuating, continually renegotiated give-and-take, a dialogue that is unequal, but not quite monologue.

Here then is the key difference between the situation of Arabs in Orientalist discourse and the situation of the working class in the discourse of the novel. "What these widely diffused notions of the Orient depended on was the almost total absence in contemporary Western culture of the Orient as a genuinely felt and experienced force." Orientalism "has less to do with the Orient than it does with 'our' world." More emphatically, it contains "all the actual human interchange between Oriental and Westerner of the Judge's 'said I to myself, said I'" in *Iolanthe*. And this is so because the Orient was "unable to resist the projects, images, or mere descriptions devised for it."[30] But where consent had to be obtained from the governed, where the dominant discourse had to speak to as well as of its Others, the existence of "interchange" distinguished the representation of the people from the absoluteness of solipsistic projection. This case has recently been argued for specific subgroups. Women, for example, had to be induced to adopt the discourse that defined them, and as recent feminist criticism has pointed out, that same discourse could thus be made to support their resistance. The position of slaves within the discourse of Southern paternalism has been described by Eugene Genovese in similar terms:

the slaves found an opportunity to translate paternalism itself into a doctrine different from that understood by their masters and to forge it into a weapon of resistance to assertions that slavery was a natural condition for blacks. . . . Southern paternalism may have reinforced racism as well as class exploitation, but it also unwittingly invited its victims to fashion their own interpretation of the social order it was intended to justify.[31]

What then is the space within hegemonic discourse where Minby's "secret pressure" makes itself felt? If this disturbance cannot be definitively tied either to the domination of the rulers or to the rebellious initiative of the ruled, its location is not so indeterminate that it cannot be specified. What produces the touching of hands is labor. When he notices Laura, Munby notices domestic drudgery. When she, crossing a threshold defended by more than etiquette, as it were *presents herself* to Munby, Laura does so through her duties. Her affection, like that of Munby's future wife, translates itself into an eager performance of routine chores. The "secret pressure" that counterpoints the elegance of the drawing room is exerted on and by a servant's "*working* hand."

In fact, a tale of hands works its way through the entire passage. The word returns, like an obsession, in a variety of grammatical forms: the "redhanded" maid appears in order to "hand me dishes," she "hands him to the door," and of course it is her "thick broad hand" whose contact speaks louder than polite conversation. This repetition is suffused with eroticism. Throughout the diaries we read of "large thick hands, infinitely suggestive to the touch and sight," that move Munby so deeply as to justify Derek Hudson's use of the term "fetish" (p. 70). But to say this is not to reduce Munby's interest in the "comparative coarseness of servant maids' hands" (p. 154) to an individual sexual eccentricity. In the nineteenth century, as Steven Marcus has shown, the "imagery in which sexuality was represented in consciousness was largely drawn from the sphere of socioeconomic activity and had to do with concerns and anxieties about problems of accumulation, production, and excessive expenditure."[32] The shaping of Munby's sexuality around the motif of labor is a case in point. In a servant's "brawny, brickred, coarse grained (workhardened) hand" Munby admired what his age admired, as the parenthesis explains: the signs of work accomplished, productive value signified and stored up in the hand's strength, size, redness, dirt.

This is not to say, as Hegel's dialectic of Master and Slave might suggest, that the mere fact of the servant's labor necessarily produces pressure on the consciousness of the master. If it demands recognition, it is because of the special status accorded to labor within the dominant discourse. Munby's eroticizing of the working hand belongs to its Victorian context. His "dear master, Thomas Carlyle" (p. 283) demanded obeisance to a deified Labor, without qualities and without objects: "Produce! Produce! . . . Whatsoever thy hand findeth to do, do it with thy whole might."[33] Enjoined by Carlyle to open his Goethe, Munby discovered with delight the garden scene in *Faust* "where Margaret says"—the words are Munby's—"how can you kiss my hand—sie ist so *garstig,* ist so *rauch*" (p. 31). A servant's rough, work-hardened hands, unlike those of the "false white-handed wenches of modern art," bore culturally acknowledged marks of election. In *Hard Times,* which was dedicated to Carlyle, Munby might have found, in the scene where Bounderby's aged mother stops Stephen at the factory door and asks how long he has worked there, Dickens' ambivalent tribute to the ready-made synecdoche of the political economists: "'A dozen year,' he told her. 'I must kiss the hand,' said she, 'that has worked in this fine factory for a dozen year!' And she lifted it, though he would have prevented her, and put it to her lips."[34] Like Dickens and Marx, Munby takes the labor theory of value at its ambiguous word. For him, the ultimate source of all value is truly the labor of "hands."

A multi-leveled motif of hegemonic discourse, labor functioned simultaneously as a secularized faith, a modernizing ethic of industrial discipline, and a militant political slogan. Before 1832, as E. P. Thompson points out, work was the basis of the middle-class political program that "divided society between the 'Useful' or 'Productive Classes,' on the one hand, and courtiers, sinecurists, fundholders, speculators, and parasitic middlemen on the other."[35] Under the banner of "labor," the Third Estate temporarily united its contradictory elements and advanced toward the Reform Bill, proclaiming itself industrious and its opponents idle. But the same excess or overshooting of specific class interest that was necessary to achieve hegemonic universality also permitted and provoked an internal interrogation of that hegemony. The laborers whose consent had been appealed to in those terms could come to identify their capitalist masters as parasites living off their labor. And the masters themselves might be the first to make the identification. Just as Hegel and Marx followed out the subversive consequences of the labor theory of value, so a native British tradition took much the same path, from Carlyle's "Whatsoever thy hand findeth to do" to his protest, recorded by Munby in his diary, against the ideology "which appears to regard human souls simply as 'hands'" (p. 81). Thence to Munby's friend Ruskin: "the guilty thieves of Europe . . . are the Capitalists—that is to say, people who live by percentages on the labor of others."[36] And from Ruskin to Morris, who describes "the creed of modern morality that all labor is good in itself" as "a convenient belief to those who live on the labor of others."[37]

Though Munby was not one of those "rare spirits like Nietzsche and Tolstoy" who alone "recognized the false ardor and hidden nihilism" in the religion of work, his own work provoked in him "a shuddering sadness that I can neither explain nor get rid of."[38] Seeing himself as one who "finds not any work to suit him or to do good to others," his gaze wandered toward those who were visibly working for him. Contemplating the new bridges and embankments at Chelsea, he exclaims, "Well may I envy the navvies their retrospect of work!" At a performance of *Henry V,* he is most enviously impressed not with the Keans' acting but with the fact that "every man and woman of the crowds of supernumeraries . . . seemed thoroughly animated and full of individual interest in their work" (pp. 28–30). Thus, when his servant-wife cleans his chimney, his vision brightens into Hegelian transcendence: "it is not desirable to be a chimney-sweep . . . but she who becomes one in the course of her work, and from such a motive, is potentially a heroine, and is capable of all noble doings" (p. 132).

This is to say that there is a firm ideological basis for Munby's conventional parallelism of masters and servants. The discourse of labor, which joins rulers and ruled in a hegemonic bond, by the same token lays out common ground where ruptures, recognitions, and renegotiations can take place between them. In the diary passage quoted earlier, the maid is aligned with her mistress, but also, transgressing gender, with Munby himself. As the servant is ordered about by "those imperious misses," so Munby's "hero" is a "captive" rebelling against an "imperial creature." Once set in motion, the demonic machine of parallelism gets out of hand; out of bachelor anxiety it conjures up a revolt against empire. If its structure precludes the fleshing out of any individual member of the "other" class, on the other hand it orients the whole passage toward unlocalizable abstractions like society and justice. Munby stretches out parallel lines only in order to label the gap between them as unjust and thus to identify the collapse of parallelism, which he threatens by his sexual preference, with the achievement of justice. Like servants themselves, this consummation cannot be represented except as displaced and deferred. Hence the superb moment of the "real adieus," the farewell that both postpones the collapse of parallelism and, in so doing, leaves an image of it hanging in the future.

It seems paradoxical that a literary tradition as old as Cinderella should be associated with the loneliness of a life improvised outside tradition, and with a social vision that refused tradition. If Munby's parallelism can create such disturbance within ideology and if that parallelism is entirely traditional, then the unspoken political disappointment about tradition that many of us share with Orwell would appear to need reexamination. It is to that tradition, from which the novel's servants derive, that I will now turn.

I

From Odysseus' Scar to the
Brown Stocking: A Tradition

One of the few critical works that permit a phenomenon on the scale of the literary servant to be grasped all at once is Erich Auerbach's *Mimesis: The Representation of Reality in Western Literature*. Addressed to "Western literature" as a whole, *Mimesis* has a totalizing intent that matches the extraordinary pervasiveness of the servant as figure of the people's subordination. Moreover, Auerbach's democratic sympathies make him almost uniquely sensitive to the marginal, fragmentary, often almost invisible passage of the people through a literature not for, by, or about themselves. Both of these qualities appear in the book's opening chapter, entitled "Odysseus' Scar." This chapter goes back to Homer in search of a point of departure and finds there an oddly significant servant. Auerbach describes the scene in which "Odysseus has at last come home," and as the stranger's feet are being washed, "the old housekeeper Euryclea, who had been his nurse, recognizes him by a scar on his thigh."[1] In this episode, as in *Mimesis* as a whole, the presence of "reality" is signaled by randomness. That the first person to recognize Odysseus should be a lowly servant, that the long-awaited recognition should occur in a humble, domestic scene of foot-washing in which the surprised housekeeper drops the foot she is holding and tips over her basin, that the passage should be interrupted at the crucial moment by a digression of almost equal length explaining how, long ago, Odysseus had received the scar— these incongruous, disorderly, apparently insignificant facts fit Auerbach's methodological intention "to put the emphasis on the random occurrence, to exploit it not in the service of a planned continuity of action but in itself" (p. 552).

Yet the appearance of this servant in Auerbach's text is not haphazard. His definition of the real as the random, as that which escapes
predetermination and prediction, reflects both his fear of ideological
systems and his uprootedness. In Istanbul, as he says, he no longer
had the use of his library and was obliged to base his analysis on
randomly chosen passages.[2] "It is precisely the random moment
which is comparatively independent of the controversial and unstable
orders over which men fight and despair; it passes unaffected by
them" (p. 552). In exile in Istanbul, Auerbach begins with the homecoming of the archetypal wanderer. And in his treatment of that
homecoming, he registers the strange salience of another, internal
exile. Euryclea "has spent her life in the service of Laertes' family;
. . . she is closely connected with their fate, she loves them and shares
their interests and feelings. But she has no life of her own, no feelings
of her own; she has only the life and feelings of her master. . . . Thus
we become conscious of the fact that in the Homeric poems life is
enacted only among the ruling class—others appear only in the role
of servants to that class" (p. 21). This is one of the richest motifs in
Mimesis: the long exile from Western literature of what it calls, without quotation marks, the people, an exile marked by the slender,
subordinate existence of the literary servant.

Signs of the unrepresented, servants haunt Auerbach's account of
representation as they do Orwell's. When Auerbach discusses the
Bible, he finds room for the unnamed "servingmen" (p. 9) who
accompany Abraham and Isaac to the sacrifice. Hagar, also mentioned
in the first chaper, comes back in the last—in the explication of a
"random" passage in Proust (p. 543). The Renaissance theater brings
up Dorine in *Tartuffe* and, in Racine's *Iphigénie,* the scene "unique in
its kind" of "the king waking a sleeping servant" (p. 387). Discussion
of the novel moves from Sancho Panza through Julien Sorel in the role
of live-in secretary in the Hôtel de la Môle and on to the Goncourts'
Germinie Lacerteux (1864), which deals with "the sexual involvements
and the gradual ruin of a maidservant" (p. 493). Yet each of these
servants represents randomness at its unacceptable extreme, and for
Auerbach the series composes a repetitive history of exclusion. "The
very fact that *Germinie Lacerteux* is once again a novel about a maid,
that is, about an appendage of the bourgoisie, shows that the task of

including the fourth estate in the subject matter of serious artistic representation is not centrally understood and approached" (pp. 498–499). The same holds for Molière: "with him too any real representation of the life of the popular classes . . . is . . . completely out of the question. . . . All his chambermaids and servingmen, his peasants and peasants' wives . . . are merely comic adjuncts; and it is only within the frame of an upper bourgeois or aristocratic household that servants—especially women—at times represent the voice of common sense. But their functions are always concerned with their masters' problems, never with those of their own lives" (p. 365). The presence of servants signifies the absence of the people. Signposts left at random in the no-man's-land between what can and cannot be represented, they indicate only that the other side of the border is inhabited.

If Auerbach celebrates randomness, it is not for randomness' sake.[3] The assumption is that beneath the random he will one day discover the genuine historical object that it replaced for so long: "the people." As he himself makes explicit, the random is not an ultimate criterion for him but only a tactic in a larger strategy, the token of a transcendent faith. Like the modernists, Auerbach confesses, he has "confidence that in any random fragment plucked from the course of a life at any time the totality of its fate is contained" (p. 547). To trust in fate or chance for one's choice of subject is thus a calculated gesture of democratic faith, intended to liberate the critic from the ideology of the moment and to ensure an ultimate inclusive justice. In applying this methodology to a maximum of cases, Auerbach hopes to arrive at what is "common" to people of all stations—that is, at a democratic representation of reality that would otherwise be obstructed by the ideological hierarchies and priorities of the time. "The more [the random moment] is exploited, the more the elementary things which our lives have in common come to light. The more numerous, varied, and simple the people are who appear as subjects of such random moments, the more effectively must what they have in common shine forth" (p. 552). In short, what appears to be random is in fact a path to the unexplored territory of the people, a territory mapped out by the *common* and the *shared* and which in due time will reveal itself as *fate*.

What does this have to do with Homer's housekeeper? To bring the notions of the shared and the fateful to bear on what seems most random in the *Odyssey* is to break open a rich semantic cluster. For Homer the two words are in fact only one. As the dictionary indicates, *moira* "lot, fortune, fate, doom" derives from *moira* "part, portion, share, in booty of the feast, etc.," in particular "a *proper* share."[4] The historical basis of this derivation is pre-Homeric tribal society, with its collective distribution of food, land, and spoils. One's lot or fate was the share one was "allotted" by the tribe, often after an actual casting of lots (as at several points in the *Iliad*) designed to ensure impartiality.[5] Whether *moira* retained some of the force of an *equal* share, as George Thomson suggests, linking the term to the notion of primitive communism, or indicated primarily a share appropriate to the honor of the recipient, there is no doubt that it conveyed the authority of the community as a whole to distribute its wealth. Thus it constructs what is for later centuries a bizarre image of an unalienated fate, motivated if not necessarily manageable by the interests of the community.

This image coexists from the outset with the more familiar notion of fate as an alien, incomprehensible agency. As the tribe gave way to the state, as people lost their "share" in society, *moira* lost ground to *Ananke,* the dark, personified Necessity that, in Plato at least, seems to have been modeled after the dark inequality of the slave system.[6] But in Homer the earlier constellation of meanings persists, thanks perhaps to "the archaizing tendencies of the poet, who is looking back towards a lost world he is trying to recall."[7] These meanings concentrate around certain ceremonies which are sometimes clearly vestigial, like the casting of lots, and sometimes overlap inconspicuously with random everyday life. The major instance of the latter is feasting. In the Prometheus myth, the fall of man from the Golden Age into mortal strife results from an unequal distribution of shares: at a *dais* "feast"—from *daiomai* "divide, apportion, allot"—Prometheus cheats the gods out of their proper share of meat (*moira*), thus deciding our collective fate. As Gregory Nagy shows, this theme is central as well to the overall story of the Trojan War.[8] The trouble with which the *Iliad* begins results from a fateful apportionment of spoils that leaves Achilles offended with his share. And in the *Odyssey,* which opens with the improper feasting in Ithaca, there is a strong pastoral motif of restored harmony which renews the connection between feasting, fate, and the Golden Age. This motif helps explain not only Odysseus' "unusual alacrity in coming to feasts" but also why servants should figure so prominently in his recognition.[9]

Before the foot-washing scene, Odysseus has already been recognized by another of his servants, and in the course of a feast. The swineherd Eumaios tells him, "Eat now, stranger, what we serving men are permitted to eat: young pigs, but the fattened swine are devoured by the suitors." After hearing the stranger's tale of troubles, Eumaios changes his mind. They will have a fattened pig after all.

> Thereafter
> the glorious swineherd gave the word to his own companions:
> "Bring in the best of the pigs, to sacrifice for our stranger
> guest from afar, and we ourselves shall enjoy it, we who
> long have endured this wretched work for the pigs with
> shining teeth,
> while others at no cost eat up what we have worked on.[10]

Eumaios' hospitable gesture has an apocalyptic excess. In its generosity it delivers the right to enjoy the fruits of the land to everyone, Odysseus and servingmen alike. When the seemingly unturnable fate of those who do "wretched work" and the soon-to-be-ended sufferings of the man of many turns are brought together in this way on the eve of Odysseus' restitution, that restitution becomes a larger thing. One might say that it is shared, or even appropriated, by those whose hospitality prefigures it. At any rate, such an appropriation is suggested by the dormant but still dazzling pun that immediately follows. Distributing the shares of meat (*moirai*), the "generous swineherd" gives the chine, the lord's portion, to his ragged lord. In the name of the community he self-consciously represents, the servant unconsciously hands his master his "fate" (14:432–438).

Even in the popular genres, this image of the servant as agent of an archaic fate that asserts the ultimate power of the community and presses obscurely toward social inclusiveness is nowhere (to my knowledge) fully specified and elaborated. But given the analytical tool of this ideal type, it is possible to construct and construe commonplace materials that are both fragmentary and, by their very repetitiveness, likely modules for some interpretive structure. In the folktales analyzed by Vladimir Propp, for example, the hero's unrecognized return involves "serving as an apprentice" or "as a cook or a groom." Only after this stage of servitude can the hero pass his ordeal and triumph. Earlier in the tale, he acquires the powers necessary to defeat the villain—the step which, as Fredric Jameson observes, is the tale's true center, "responsible for the 'storiness' of the story in the first place"—only by acquiring a "magic helper," and in order to obtain the magic helper he again has to go through a stage of social descent or dependence.[11] Hero and donor meet on terms of equality, and it is at this moment that the hero receives the strength he lacks at the outset.

This commonplace shapes the scene with Euryclea as well. The ragged, as-yet-unrecognized master has sunk to a low point, and when recognition occurs, there is a sudden, exceptional moment of equality or identification between the temporarily dispossessed Odysseus and a servant who, as we are abruptly encouraged to see, is structurally dispossessed. Power has been redistributed. As Odysseus acknowledges, Euryclea holds the power to destroy him: "Nurse, why are you trying to kill me?" (19:482). This is not an isolated instance. Momentary dissolutions of hierarchy on the same model fill the second half of the *Odyssey*. Tracing what he calls an "attendance motif" through "the whole episode of Odysseus' revelation-and-enactment of his identity, the dénouement of the epic," Michael Nagler concludes that "symbolic change of position with the servants" is at the heart of "the hero's resumption of his social authority." In fact Nagler identifies "a key interchange of master and servant as the center of the *anagnorisis*": "in his beggar's role, just at the point where he first asserts his authority to rectify the social disorder of his house, [Odysseus] 'bears' a torch for his own vassals: . . . 'I shall furnish the light for all these' (18:317)."[12]

In sociological terms, this motif traces the coordinates of those who by virtue of their rank are customarily attended—*ouk oios,* "not alone." But it clearly does something else as well. From a historical perspective that does not assume, as Auerbach does, the calm stability of the Homeric world, the servants who so oddly surround Odysseus' homecoming might appear as oblique defenders of the dying system of kingship, which was "the agent of the community principle."[13] In defending Odysseus against the suitors, his servants would also be defending the people of Ithaca against a rapacious, expropriating aristocracy. Odysseus would in fact be the agent of his servants, then, both in the formal sense—their recognition places him back at the head of the community, restores to him his *moira,* empowers him— and in the sense that his restoration could be associated with the return or renewal of traditional popular rights to the land. Eumaios' complaints have a historical basis; already the pressures of debt, expropriation, and the monopolization of agrarian property were growing that would make "the debt-ridden farmer" a "universal figure" and would lead to the later slogan of *isomoiria,* equal shares and equal fates.[14] From the time of Homer on, M. I. Finley writes, "the poor man's counter-ideology" remained constant: "With absolute regularity, all through Greek history, the demand was 'Cancel debts and redistribute the land.'"[15]

Popular indignation at the mortgaging and alienation of land can be documented beginning at the point when these practices were a fresh scandal. Indeed, in the light of Homer's recognition scene it is intriguing that this outrage expressed itself precisely by identifying debt-ridden farmers with humiliated slaves: someone whose land was mortgaged was called *stigmatias,* a branded slave.[16] And it is also intriguing, in the light of the extraordinary repetitiveness of the recognition scene, that this outrage is also so repetitive. If the transition from kingship to aristocracy is specific to the early archaic period when the *Odyssey* was composed, and thus is disqualified from accounting for so repetitive a phenomenon as the recognition scene, the distress of small farmers threatened with expulsion from their ancestral lands is, as Finley says, regular and even universal. And the same terms apply to the appeal by such farmers against their expropriators, an appeal backwards to a traditional image of social justice that is seen as an ultimate arbiter whose real if latent powers remain greater than those of the strongmen of the moment. This appeal could remain relatively constant over the centuries because the hegemonic system that upheld it, which both articulated a ruling-class ideology and gave those who appealed against it some ground for hope and resistance, also remained relatively constant. The lack of minute historical differentiation takes nothing away from its historical reality. Thus there is no scanting of history when, for example, we detect a whiff of archaic justice pervading the brief moments when Euryclea and Eumaios live out their literary existence, or when Ernst Bloch suggests that Odysseus' homecoming as "a savior in the form of a servant" stretches out "a tenuous reference to the Golden Age."[17] Like the pastness of other alternative societies, the Golden Age belongs to the realm of rhetoric. As Bakhtin says, "a thing that could and in fact must only be realized in the *future* is here protrayed as something out of the *past,* a thing that is in no sense part of the past's reality, but a thing that is in its essence a purpose, an obligation."[18] But this rhetoric is itself part of the reality of the past as well as the present, attached both to the distress it represents and to the shared tradition, or residual ideology, that gives it force.

CRITICISM OF THE COMMONPLACE

I am proposing that in leveling servant and master at the threshold of the master's restitution, the recognition scene produces an abridged, transient utopia—a place of displacement, a "nowhere" emerging within ideology and yet prefiguring very different social arrangements. This utopia is also a *topos,* a commonplace. And its recurrence can in some measure be understood by relating it to the recurrence, on the same historical scale, of a traditional rhetoric of popular self-defense. This interpretation connects an ultimate sharing in common to an ultimate fatefulness in order to compose precisely what Auerbach is looking for: a literary representation of the people. And yet it can do so only by breaking up the reciprocal definition of the "real" and the "historical" that guides his quest for the people.

In his exile, Auerbach tried to see Western literature as a single historical entity, a whole, and much of the power of what he has to say about individual texts stems from the overarching narrative of European literary and social destiny in which he makes those texts participate. From Homer to Virginia Woolf, literature has gradually overcome barriers of prejudice and convention. Despite some areas of lingering neglect, it continues to pursue its inexorable, progressive inclusion of hitherto excluded realities, aiming finally at the most excluded reality of all, the people. This is not a mere parallel with the extension of European democracy. The real is invested with value for Auerbach not for itself alone but because it leads to a democratic finale, because of the providential history that, for him as for Orwell, associates the progressive assimilation of the real to a progressive movement toward egalitarianism. But providential history also devalues and suppresses premature or untimely manifestations of that which it reserves for the end. There exist resources of political precedent that cannot be perceived at all if they cannot be neatly placed in an upward trajectory. Inattentive to the contingency of history, this vision squanders its available energies. These are often to be recovered only by searching out a logic, like Foucault or the *Annales* historians, in what appear to be trivial, unbearably repetitive patterns of everyday life, in the sub-historical constants usually canceled out in favor of more momentous variables. The difficulty lies in learning to conceive of history in such a way that the concept no longer excludes repetition, but registers its vitality. As Edward Said writes, "repetition is useful as a way of showing that history and actuality are all about human persistence, and not about divine originality."[19]

A providential scheme of history both defers and guarantees the value to be salvaged from the literature of the past. The absence of the people, for example, is compensated by an ultimate and continuously guiding presence of the essentially human. But if history is no longer to be organized around a final, blindingly transcendent consummation that throws so much inessential human effort into the shadow, then we have to learn to find value in unaccustomed things and out of the way places. This accounts for certain differences between the approach here and earlier criticism of the literary servant. Among the formal consequences of accepting this challenge, for instance, is the impossibility of ordering the study around individual authors. Floating freely in literary tradition, servants are unusually difficult to anchor in an authorial origin. Though I began with the *Odyssey,* the search for a collective origin might be pushed farther back. (In *Gilgamesh,* the character who kills the monster Huwawa, provoking the wrath of Enlil and turning folktale into tragedy, is the hero's companion in the Babylonian version but his servant in the earlier

Sumerian version.) In Plautus and Terence servants are Greek, in Shakespeare and Molière they advertise their descent from Plautus or the *commedia dell'arte* or popular folklore. In the novel, they are borrowed from all of these sources. A sort of permanent residue, always already anachronistic, they seem inseparable from precedent, convention, self-conscious literariness.

To locate value in an author's privileged perception or original transformation of his or her materials is not necessarily to ignore the fact of recurrence. But it is to limit criticism's moves. Most often, recurrence is simply formalized as "influence." The effort is to distinguish the elements in author X that can be attributed to the influence of literary models from those elements that faithfully transcribe the actuality of the time, for which credit is alone awarded. Thus Shakespeare receives praise for "Anglicizing" the Roman and Italian servant types at his disposal, and Plautus is denigrated as a mere translator of (or esteemed for transcending) his lost Greek originals. The author's "borrowings" must either be acknowledged at his expense (perhaps mitigated by the notion that after all subordination is everywhere alike) or else minimized, and as much as possible attributed to the author's realism. These answers seem to wander away from the more interesting questions.

It is true that servants seem to enjoy a strange intimacy with their authors. Many have been taken for their author's mouthpiece: didn't Molière act the part of Scapin? didn't Jacques speak for Diderot? They have even been confused with their author: Figaro equals "fils Caron" equals Beaumarchais. But this peculiar authority is too generalized, too regular, and too provocative to be attributed to the whims of individual authors. Its sources must be sought elsewhere. And it is because of this authority, along with other effects which are equally repetitive and equally uncanny, that this study also cannot seek its coherence in servant *characters*. It is not that characters do not recur. They do, as a glance at the critical literature of the great comic periods will attest. The problem is that, forced into the mold of character, servants reveal so little worth investigating. Criticism on the subject is like a stroll down an endless gallery of look-alikes: each portrait is the same all-too-loyal retainer, sharing his master's conviction of natural hierarchy and aiming complaints only at his own somewhat ambiguous place in it. A recent critic of Shakespeare goes to the trouble of declaring that the servants of the comedies "make possible the continued liberty of the aristocrats while relinquishing [their] own autonomy," that the fairy servants of *A Midsummer Night's Dream* "demonstrate pure service," and that old Adam in *As You Like It* "endorses the aristocratic ideal of a static social hierarchy."[20] These are partial truths, but they would be worth repeating only if there were good reason to expect something quite different. It is only if literature can be expected, for example, to display "collective popular activity" as "capable of sophisticated organization, political analysis, and of articulating the need for change" that it is possible to dismiss the rebellious servant who joins the Gordon Riots in *Barnaby Rudge* as "a comic but reactionary character seeking not to change the nature of society but merely to reverse the familial roles."[21]

The absolute fixity of these results invites us to relativize the perspective that generates them. Why *characters*? What is hidden in Auerbach's and Orwell's identification of "reality" with character? In the representation of the people, the call for decorous consistency of character has commonly meant nothing more than conformity to certain pre-established and reassuring models. It was the revolutionary absence of character in this sense that so irritated the neo-Aristotelian Francis Jeffrey when he encountered the poor folk of the *Lyrical Ballads*. Character was the mask the people were expected to don in the face of power; it was a way of making them hold still and be judged. It seems more than coincidence therefore that from the time of Pope and Addison, when modern criticism took shape, a "character" was a statement in which one employer described to another employer the habits and qualities of a servant, vouching for and thus controlling such key traits as honesty, chastity, sobriety, and industriousness. Fielding, who set up with his brother a Registry Office where, they claimed, reliable servants could be hired, joined Defoe in the general outcry for stricter controls over these testimonials. He denounced "the unjust Characters given of Servants; an Order of People, who are moved out of one Station into another, and are admitted into Places of Trust according to their Recommendations": "one would imagine that half of the Masters and Mistresses of this Kingdom, by the Characters they give of their Servants, live in fear of, and are dependent upon them. I declare for the Future, that whoever acts in my Family in the Capacity of Servant shall, when he or she leaves it, have that Character from me which their Behavior entitles them to, be it good, bad, or indifferent."[22] Characters must be made standard, obligatory, exact; how else could employers feel safe from the strangers they were taking into their homes? The character was—and the first English novelists acknowledged it to be—a "labor passport," a means of policing the borders of respectable society by restricting the movements of class aliens.

In view of the fact that, as far as the people are concerned, criticism's demand for "character" has been a demand for social immobility, it becomes more interesting to note that this demand has gone unsatisfied. Histories of the great comic periods, in an effort to trace a movement from one sort of servant character to another, have tended to break their material down into two psychologically or morally consistent types—most often, some version of the trickster and the buffoon, the self-conscious wit and the unconscious butt. Around these hypothetical poles they have built their classifications and sequences. In the comic valets of Molière's century, Jean Emelina observes "an incontestable rise of knavery . . . to the detriment of stupidity and churlishness," the same development that Charles Mauron finds in the slave role from the Old Comedy of Aristophanes to the New Comedy of Menander, including Plautus and Terence.[23] The reverse trajectory, from servant-as-trickster to servant-as-dupe, is given by Victor Bourgy as characteristic of the English comedy of the sixteenth century: "the growing fashion for a buffoon-type opposite to the Vice, namely the simpleton, the ridiculous lout who is easy to dupe." It is also, according to a number of authorities, part of Terence's revision of Plautus as well as a disputed version of Terence's own career.[24]

However, these attempts to impose distinct and consistent "characters" on their servant material run into stiff resistance. In almost every case, classifications and sequences founder at one point or another over the servant's apparently irreducible inconsistency. Commenting on the usual praise of Terence "for his unconventional treatment of the intriguing slave"—for example, keeping the slave deceived or offstage—Duckworth tries to defend the purity of the type of transferring impurities to another: "A slave like Parmeno in the *Hecyra* derives, not from the traditional intriguing slave, but from the loyal slave." On the other hand, he also admits that loyalty always coexisted with intrigue, and, finally, that the type itself was always mixed: "Slaves are deceived in Plautus."²⁵ In a similar defense of consistency, Bourgy denies that there are buffoon-like "traces of gluttony and lasciviousness" in the Vice and refuses the idea of a link between "the fundamental simplicity of the clown" and "the cunning and intriguing spirit" of the Vice and his descendant, the "tricky servant." But he also concedes that there is "a whole current of protest, and even of social demands, that is expressed by . . . the clowns," and of course that the Vice, carried off at the end on the devil's back, is the dupe of the Christian dénouement.²⁶ The *commedia dell'arte* furnishes a final example. K. M. Lea distinguishes between two *zanni*—"one astute and witty servant to attend to the plot and another to play the awkward booby"—and then reproachfully traces their merger. But not before confessing that "the parts are not thus stably related. The fool has flashes of ingenuity, the knave his blind side. In practice, the zanni are to each other as the two parts of an hour-glass; there is just so much wit, or sand, between them, and as time and place shall serve it is variously distributed."²⁷

In the period of the novel, as "character" is assuming an ever more privileged critical position, the rationale for this resistance to characterization becomes more obvious. The hermeneutic openness of *Pamela,* for example, which criticism sought to close off by constructing a "Shamela" it could then indict, is a structural fact of servitude. As in the other servant-narrated works of the picaresque tradition, like *Lazarillo de Tormes,* it stems from "the necessary dissimulation of the poor when obliged to give an account of themselves . . . to the rich and powerful."²⁸ This is why, as a critic notes about Lázaro, the "reader's interpretation . . . oscillates between two views of what is there—the inadvertent admissions of a dehumanized victim or the contrivances of a mask-wearing trickster": "Lázaro must be seen either as a victim or as a deceiver; in the reader's eyes, the narrator cannot be both at the same time, and yet both interpretations of the text are possible."²⁹ Characterlessness cannot be read, in other words, simply as a deprivation or failure of representation. Its consequences are such as the poor and powerless might have willed: to evade critical surveillance, to smuggle expressive possibilities around those checkpoints that criticism has most vigilantly guarded. The convention that William Empson calls "Comic Primness," which rules out questions of whether the "comic people" mean what they say or of "how much they and how much the author has put into their ironies," means that the servant cannot be held responsible for his or her barbed puns and mockeries.[30] Historical criticism of a strictly referential sort, which demands a hard-and-fast distinction between "the jokes of the simpleton" and "those of the sham," must usually confess that in practice this distinction is "very badly respected."[31] In the words of *Rob Roy*'s Andrew Fairservice, "Drunk or mad? nae doubt . . . ane's aye drunk or mad if he tells what grit folks dinna like to her." The radical indeterminacy of servant character at least permits, if it does not oblige, the articulation of "what grit folks dinna like."

This brings us back to the problem of recurrence. How can "what grit folks dinna like" be both historically specified and made pertinent to the literature of widely separated times and places? Faced with so much recurrence, the temptation has been strong to conclude that there cannot be any pointed or offensive questioning of the powers that be. Thus critics who have corrected judged these materials incoherent at the level of referentiality and character have tended to move their interpretations away from history altogether, or—the two are not mutually exclusive—to take the absolute dominance of the status quo for granted. One of the most familiar readings in this vein is that which passes from the indeterminacy of servant characterization to the conclusion that indeterminacy or relativism is precisely the point.

A precocious instance is the influential work of William Empson. Looking back at the literature of Europe from the Far East, as Auerbach was to do from Istanbul, Empson saw (again like Auerbach) that the breakdown of distinct genres and stylistic levels could be correlated with the rise of the lower classes. In *Some Versions of Pastoral* (1935) he showed that the penetration of pastoral into a variety of genres had been accompanied by pastoral's characteristic theme: the tension between the rich and the poor. A prime example was the double plot of Renaissance drama, in which masters were "doubled" by their servants. But in Empson's interpretation the double plot is less a step toward literary democracy than a formal stronghold for his skeptical relativism. When servants duplicate their masters' doings, he says, the criticism of the masters is only apparent, a "pseudo-parody to disarm criticism." The real aim is to convince the reader "that he can rely on your judgement because you know both sides of the case." Which means that pastoral is arguing, finally, against all partisanship ("a plague on both their houses") and against all certainties—in short, for the ultimate ambiguity of all values. At the same time, however, Empson can speak of servant-master doubling as representing "a proper or beautiful relation between rich and poor."[32] In the meantime, for the (seemingly limitless) duration of our present uncertainty, he puts the weight of the impartial, relativist author behind an idealization of the present social order. His relativism is thus a detour: by walking resolutely away from historical partisanship, Empson arrives back at the status quo.

Without a better hold on history, the interpreter can only, it seems, surround the status quo with a philosophical generality that will then crumble away, leaving behind the solid social hierarchy it began by relativizing. The same process can be observed in Leo Spitzer's "perspectivist" reading of *Don Quixote*. Spitzer declares:

the numerous dialogues between the knight and the squire . . . are inserted into the novel in order to show the different perspectives under which the same events must appear to two persons of such different backgrounds. This means that, in our novel, things are represented, not for what they are in themselves but only as things spoken about or thought about. . . . There can be no certainty about the "unbroken" reality of the events.

But Spitzer at once goes on to argue that "perspectivism suggests an Archimedean principle outside of the plot—and the Archimedes must be Cervantes himself." "Cervantes" then resolves into "the teachings of the Catholic Church and the established order of state and society."[33] The point is worth stressing, since some form of "perspectivism" has continued to be one of the critic's first reflexes when confronted with the literary servant—for example, in Robert Alter's account of *Jacques le fataliste* or Milan Kundera's more recent treatment of both it and *Don Quixote*.[34]

If the elision of history encourages criticism to slide from a philosophical relativism to an affirmation of things as they are, an insistence on historical specificity is no guarantee of more satisfactory results. The sort of nineteenth-century scholarship that declared it had found the inspiration for Molière's soubrettes in Molière's maidservant La Fôret is only an extreme case of the tendency to achieve specificity by falling into triviality. A more frequent version is the answering of questions such as whether servants were under-represented or over-represented, in proportion to their numbers in society, by the theater of a given author. And where the results are not simply trivial, a determination not to let go of historical particulars often finds itself plunged into recurrence of a inadvertent and embarrassing kind. The servants of Shakespeare for instance are described as faithful reflections of the servants of Elizabethan England, who were "in transition from a feudal to a modern basis."[35] But this transition had been going on for some time, and it did not end with Shakespeare. An acute essay on the servants of Dickens comes to the same conclusion, but this time makes it specific to Victorian England: "his portrayals of domestic servants and their masters embody the contradictions in the actual historical predicament of the domestic servant in Victorian England, the conflicting pulls of paternalism and the 'free market in labor' which at that historical moment created this extreme class tension."[36] That the collapse of a paternalistic model of mutual obligation and the rise of a self-interested, contractual view can be observed both in Dickens and in Shakespeare is not an insuperable objection to the argument about either one. But it does seem to call for a change of focus. It is when the critic stakes everything on claims for what is specific to one "historical moment" that the reader's conviction is liable to falter. If misleading exactitude is not to weaken the persuasiveness of historical criticism as a whole, the vast, gradual, repetitive nature of the social process in question should be conceded, and conclusions about it should be generalized accordingly or reformulated.

UNTIMELINESS AND THE NOVEL

As the critic of Dickens quoted above confesses, Dickens' novels "most often" do *not* represent the contradictory position of the mid-Victorian domestic. What they do with servants is for the most part closer to "farce."[38] Most of the servant's literary existence, that is, belongs to that level of "non-representational" functionality that realism can only dismiss, the "farce" together with the recognition scene. But this is what is there, and what demands to be accounted for, all the more because of its paradoxical persistence into the realist novel itself.

For the purposes of the novel, as for the literary tradition that precedes it, the field of objects that I call "servants" refers less to an occupational group defined, outside of slavery, as non-kin paid to perform menial work in the house than to the conjunction of that group with a certain body of aesthetic functions, a repertory of gags and tags, expedients for pointing a moral or moving a plot, that cling to it with uncanny fidelity. The use of master-servant dialogue to provoke laughter, while more subdued in print than on the stage, is one clear continuity. Another is the use of all those surrogates, doubles, parallels, and parodies who extend the protagonist's identity, duplicating but also displacing and amplifying it. The recognition scene reappears in all those plots where a crew of missing heirs, as Kipling put it, "shipped as Able Bastards till the Wicked Nurse confessed,/and they worked the old three-decker to the Islands of the Blest." Among the most familiar and, upon reflection, the strangest narrative devices bestowed upon social subordinates is the transmission of the story: the bits of useful exposition scattered as the curtain rises, the crucial confidences stage-whispered or fished out via *ficelle,* the narrators, observers, informants, and messengers who embody the classical adage that "no man is a hero to his *valet de chambre*" so successfully that the point of view of the novel itself, as Harry Levin notes, "has often been associated with the servant in the house."[38] Finally, there is intervention in the story: the slave or servant who interferes with superb arbitrariness in plots devoted to the destinies of his or her superiors. When Coleridge praised *Tom Jones* along with *The Alchemist* and *Oedipus Tyrannus* as "the three most perfect plots ever planned," he was speaking, strangely enough, of three plots in which the fate of the masters is placed in the hands of their servants.[39]

The extraordinary scale of this conjunction has become visible thanks in large part to Auerbach's grandiose project of chronicling the democratization of Western literature. But as a repetitive, non-representational disturbance within his history, it could only appear as an affront to historicality itself. And all the more so in the novel, initially defined as a bearer of news and novelty and still one of our central monuments to modernity and progressiveness. The double challenge taken up here is to establish connections between servant functionality and history, and at the same time to establish these connections such that they remain relevant to the presence of that functionality both in the novel and in the literary tradition from which the novel borrowed. The suggestion that a popular appeal to old traditions against new threats is the background of the servant's otherwise inexplicable involvement in the recognition scene attempts to satisfy the first requirements. But to what extent can it satisfy the second? Across such a temporal span, can it be relevant in any way to the servant functionality of the novel?

Aggressively vestigial, reminders of earlier literature and earlier society, servants might be described in general terms as repetitions of the premodern within and against the novel's modernity. But this congenital backwardness can be made more precise. Eric Hobsbawm writes, "the proletarian whose only link with his employer is a 'cash nexus' must be distinguished from the 'servant' or pre-industrial dependent, who has a much more complex human and social relationship with his 'master,' and one which implies duties on both sides, though very unequal ones. The Industrial Revolution replaced the servant and man by the 'operative' and 'hand,' except of course the (mainly female) domestic servant, whose numbers it multiplied for the benefit of the growing middle class.[40] In precapitalist society, *all* subordination was articulated by forms of personal, reciprocal obligations; all laborers were servants. In the process of creating a landless working class, free (that is, compelled) to sell its labor and thus ruled by the impersonal forces of the market, capitalism and its "harsh profit-and-loss purgatives"—in E. P. Thompson's words—voided the body politic of old notions of duty, mutuality, and paternal care."[41] The modern domestic, whose position continued to be defined by such notions, became an anachronism: the most conspicuous surviving type of preindustrial dependency.

Little by little this anomaly disappeared. Servants too began to be assimilated to contractual, "cash-nexus" thinking, and even at times to take it over as a weapon. Like recent feminists who have sought an acknowledgment of the value of housework by demanding wages for it, wages being our society's acknowledgement of value, some servants advanced the political economists' "labor-as-commodity" thesis in an effort to protect themselves against the degradations that paternalism had helped obscure and protect.[42] But the parallel goes one crucial step further. As Joan Scott and Louise Tilly show in "Women's Work and the Family in Nineteenth-Century Europe," domestic servants came from the country to the city. "Two-thirds of all the domestic servants in England in 1851 were daughters of rural laborers." They brought with them a powerful set of familial, preindustrial values. But these values did not hold them back from entering the new industrial world, as one might have expected; they helped make it possible for these women to confront it. If these servants are exemplary participants in the transition to modernity, they are also exemplary of "the continuity of traditional values and behavior in changing circumstances. Old values coexists with and are used by people to adapt to structural changes.[43] The village traditions that Scott and Tilly call "familial" might as well be described as "paternalistic" or even "feudal," to use the terms most often evoked in ideological characterizations of the servant. And their reversal of unthinking progressivism holds here as well. There was certainly much truth in the familiar conservative stereotype of the servant: unquestioning acceptance of constituted authority, insistence on the marks of precedence, appeal only to the master's personal, paternal benevolence. And there is no doubt that it was comforting for the masters to believe the working class as a whole was nothing more than a nation of servants. But it is also true that such beliefs on both sides were a double-edged sword. An ideology that, like "paternalism," takes the family with its reciprocal obligations as well as its hierarchy for a social model can then be appealed to by the lowly (without incurring the risk of calling their lowliness into question) as a standard to judge present abuses and a source of retribution against them. If the cash nexus served as a weapon against paternalism, paternalism also served as a weapon against the cash nexus.

As Scott and Tilly point out, the widely dispersed and otherwise quite different areas of Europe where there was a "peasant or familial economy . . . offer strikingly similar descriptions of peasant social organization." There was little variation in the "solidarity" that pro-vided "the basic framework for mutual aid, control, and socializa-tion," a model of authority that could be invoked so as to put pressure on those in authority (p. 44). Focusing on the continuities of peasant life, it is a reasonable hypothesis—though this is *longue durée* with a vengeance—that what was said about the *Odyssey*'s recognition scene may well be pertinent to the many scenes and devices in later literature that resemble it. There is a level of history on which the vitality of repetitions, especially in the service of lost causes, has to be acknowledged. In *The Country and the City,* one of the rare books that can compare with *Mimesis* in scope and power, Raymond Williams shows that the demise of the "organic community" of rural England, which Leavis and others had taken for a recent, dramatic event, is in fact a historical constant. Climbing on an "escalator," Williams fol-lows this supposed event further and further away, moving "'Old England' and its timeless agricultural rhythms back from the early twentieth century to the middle of the eighteenth century" and then back to Virgil, Hesiod's *Works and Days,* and finally Eden. "Is it any-thing more than a well-known habit of using the past, the 'good old days,' as a stick to beat the present?"[44] In Williams' view it is. Hesiod's myth of a Golden Age exists in tension with his own "iron age," which "determines his recommendation of practical agriculture, social justice, and neighborliness" (p. 24). In Virgil's *Eclogues,* "the pastoral singing is directly related to the hopes and fears of the small farmers under threat of confiscation of their land" (p. 27). Which is to say that when the idyllic or idealizing use of the rural past becomes an image "of the future: of a restoration, a second coming, of the golden age," we must read backwards to the "threat of loss and eviction" (pp. 27–28). The effect of Williams' critique of the idealiza-tion of the land and its vanished traditions is not simply to differenti-ate this homogeneous mass. Though he adds unpleasant realities to the picture, close attention to historical detail leads him on the contrary to compose and substitute an alternative picture that is nearly as constant: the picture of what E. P. Thompson calls a "moral economy" of mutual charity and protection, insistence on "fair" wages and prices, appeal to the authority of the community, a tradition which was threatened, continually and repetitively, with "loss and eviction" and yet which remained a source of possible appeal to rural inhabitants from Hesiod through the nineteenth century.[45]

It is less outlandish than it seems, therefore, to suggest that the recurrence of the literary servant can be linked to comparably persistent facts of long-term disturbance in traditional society and traditional ideology. Bakhtin has traced the servant's formal continuity through what he calls "idyll": "The most recent influence of the idyll on the novel," he writes, is the "fragmentary penetration of isolated elements" like the "'man of the people.'" "Of just such a sort is the servant in Walter Scott . . . in Dickens, in the French novel (from Maupassant's *Une Vie* to Françoise in Proust)."[46] The point is an important one. Despite the enormous stretches of time and space over which Bakhtin effortlessly glides, his identification of Dickens' servants with "idyll" in fact produces a more precise and convincing reading of Dickens' rhetoric than those descriptions of the "feudal type," in Orwell and elsewhere, that make a show (or a fetish) of historical specificity.

Consider for example the functions of servant regressiveness in *Our Mutual Friend*. Silas Wegg, servant of sorts to Mr. Boffin (himself a former butler), begins the novel as a seller of ballads and gingerbread on a London street corner. However, he prefers to imagine this place on the unprotected market, open to the winds of supply-and-demand, in the cosily anachronistic terms of fedual patronage:

He had not only settled it with himself in course of time, that he was errand-goer by appointment to the house at the corner . . . but also that he was one of the house's retainers and owed vasselage to it and was bound to leal and loyal interest in it. For this reason, he always spoke of it as 'Our House,' and, though his knowledge of its affairs was mostly speculative and all wrong, claimed to be in its confidence. . . . Yet, he knew so little about its inmates that he gave them names of his own invention: as 'Miss Elizabeth,' 'Master George,' 'Aunt Jane,' 'Uncle Parker.'[47]

When Boffin takes over "Our House," Wegg does in fact become one of its retainers. Unsatisfied by this arrangement, he drops his feudal devotion to assume the role of would-be villain, plotting to expropriate his master. His efforts to move the plot are foiled, and Boffin tries to dismiss him at the end of the novel with a small present. Like other comic entertainers, however, Wegg seems to have an invisible hold over both his master and his author that makes him difficult to dispose of.

"I shouldn't like to leave you, after all said and done, worse off in life than I found you. Therefore say in a word, before we part, what it'll cost to set you up in another stall."

"Mr. Boffin," returned Wegg in avaricious humiliation,: "when I first had the honor of making your acquaintance, I had got together a collection of ballads which was, I may say, above price."

"But it's difficult to name what's right," said Boffin uneasily, with his hand in his pocket . . .

"There was also," Wegg went on, in a meditative manner, "a errand connection, in which I was much respected. But I would not wish to be deemed covetous, and I would rather leave it to you, Mr. Boffin."

"Upon my word, I don't know what to put it at," the Golden Dustman muttered.

"There was likewise," resumed Wegg, "a pair of trestles, for which alone a Irish person, who was deemed a judge of trestles, offered five and six—a sum I would not hear of, for I should have lost by it—and there was a stool, a umbrella, a clothes-horse, and a tray. But I leave it to you, Mr. Boffin. . . . There was, further, Miss Elizabeth, Master George, Aunt Jane, and Uncle Parker. Ah! When a man thinks of the loss of such patronage as that; when a man finds so fair a garden rooted up by pigs; he finds it hard indeed, without going too high, to work it into money. But I leave it wholly to you, sir." (bk. 4. ch. 14)

As this inventory of sacrifices goes on—and we are not at the end yet—it acquires a significance that is independent of Wegg's character and motives. Wegg's archaic attachment to Miss Elizabeth and her family is of course a bargaining point which permits a certain ridicule of the paternalist version of master-servant relations. On his corner or in the house, Wegg is in fact ruled not by deference but by money; the feudal tie is a figment of his imagination. On the other hand, the awkwardness and profundity of the humor here have to do with the impossibility, in this dialogue, of not supporting the figments of imagination against the (corrupting) power of money that is opposed to them. Boffin, who is on the side of silence, is trying to close off a human relation with "a couple of pound"—to substitute for his servant's loquacious, seemingly infinite demands a sort of "cash nexus." Against this background, the reader is provoked into alliance with imagination, which gives Wegg all the good lines along with Dickens' own power to lift the housetops off, and the paternalist fantasy of "Our House." Though it is only a fantasy, and an anachronistic one, though our complicity with it is only momentary, there is more for us in "Our House" than in the "cash nexus" that supersedes it. In the entertainer's loving pause over Miss Elizabeth, Master George, Aunt Jane, and Uncle Parker, the incongruous rhetoric of comedy carries with it the disturbing incongruity of the old non-contractual reciprocities, and thus shakes up the ending with the glimpse of an end that has not been achieved.

My point here is that in addition to the scene's historically specific elements—Boffin's *nouveau riche* vulnerability, Wegg as the "new" servant who defends himself by playing the capitalist game, converting everything into commodities—recurrent elements that are more difficult to specify, yet indispensable for an understanding of the politics of the literary servant, are introduced by the functioning of comic archaism. The fantasy of "Our House" may be factually regressive, but when comedy forces it on us the effect can be critical, anticipatory, progressive. Ernst Bloch calls such effects "non-synchronous" (*ungleichzeitig*).[48] In making room for them within the political representations of realist fiction, I am trying, like Bloch, to make room beside the "real" for the positive unreality of utopianism, a contribution to social cognition that relativizes and de-realizes in order to recall that things might well be otherwise.

THE BROWN STOCKING

The first two hundred years of the English novel, let us say from *Robinson Crusoe* (1719) to *To the Lighthouse* (1927), make up a unit large enough to permit me to generalize about the literary servant's persistence without being so large as to require detailed differentiation or periodization. To make recurrence my focus is not of course to suggest that nothing of significance changes from Defoe to Woolf. For Woolf, indeed, servants are a crucial (if also comic) indicator of how much *has* changed. In her modernist manifesto, "Mr. Bennett and

Mrs. Brown," she writes: "In life one can see the change, if I may use a homely illustration, in the character of one's cook. The Victorian cook lived like a leviathan in the lower depths, formidable, silent, obscure, inscrutable; the Georgian cook is a creature of sunshine and fresh air; in and out of the drawing room, now to borrow the *Daily Herald,* now to ask advice about a hat. Do you ask for more solemn instances of the power of the human race to change than that?"[49] The world that had furnished Crusoes with submissive Fridays seems to be finished, and servants usher in an apocalyptic modernity: "The nineteenth century going to bed, Martin said to himself as he watched her hobble down the steps on the arm of her footman."[50]

In order to trace this curve, Auerbach's narrative frame is still useful. In the eighteenth century the emergent novel inherited a stock of popular types and devices from the comic stage, where novelists like Fielding, Lesage, and Marivaux had done their apprenticeship. This vestige of the separation of styles persists. Scott and Dickens were still borrowing their servants from Elizabethan drama directly as well as indirectly through preceeding novelists. The tradition is dense, rarely interrupted, and almost exhaustive.[51] It is not until the late nineteenth century that there is a decisive break in the equation of the people with theatrical functionality—first, when naturalism discovers the servant's *life* as a subject (e.g., George Moore's *Esther Waters*) and then when modernism throws out theatricality, servants, and "real life" all together. "Living? our servants will do that for us."[52]

Aside from other awkwardnesses, the trouble with this trajectory is that its ends meet. The modernist disdain with which Axel hands down the worn garment of worldly existence to the servants in fact clings to their surrogacy from the beginnings of theatrical tradition. In this domain, the horizontal progressiveness of literary history is overridden by the vertical invariant of social hierarchy. According to Coleridge, Fielding dissociates Tom Jones' character from his conduct in the same spirit: conduct, or action, is for the servants. "If I want a servant or mechanic, I wish to know what he does:—but of a friend, I must know what he is."[53] This is not substantially different from Thackeray's rationale for his own deployment of functional servants. "I give you my word," he writes in *The Roundabout Papers,* "there seem to be parts of novels—let us say the love-making, the 'business,' the villain in the cup-board, and so forth, which I should like to order the footman to take in hand, as I desire him to bring the coals and polish the boots. Ask *me* indeed to pop a robber under a bed; to hide a will which shall be forthcoming in due season . . . !"[54] Thackeray is willing to bestow the business of robbers and wills on the servants—as he does for example in *Pendennis* and *The Virginians*—because he finds it absurd. Moving to the end of the two hundred year period, E. M. Forster makes a similar remark about Scott's *The Antiquary,* where the truth comes out thanks to the revelations of two servants: "There are indeed plenty of reasons for the *dénouement,* but Scott is not interested in reasons." Since Forster takes the usual causal sequences to be an absurd tyranny—he imagines them as "a sort of higher government official" who bullies interesting characters into making "a contribution to the plot"—the servant who appears, like a *deus ex machina,* solely in order to contribute seems the ultimate absurdity.[55] But when Forster codifies this attitude in *Aspects of the Novel,* he is not just speaking for his fellow moderns. He is defining a tradition of absurdity that extends throughout the English novel. From the beginning, the functional, secondary, second-hand presence of servants in the novel is extraneous, absurd, modernist.

With its high respect for randomness and discontinuity, *Mimesis* is another classic of modernism. Auerbach does not entirely approve what he sees as the modernist demotion of exterior action in favor of inward, subjective life, but he is generous enough to present it as a victory for the randomness he himself believes in. Thus, in the concluding chapter, devoted to *To the Lighthouse* and entitled "The Brown Stocking," he explicates a passage in which Mrs. Ramsay is fitting a stocking on her fidgety son in order to show "the randomness and contingency of the exterior occasion" with respect to the flood of subjectivity it releases. "Nothing of importance in the dramatic sense takes place" (pp. 538–539). But again, as in "Odysseus' Scar," what is offered as random discloses patterns that are shared and fateful and that lead toward an unacknowledged representation of the people. It is clear for example that the "digressions" which fascinate Auerbach here as well do not wander aimlessly away, but circle obsessively around an uncommented center he finds deeply moving. Here the exiled Auerbach's lingering attention to the homecoming of the exiled Odysseus is echoed in the repeated sentence whose force helps close the digression: "At home the mountains are so beautiful." The words are spoken by Mrs. Ramsay's Swiss maid, who has the power to interrupt this digression just as Euryclea provokes the other. She too is in exile, and her exile motivates the apparent randomness of her spare, functional literary presence.

Let us look at the center of the three-and-a-half-page passage that Auerbach explicates. While mending the stocking for the lighthouse keeper's son, Mrs. Ramsay complains to herself of how children and servants are forever leaving the doors of the house open. Then she remembers one of those servants, the Swiss maid, standing at the open window—unlike the others, she insists on leaving her window open, and Mrs. Ramsay approves—and thinking of her father, at home, who is dying of cancer. She recalls the maid saying that the mountains at home are beautiful and that there is no hope. Complaint about the state of the household slips out of Mrs. Ramsay's mind, and her thoughts return to her charitable mending.

Auerbach notes that this is a decisive moment: "it is only when the switch from the open windows to the Swiss maid's words comes, that something happens which lifts the veil a little" (p. 537). What is it that the reader glimpses behind the veil? Presumably what Auerbach has declared several pages earlier: "the cruel meaninglessness of a life whose continuance [Mrs. Ramsay] is nevertheless striving with all her powers to abet, support, and secure" (p. 531). But this meaninglessness is saturated with social logic that seizes upon doors and windows in order to oppose inside and outside, ours and theirs, masters and servants, a wishful openness and a forced enclosure. The passage begins with James fidgeting deliberately because he is jealous, "not liking to serve as measuring-block for the lighthouse keeper's little boy" (p. 525). The central section ends with Mrs. Ramsay's "spasm of irritation" at him, provoked by the memory of the maid at the window. A motif of social exteriority ties together the stocking and the servants. This is to say that subjectivity here is not random; it takes off from and elaborates a confrontation of upper and lower classes. Mrs. Ramsay has been worrying about the degradation of the house, exposed to the open air as it is by a wanton opening of doors for which servants are largely responsible. Why should servants want to open doors, or stand at open windows? Through the exiled maid, the passage transmutes her desire to close off into a desire to open out.

In a closed world, the technique of subjectivism by which ideas "cut loose from the present of the exterior occurence and range freely through the depths of time" (p. 540) might be said to acquire a social or even a utopian function. Here, at any rate, the escape in time converts images of everyday complaint into images of an alternative space: "if every door in a house is left perpetually open . . ." (p. 526). The crucial point is that the modernist disconnection that makes such utopian reconnections possible is not a peculiarly modernist technique at all. It parallels and continues the apparently random, absurd disconnectedness of the whole line. If modernism stands outside literary tradition in time, servants are placed at the margins of its social space. The two share a powerful, destabilizing exteriority.

Woolf may seem an unlikely author in whom to find a servant-specific utopianism, and yet there are places where hints of the recognition scene's ultimate utopian inclusiveness are hard to ignore. Here for example the Pargiters are chatting idly, and the mere entrance and exit of the maid, framing and rearranging the conversation, give Eleanor something of an epiphany:

"But that reminds me of Ronny; and I don't like Ronny. We had a stable boy called Ronny."

"Who stole the hay," said Peggy. They were silent again. "It's such a pity—" Celia began. Then she stopped. The maid had come in to clear away the coffee.

"It's a wonderful night, isn't it?" said Celia, adapting her voice to the presence of servants. "It looks as if it would never rain again. In which case I don't know. . . ." And she went on prattling about the drought; about the lack of water. The well always ran dry. Eleanor, looking at the hills, hardly listened. "Oh, but there's quite enough for everybody at present," she heard Celia saying. And for some reason she held the sentence suspended without a meaning in her mind's ear," . . . quite enough for everybody at present," she repeated. After all the foreign languages she had been hearing, it sounded to her pure English. What a lovely language, she thought, saying over to herself again the commonplace words, spoken by Celia quite simply, but with some indescribable burr in the r's, for the Chinnerys had lived in Dorsetshire since the beginning of time.

The maid had gone.[56]

When the maid enters, their topic of conversation adapts along with their voices. Under the silent pressure of her presence, the subject of servants who steal the hay disappears, and what takes its place in Eleanor's mind is the phrase "quite enough for everybody"— a reference to the drought, but taking on a particular beauty when removed from its context, and a beauty that does not depend solely on its "pure English." Four pages later Eleanor chances upon some of Dante's Italian that explains for us, if not for herself, the disconnected happiness she felt while, disconnected from ordinary opinions by the maid who was quietly gathering up the coffee cups, she held a few "commonplace words" suspended in her mind:

> cheè per quanti si dice più lì nostro
> tanto possiede più di ben ciascuno

What did that mean? She read the English translation.

> For by so many more who say "ours"
> So much the more of good doth each possess.

It is remarkable that the silent maid, so far removed from the garrulous soubrettes of the theater, can occasion such an eloquent rephrasing of the utopian burden of their many expositions and recognitions, and in such "commonplace words."

2

Impertinence:
The Servant in Dialogue

Impertinent
1. Not appertaining or belonging (to); unconnected, unrelated, in-
consonant. Obs.
Wycliffe, *Sermons* (1380) Many men in this world ben impertinent to
ertheli lordis, for neither thei ben servantes to them, ne thes lordis
their worldly lordis.

Oxford English Dictionary

THE "PLACE" OF THE PEOPLE

To define the subject of this essay as the "place" of the people in
literature and to begin by suggesting that this place, such as it is, has
largely been filled by servants, is to provoke an unfortunate collision
of connotations. According to common usage, servants did not look
for work, like other members of their class, but for a "place." Static,
intransitive, and hierarchical, less an activity than a dependence, this
way of conceiving labor clearly helped to restrict social mobility. To
"know" your place was to be put in your place. As far as the project
of "knowing" the place of the people in literature is concerned, the
risk is again that of perceiving only what has stayed put, of collaborat-
ing in a normative view that registers only the people's subordination,
and thus perpetuates and even extends that subordination.

It is against this immobilizing effect of topographic metaphor that
the previous chapter offered the paradox of a utopian *topos,* a commonplace that is also a "no place." In using the term "utopian" to

shake loose from a certain historical narrowmindedness, I do not mean to imply that history can be replaced with an ardent impracticality. My intention is to help preserve and renew Auerbach's drive toward social amelioration by removing it from its entanglement in the trans-historical essence of "the people"—where it is "utopian" in the weak, merely wishful sense—and to restore it to the world of real contingency. By shifting attention from "the people" to servants, the argument moves from the abstract essence or identity of the former to the sliding, indeterminate ideological position of the latter—a position which is both popular and political to the extent that it articulates a variety of ideological aspirations and disturbances that "represent" the people without being exclusive to or defining them. The next and crucial step in this argument is to demonstrate that such aspirations and disturbances are indeed transmitted, as has not seemed evident to previous commentators, by the recurrent functionality of servant *topoi*. It is to these individual *topoi* that I begin to turn in this chapter.

One graphic and highly appropriate instance of how servant commonplaces can be thought of as the literary place of the people appears in the revisionary account of medieval stagecraft offered by Robert Weimann in *Shakespeare and the Popular Tradition in the Theater.* "The mysteries were not only performed on the big four- or six-wheeled pageant wagons or moveable stages, such as those used at Chester and York," Weimann writes, "but also in stationary acting places—sometimes in the round—where actors spoke from atop scaffold structures or descended to perform at ground level on the 'place.'"[1] For other sorts of medieval drama as well, it is necessary to make "the distinction between a 'place' or platform-like acting area (the *platea*) and a scaffold, be it *domus, sedes,* or throne (the *locus*)" (p. 74). Farther away from the audience, the *locus* is where the "realist" convention of ignoring the audience first develops, and with it the need to provide psychological motives for the movements of the actors. It is the birthplace of the representational. By the same token, it is where allegorical figures like God the Father, kings, priests, and judges sit and where consistent allegorical interpretation of the drama in terms of Christian orthodoxy is encouraged. The *platea* or "place," on the other hand, is closer to or even shared with the audience. "The

Latin word *platea* (Gr. πλατεια, Ital. *piazza*) originally indicated the open space between houses—a street or public place at ground level. As Italian usage suggests, the *platea* developed into the ground floor of an auditorium. But, before the separation of actors and audience was taken for granted, the *platea* or 'place' corresponded to the 'plain' in the Cornish Round or the 'green' in Lindsay's *Satire of the Three Estates*" (p. 79). This is where the participatory festivals of an older community had been held, and its peculiar dramaturgy preserved a participatory emphasis. "Unlike [the] *loca,* which could assume an illusionary character, the *platea* provided an entirely nonrepresentational and unlocalized setting" (p. 79). At the edge of the dramatic illusion, the actors in the *platea* could recognize the time and space of the audience, and the audience in turn could recognize itself in those actors who gravitated to the *platea.* As the border zone where the symbols and hierarchies of official representation could be ignored or undercut, it tended to be occupied by figures of questionable moral stature and low social position, like fools and servants. In a good deal of medieval theater, that is, the place of the people is literally the "place."

One example is Medwall's *Fulgens and Lucrece,* "the earliest extant interlude" (p. 106). Here the traditions of outdoor popular festivity intrude into the aristocracy's indoor entertainment by means of a servant subplot. The two suitors for the hand of Lucrece are provided with two servants, "A" and "B," who parallel their masters by wooing Lucrece's maid:

All through the play "A" and "B" rub shoulders with the humble folk in the hall; in fact, their social identity is dramatically stylized in a brilliant induction. Before the play begins they stand idly about the hall, but since they are "maysterles" (I:398), and so in search of work, they hire themselves out to the gentlemen suitors in the interlude. The performance begins before they cross the borderline between the real world and the play world, for such a crossing assumes, at the outset, the function of a dramatic effect and indicates the first phase of a significant movement: "spectators" become actors, the masterless servants in the hall become servants acting on the "place." This extradramatic counterpoint is ironically underlined when "B" energetically denies that he is an actor (46 et. seq.), so that "A" then fears he will "disturb the play" (363). (pp. 107–8)

The externality to the dramatic illusion associated with the "place" does in fact "disturb the play": "they reflect a *platea*-like position from which the everyday experience of ordinary people can be invoked against the illusions (both theatrical and ideological) of the stage world. . . . The direct appeal to the 'gode women' in the audience, asking whether they would also choose their husbands according to these standards, contains a veiled challenge to, if not a direct inversion of, the moral authority of the ruling class" (p. 110).

In the literal sense, the "place" does not survive beyond the medieval theater. With the new stagecraft that accompanies the new courtly, literate public, there is an obvious end to the Vice of the moralities (also a servant) who warns the spectators against his cousin the cutpurse. The servant who opens a Mummers' Play with the traditional call for room ("My master sent me here, some room for to provide, /So therefore gentle dears, stand back on every side") becomes an isolated vestige.[2] Nevertheless, "certain conventions of speech and movement that roughly correspond" (p. 83) to the dramaturgy of the *platea* can be traced into the comic subordinates of Shakespeare, as Weimann shows—and, beyond them, into those theatrical servants who do so much of the work of representing the people in the novel. It is a privilege of servant commonplaces to manifest Western literature's strangely lingering respect for the (dis)unity of "place."

Nothing could be more characteristic of theatrical servants than some association with the knowledge that "it's only a play." Even where direct address to the audience is out of the question, they continually pop up at boundary points between play and public in order to take their distance from the former in the name and in the accents of the latter. And if a knowing wink at the audience is possible within local conventions, it is likely to be perpetrated in one of their prologues, epilogues, exits, or entrances. Mercury's entrance in Plautus' *Amphitryo* is typical of an extradramatic effect that should be familiar:

Out of the way, out of the way, everybody . . . excuse me, please . . . let me pass, will you . . . urgent business . . . don't stop me . . .

Well, I suppose a god can order people about if a slave can; you know,— those slaves in a comedy who rush in to announce that the ship has just come in or the angry old man is on his way. I'm here on Jupiter's orders and business, so I can surely expect people to get out of my way and let me pass.[3]

Mercury is alone on stage. The "everybody" with whom this slave acting the part of a god imitating a slave is so familiar is the public, and the space that his authority opens up among them is in a sense their space.

The scale and continuity of this privileged audience-contact are difficult to overstate. Terence, much more concerned for psychological verisimilitude, nevertheless does not drop the convention of the slave as the audience's delegated truth-teller but only gives it a psychological coloring. In The *Eunuch,* Parmeno's inability to hear "a lie or an invention or a trumped-up tale" without venting his disbelief aloud is naturalized as a mildly humorous quirk of his character; Parmeno becomes a bit of a buffoon, but the convention continues to operate.[4] And further naturalizations and sophistications seem to have just as little effect on it. In French comedy of the seventeenth century, "valets and maidservants sometimes remind us clearly," as Jean Emelina comments, "that they are actors." It is they who concentrate in themselves a "complicity with the house," who create "a sort of humor that allows it to be understood that the comedy *is* a comedy."[5] Finally and more surprisingly, it is servants who prove that this sort of humor can be reproduced in print: "I am Don Quixote's squire who is also to be found in the story and who is called Sancho Panza—unless they have changed me in the cradle—I mean to say, at the printer's."[6]

Certain themes tend to cluster with surprising promptitude around even the slightest gestures toward the restoration of the servant's privileged immediacy to the audience. Notice for example how Susan, the cook in Fielding's *Grub-Street Opera,* slides back and forth between a self-introduction that mimics the old audience-contact and the congruent theme of solidarity:

Fie upon't, William, what have we to do with Master's losses? He is rich and can afford it. Don't let us quarrel among ourselves. Let us stand by one another, for let me tell you, if matters were to be too nicely examined into, I am afraid it would go hard with us all. Wise servants always stick close to one another, like plums in a pudding that's over wetted—says Susan the cook.[7]

Both her emphatic self-reference ("says Susan the cook") and her uninhibited sharing of professional secrets with the audience involve a stepping out of the play world/social world. Similarly, Susan's aphoristic urge ("Wise servants always stick together") lifts her words out of their immediate context. In each of these subdued but distinct twists of language, we can detect a reaching out for the old participatory public. And this is translated into thematic terms: a reaching out for lost community.

SUSAN: So, as the smell of the old English hospitality used to invite people in, that of the present is to keep them away.
LADY APSHINKEN: Old English hospitality! Oh, don't name it; I am sick at the sound.
SUSAN: Would I had lived in those days! I wish I had been born a cook in an age where there was some business for one (3:3).

In the next chapter I will have more to say about the novel's transformation of servant reflexivity. But there as here my interest is less in mapping the survival route of what Weimann call an "atavistic link" than in describing the survivor's continuing functions. More precisely, the suggestion that the servant can still "break through the 'fourth wall' (at a time when it already seems impenetrable), and again conjure and renew the old audience-contact" (p. 12) seems a useful way of contesting two of the most frequent and facile opinions about what archaic servants are doing in modern texts. First, that they are there in order to demonstrate the proper deference of their class or to soothe and contain the tensions of its subordination. And second, that their *raison d'être* is simply to provide entertainment of "comic relief."

Let us begin with the example of verbal equivocation, whether as witty wordplay or witless bumbling. The latter can of course be accounted for as a mark of uninstructed ignorance, and both could be seen as mechanisms for the production of laughter. But in order to feel that neither explanation exhausts their significance, one need only consider them for the moment as compromised, vestigial forms of the right to violate the dramatic illusion. If the servant can no longer address the audience directly, he or she can at least, rather than simply addressing other characters, comment *on* their words. If his or her own words can no longer acknowledge that they move in two directions, toward the audience as well as toward the other characters, they can at least reveal the hidden multi-directionality of the words of others. It is as if the public and its interests exerted an invisible gravitational pull on any words pronounced by the servant or in the servant's vicinity—that is, close to itself.

Organized around the massive fact that one speaker is powerful and the other powerless, dialogues between master and servant can be reduced to a handful of standard types. Among the servant *topoi,* they are perhaps the form in which it is most difficult to find anything other than unrelieved "comic relief" and degrading class stereotypes. And yet lexical quibbling in effect includes the audience as an implicit third term, shifting the balance of power. As in the first clown scene from *Doctor Faustus,* where Wagner enlists the ragged clown in his service:

WAGNER: Sirra, hast thou no comings in?

CLOWN: Ay, and goings out too, you may see sir.

WAGNER: Alas, poore slave, see how poverty jests in his nakednesse. I know the Villaines out of service, and so hungry, that I know he would give his soule to the devill, for a shoulder of Mutton, tho it were bloud raw.

CLOWN: Not so neither; I had need to have it well rosted, and a good sauce to it, if I pay so deere, I can tell you.

WAGNER: Sirra, wilt thou be my man and waite on me? and I will make thee go, like *Qui mihi discipulus.*

CLOWN: What, in verse?

WAGNER: No slave, in beaten silk, and staves-aker.

CLOWN: Staves-aker? that's good to kill Vermine; then belike if I serve you, I shall be lousy.[8]

On the Elizabethan stage, the audience could still be addressed directly. Both servants command it to "Beare witness." And one should note that the clown overhears Wagner's attempt at an aside. He is still too close to the audience to be effectively governed by the "fourth wall" convention and thus excluded from its confidence. But equivocation sustains this audience-contact as well. Each play on words ("goings-out," "well rosted," "staves-aker") marks a slight rise in the clown's dignity. It is as if he found the strength to stand apart from his poverty and from his new master in the collective apartness of the public.

There is a another illustration in Greene's *Friar Bacon and Friar Bungay* when the servant Miles, left alone with Friar Bacon's brazen head, spoils it by his comic blundering. If the head is declared to be good for England, it is not clear that it will be good for English people: Bacon emphasizes its uses in wartime, and when Miles furnishes himself with weapons to guard it, he hurts himself. But it is in the language of *double entendre,* appropriate both to his subservience and to his liminal position alone on stage between symbolic head and popular audience, that best explains the unconscious intentionality beneath his clowning. "Now, Jesus bless me, what a goodly head it is! And a nose! You talk of *nos autem glorificare;* but here's a nose that I warrant may be called *nos autem populare* for the people of the parish."[9] What Miles is saying is that the nose is not for us (*nos*). Or, more pointedly, that it is not for the people but rather "to destroy" (*populare*) us. Through this piece of misquoted Latin the people, or the audience, has its say.

As William Empson—who pointed out the pun above—has suggested, wordplay can be thought of as one version of pastoral. Its intermittent reach outside the semantic field of the drama, responding to the extra-dramatic presence and interests of the audience, is like a brief subliminal glimpse of another society. This perspective on the impertinence of servant speech is especially pertinent to dialogues between servant and master. The existence of such dialogues in the first place corresponds to a kind of pastoral: it embodies a toleration of "answering back," a temporary, conventional suspension of the master's expectation of obedient silence and of his power to enforce it. This formulation may sound most relevant to the Victorians, who were in fact most anxious to enforce silence. But the *Schwellendialog* between Wegg and Boffin, with its focus narrowed to bargaining over an expulsion and its final recourse to mute violence (still trying to raise the price of his departure, Wegg is flung into a dust cart), is characteristic of the structure underlying all master-servant conversation. One explosive dialogue between Joseph Andrews and Lady Booby nearly clears the house of its servants. Putting the servant before his master is very much like putting him before a magistrate; Fielding, Scott, and Dickens naturalize the convention by doing just that.

This structural defensiveness nonetheless permits paradoxical effects. In Fielding's *The Intriguing Chambermaid,* for example:

OLDCASTLE: Hold your impudent, saucy tongue!
LETTICE: Nay, sir, don't be angry with me. I only deliver my message.

The message follows: "she only bids me tell you, she hates you, detests you more than any creature upon the earth."[10] The messenger, speaking in the name of another, is freed of responsibility for whatever verbal aggression she or he may deliver, and yet will be associated with it and perhaps also take satisfaction in it. By speaking on behalf of someone or something else, the servant can say something for herself; her instrumentality authorizes subversive, multidirectional speech. And in dialogue the servant is always the messenger of absent authorities.

The principle is more or less the same whether on the stage, in a didactic pamphlet, or in the novel. Consider for instance the following slice of conversation, included in one of Defoe's irritated anti-servant broadsides, in which mistress takes maid to task for indulging in a Sunday walk:

LADY: Did I ever refuse you, Mary, when you asked me for a day for yourself.
MARY: I never troubled you much with asking.
LADY: I had rather you had, Mary, than take God's time for yourself.
MARY: God's time, madam; all our time is God's time, I think.[11]

The power relation is evident in the way the servant can only echo her mistress' words, inflecting them slightly. It is not herself that she expresses. On the other hand, repetition strengthens her replies. When she echoes and extends her mistress' thought ("all our time is God's time"), she conceals herself—the responsible, punishable self addressed by examining magistrates—in the interstices of official belief and speaks, irresponsibly, on its behalf. At the very least, her brief but poetic melding of Defoe's Puritanism with his Enlightenment rationalism frustrates his desire for subordination. One of Defoe's proposals for remedying the sort of insubordination he here describes was to oblige servants to present certificates of character, but here the servant *has* no character, presents no target, and slips out of control.

In the novels of Fielding, it is easy enough to see that the comic servants derive from the theater and throw their voices to their author's old audience.

The lady, who began to admire the new style in which her waiting-gentlewoman delivered herself . . . called her back and desired to know what she meant by the extraordinary freedom in which she thought proper to indulge her tongue. "Freedom!" says Slipslop, "I don't know what you call freedom, madam; servants have tongues as well as their mistresses." (*Joseph Andrews,* bk. 1. ch. 9)

When Slipslop says "Freedom!" it is as if she were responding directly to the narrator, who has (presumably) paraphrased her mistress. This foothold outside the dialogue raises her, if only briefly, to a higher level of discourse. Moreover, the repetition itself casts her in the superior role of commentator. It is remarkable what small turns of phrase will serve to identify the servant's point of view with the authority of narrator and reader:

". . . I assure you I shall bear no such impertinence." "Impertinence! I don't know that I am impertinent," says Slipslop. "Yes indeed you are," cries my lady, "and unless you mind your manners, this house is no place for you." "Manners!" cries Slipslop, "I never was thought to want manners."

As Lady Booby says, "the surest way to offend me" is "repeating my words." This minimal impertinence brings the perspective of an outsider into their very heart, suggesting the presence in the servant's thought of some monster too hideous to be shown.

In *Robinson Crusoe,* the dialogues between Crusoe and Friday may or may not depend directly on theatrical models, but they offer an extraordinary gloss on what the comic tradition is up to.

After this, I had been telling him how the devil was God's enemy in the hearts of men, and used all his malice and skill to defeat the good designs of Providence, and to ruine the kingdom of Christ in the world; and the like. "Well," says Friday, "but you say, God is so strong, so great, is he not much strong, much might as the devil?" "Yes, yes," says I . . . "But," says he again, "if God much strong, much might as the devil, why God no kill the devil, so make him no more do wicked?"

I was strangely surprized at his question, and after all, tho' I was now an old man, yet I was but a young doctor, and ill enough qualified for a casuist, or solver of difficulties; and at first I could not tell what to say, so I pretended not to hear him, and asked him what he said. But he was too earnest for an answer to forget his question; so that he repeated it in the very same broken words, as above. By this time I had recovered my self a little, and I said, "God will at last punish him severely; he is reserved for the judgment" . . . This did not satisfie Friday, but he returns upon me, repeating my words, "*Reserve, at last,* me no understand; but why not kill the devil now, why not kill great ago?" "You may as well ask me," said I, "why God does not kill you and I, when we do wicked things here that offend Him. We are preserved to repent and be pardoned." He muses a while at this. "Well, well," says he, mighty affectionately, "that well; so you, I, devil, all wicked, all preserve, repent, God pardon all." Here I was run down by him again to the last degree. . . . I therefore diverted the present discourse between me and my man, rising up hastily, as upon some sudden occasion of going out; then sending him for something a good way off.[12]

With a charming, self-forgetful frankness, Crusoe admits to the ruses by which he tries to avoid ideological embarrassment—ruses that fall back on the power differential between them. Stuck for a reply, he feigns deafness or sends Friday "for something a good way off."[13] He even hints hopefully that the mind of the savage may be too weak to recall the difficult question it has posed. All of these factors—deafness, faulty memory, sudden occasions of going out—will be exploited (less openly) by the novelists who follow Defoe in order to protect their protagonists against too free an exchange of ideas. And yet all this comic distraction doesn't preclude a revolutionary refocusing. Before terminating the conversation, Crusoe adds by way of apology for the feebleness of his defense of Christianity that Friday's reasoning has remained at the insufficient conclusions to which "meer notions of nature" will take "reasonable creatures." Friday has not had access to revelation, in other words, but he is certainly "reasonable." And Reason, isolating the democratic impulse in Defoe's Christianity, can thus give him a rather extraordinary utopian moment: the vision of a promiscuous pardon in which "you, I, devil" reach an endpoint of happy equality.

FORMULAS OF DIALOGUE

These examples are perhaps sufficient to suggest that when the novel appropriated its master-servant dialogues from the theater, it took over something more than a set of commonplaces made safe by centuries of repetition. This needs to be said, for given the conventions of realism, it is even more evident in the novel that the moral and intellectual qualities to be inferred from the servant's part in these dialogues do not compose a flattering portrait of the class. And because of the *topoi* that constitute literary servants, dialogue provides their most extended opportunity to articulate their own concerns—all the more so in that the usual interference of the narrator is less—it is perhaps less evident in the novel why such a class portrait is not everything that master-servant dialogue produces. But in the novel, as in the theater, the servant is not speaking only to the master. Even where aesthetic self-consciousness is severely restricted by the ground rules of realism, the servant's traditionalism, his shameless indebtedness to Cervantes, Lesage, Molière, and Marivaux, makes the figure stand out from prose whose tendency is to assert its unmediated relation to social reality. Wilkie Collins and Elizabeth Gaskell, whose hard-nosed realism about the institution of domestic service was cited above, are exemplary in allowing servants, unlike other characters, to acknowledge their own status as literature. In *The Moonstone* Gabriel Betteredge, himself a delegated story-teller, family chronicler, and surrogate for the novelist, opens his narrative and the novel by citing a literary source—*Robinson Crusoe,* itself a seminal text of the master-servant line. And Gaskell's *Ruth* was published with an appendix containing further gleanings from the quotable and much-quoted Sally, as detached from the novel as Sancho's proverbs and the Wellerisms of *Pickwick Papers.* In such diminished but recognizable forms, the servant's authoritative exteriority intrudes into realist fiction. And in the light of this textual extraterritoriality, the gamut of banal servant deficiencies—superstition, sloth, feeble-mindedness, and so on—no longer seems definitive.

No more definitive, one might say, than another item on the same list: deafness. The argument that the lower classes are congenitally or vocationally hard of hearing has yet to be made. But time and time again in the midst of dialogue novelists will strategically plug up servants' ears. Clearly this deafness is functional, an expedient called upon to relax discipline or ensure the voicing of suppressed ambiguities. Servants in general are in the position of Caleb Balderstone in Scott's *The Bride of Lammermoor,* who, his master apologizes, "is somewhat deaf amongst his other accomplishments, so that much of what he means should be spoken aside is overheard by the whole audience, and especially by those from whom he is most anxious to conceal his private maneuvers" (ch. 7). The metaphor is very much to the point; like the theatrical aside, from which it derives, deafness permits the servant to preserve the role of decorous subservience while also stepping out of it to appeal to the higher court of the "whole audience."

In particular, the servant is thus enabled to address his master with words otherwise out of character or entirely out of the question. When Andrew Fairservice hastens over the border with a stolen mare, a hint of deafness protects his disobedience. In *Nicholas Nickleby,* it is the enabling convention for Peg's opposition to her elderly master's mismarriage:

"Why don't you wear your everyday clothes like a man—eh?"

"They ain't becoming enough, Peg," returned her master.

"Not what enough?"

"Becoming."

"Becoming what?" said Peg sharply. "Not becoming too old to wear?"

Arthur Gride muttered an imprecation upon his housekeeper's deafness, as he roared in her ear:—

"Not smart enough: I want to look as well as I can."

"Look?" cried Peg. "If she's as handsome as you say she is, she won't much look at you, master, you can take your oath of that" (ch. 51).

Deafness performs roughly the same function here that is elsewhere performed by drunkenness, epileptic fits, terror, somnolence, and others of the servant's habitual lapses into incomplete awareness. It frees her speech, allows her to comment against the grain instead of responding submissively. This is the constant. The moral and even physiological attributes that surround it are secondary, interchangeable, and often self-contradictory. Gride tells himself complacently, "it's no use her listening at keyholes for she can't hear." But on the other hand he also seems "half afraid that she might have read his thoughts" (ch. 51). And his fears are realized when her conventional curiosity is the instrument that publishes his misdoings to the world. As Gride tells his co-villain, "clerks and servants have a trick of listening" (ch. 47), and their deafness does not interfere with it.

Significantly, Ralph Nickleby too will be foiled by his clerk-servant's conventionally distended earshot. The two conventions, indiscreet listening and impaired hearing, are in fact parts of a single whole. They give private dialogues a public hearing, enlist the public on the servant's side in unequal dialogue. Their unity is crystallized in an anecdote Gaskell tells of the Brontës' servant Tabby, who "expected to be informed of all the family concerns, and yet had grown so deaf that what was repeated to her became known to whoever might be in or about the house."[14] Literary emblems of this function surround the servant, from the fact that Lazarillo de Tormes ends the novel as town crier to the maid in Ford Madox Ford's *Parade's End,* nicknamed "Hullo Central." Not the least exact is the epithet given to Sally in *Ruth:* "people."

The several formulas of dialogue that the novel took over wholesale from the comic stage, including, for example, flattery, consolation, and the garrulous delayed delivery of messages, make up a sizeable proportion of its total verbal interchange between the classes. The formal conservatism of these dialogues is probably one reason why, if they have been noticed at all, they have been felt to convey an uninteresting and unchallenging picture of the social order. Since, in addition, functions like flattery and consolation are constructed around the servant's subsidiary status, if not his or her enthusiastic espousal of things as they are, it is no surprise that they have helped consolidate the literary image of the "faithful family retainer." We need to be reminded therefore how partial this truth is.

Flattery of master by servant, one of the dialogue forms that persist into the novel most abundantly, would seem to display the servant at his or her most servile. But nothing is more faithful to comic tradition than a sudden involuntary stumble from the heights of praise into a pointed disservice. Witness the treacherous defense of her mistress by Mrs. Western's maid:

"And, madam," continued she, "I could have despised all she said to me; but she hath had the audacity to affront your ladyship and to call you ugly— Yes, madam, she called you ugly old cat to my face. I could not bear to hear your ladyship called ugly."

"Why do you repeat her impudence so often?" asked Mrs. Western. (bk. 7. ch. 8)

Defense of the superior is itself an enabling convention; the duplicity that Fielding wittily underlines here is traditional. The convention naturalizes, excuses, permits what amounts to its contrary: the maid taking the side of the attacker.

The closer one looks, in fact, the more numerous are the slips for which fidelity has prepared the ground. The servant who seems more royalist than the king often brings out into the open values that his majesty may hold but prefers not to hear proclaimed. A loud endorsement of that which ought to go without saying can of course amount to a reversal, for it precipitates a collision between contradictory beliefs that polite silence would otherwise cover over and keep apart. As when the memorable Miggs uses her flattery to foment discord between husband and wife:

"Come, Martha, my dear," said the locksmith cheerily, "let us have tea, and don't let us talk about sots. There are none here, and Joe don't want to hear about them, I dare say."

At this crisis Miggs appeared with toast.

"I dare say he does not," said Mrs. Varden; "and I dare say you do not, Varden. It's a very unpleasant subject, I have no doubt, though I won't say it's personal"—Miggs coughed—"whatever I may be forced to think"— Miggs sneezed expressively. "You never will know, Varden . . . what a woman suffers when she's waiting at home, under such circumstances. If you don't believe me, as I know you don't, here's Miggs, who is only too often a witness of it—ask her."

"Oh! she were very bad the other night, sir, indeed she were," said Miggs. "If you hadn't the sweetness of an angel in you, mim, I don't think you could abear it, I raly don't."

"Miggs," said Mrs. Varden, "you're profane."

"Begging your pardon, mim," returned Miggs, with shrill rapidity, "such was not my intentions, and such I hope is not my character, though I am but a servant." (ch. 13)

Any discord makes a breach through which the servant's self-assertion can pass, and Miggs, with her theatrical self-consciousness, is always ready. The comic motif of "though I am but a servant" (quoted from Fielding) leads directly into Miggs' open rebellion later in the novel, where she continues to use her mistress' Protestantism against her master and to expose her mistress' vanity to the reader. The aspiration expressed in her wanton plurals, even in the timing of her coughs and sneezes, can supply the place of ideology.

Strangely enough, it is often when the servant's opposition is most loyal, when it emerges neither into consciousness nor into the plot, that it makes its most radical statements. In *North and South*, for example, the extreme of Dixon's feudal deference shields an unusually forthright extreme of class complaint. Margaret, having discovered that the maid alone knew (as she herself did not) the secret of her mother's impending death, apologizes for her harshness:

"Oh, Dixon!" said Margaret, "How often I've been cross with you, not knowing what a terrible secret you had to bear!"

"Bless you, child! I like to see you showing a bit of spirit. It's the good old Beresford blood. Why, the last Sir John but two shot his steward down, there where he stood, for just telling him that he'd racked the tenants, and he'd racked the tenants till he could get no more money off them than he could get skin off a flint." (ch. 16)

Once one has picked up this latent level of servant self-reference, its traces are visible everywhere. "Many's the time I've longed to walk it off—the thought of what was the matter with her," Dixon goes on to say—just after recommending that Margaret herself, now that she too knows her mother's secret, take a stroll. Is it possible that there is no reminder here of the fact that servants, unlike their mistresses, cannot come and go as they please? In *Ruth*, the comedy of snobbish mistress seconded by snobbish maid—what Thackeray once called "the servants' ditto"—works by the same indirection. The maid eagerly joins the mistress' attack on our heroine, but she unwittingly concludes by first defending Ruth and then offending her mistress; "the maid's chattering had outrun her tact" (ch. 10). Such procedures might be thought of, in Dickens' phrase, as "the diplomacy of Miss Miggs"—that is, rhetoric that generates or allies itself with class conflicts even where the rhetor is too unconscious of her or his own interests even to imagine actually participating in them.

Consolation, like flattery, both ministers to the master's needs and simultaneously allows the servant, at a moment of relative strength, to get some of her own back. For one thing, it is impossible for the sympathizing servant to put herself in her mistress' shoes without evoking the eventuality of walking away in them. As in *Tom Jones*:

"Indeed, ma'am," cries Honour, "I wish your la'ship and I could change situations; that is, I mean, without hurting your la'ship, for to be sure I don't wish you to be so bad as to be a servant; but because if so be it was my case, I should find no manner of difficulty in it; for in my poor opinion, young Squire Blifil is a charming, sweet, handsome man." (bk. 7. ch. 7)

This is not so much bad taste as the wish not to be "so bad" as a servant. Note that the prospect of "hurting your la'ship" is explicit. Beneath the husk of tactless inconsistency one can usually find a kernel of complicity with the agents of the master's or mistress' suffering. To imagine eventualities can be an excuse for delivering hypothetical bad news in advance. Moreover, the conventional plurality of contradictory consolations of course detracts from the efficacy of them all, and thus makes the consoler into a surrogate inflicter of pain. This may be suggested by Scott's simile (in *Old Mortality*) for "the multitudinous grounds of consolation which Jenny Dennison brought forward, one after another, like a skilful general who charges with several divisions of his troops in regular succession."

First, Jenny was morally positive that young Milnwood would come to no harm—then, if he did, there was consolation in the reflection, that Lord Evandale was the better and more appropriate match of the two—then, there was every chance of a battle, in which the said Lord Evandale might be killed, and there would be nae mair fash about that job. (ch. 19)

In the initial simile Jenny incarnates the army that is endangering the life of her mistress' Intended. She then proceeds to decimate gaily the whole stock of available males. Finally, to draw her mistress' attention to "other fish in the sea," as is standard practice—"There wad be aye enow o' young men left, if they were to hang the tae half o' them"—is also to express, if only tangentially, a general impatience with exclusiveness and a vivid apprehension of the reality of invisible "others," and both of these sentiments bear a distinct relation to the servant herself. They do not form an ideological position, but they are foundation blocks on which the edifice of democratic thought can rise.

The examples of flattery and consolation are sufficient, I think, to indicate that master-servant dialogue cannot be dismissed as a hegemonic syllogism, supporting class rule by foregrounding the inferiority or complacency of the ruled. The point may seem overly obvious, but it is after all one of the two critical assumptions that in practice tend to cover, or to justify the neglect of, an extensive and socially significant body of literary materials. The other assumption holds simply that these materials can be classed as entertainment. If the *non sequitur,* for example, is clearly not intended as a sign of mental debility, and if parallel-hunting does not flush any interesting game from the thickets of gratuitous inconsequence, then one should perhaps be content to speak of simple mechanisms of amusement.

This reading can be confronted on different levels. It can certainly be disputed on theoretical grounds, for instance by asking whether (but for the laziness or "resistance" of the reader) there in fact exists any such thing as "pure" amusement. But it seems more to the point to begin simply by noticing how again and again humorous irrelevance conceals a razor edge of self-assertion or lays out for future workers the scattered building blocks of an alternative world view. As one illustration, we can appeal to another conventional dialogue form: the servant's long-winded, digressive delivery of a message to an impatient interlocutor, a set piece that goes back as far as the tragedies of Sophocles and that is still going strong when Macbeth hears from a servant that Birnam Wood is approaching Dunsinane. The least one finds in dialogue of this sort is the servant interposing the pressing fact of his own existence between the master and his news. As for instance when Partridge brings Tom Jones word of Sophia after encountering Black George in London:

"Well, but what is your good news?" cries Jones, "What do you know of my Sophia?"—"You shall know it presently, sir," answered Partridge, "I am coming to it as fast as I can" . . . "Well, pray go on in your own way," said Jones, "you are resolved to make me mad, I find." "Not for the world," answered Partridge, "I have suffered enough for that already; which, as I have said, I shall bear in my remembrance the longest day I have to live."—"Well, but Black George?" cries Jones,—"Well, sir, I was saying, it was a long time before he could recollect me; for indeed I am very much altered since I saw him. *Non sum qualis eram.* I have had troubles in the world." (bk. 15. ch. 12)

Walpole's equally theatrical variation in *The Castle of Otranto* achieves a more original effect:

"Where is my lord? where is the prince?" "Here I am," said Manfred, as they came nearer; "have you found the princess?" The first that arrived, replied, "Oh! my lord! I am glad we have found you!" "Found me!" said Manfred, "have you found the princess?" "We thought we had, my lord," said the fellow, looking terrified, "but"—"But what?" cried the prince; "has she escaped?" "Jaquez and I, my lord"—"Yes, I and Diego," interrupted the scond, who came up in still greater consternation—"Speak one of you at a time!" said Manfred; "I ask you where is the princess?" "We do not know," said they, both together. (ch. 1)

More than their terror, it is their common insistence on "we"—a word that will have a special resonance throughout this book—on neither speaking if both are not included, that delays the news. And it does not seem coincidental that this "we" should serve as the obstruction to Manfred's overwhelming egotism. In *The Bride of Lammermoor* this formula is so overtly ideological that a term like "comic interlude" would not even come to mind. Ravenswood's Hamlet-like interrogation of an old family retainer—now a gravedigger—allows the latter all the good lines. A trumpeter who was present but failed to play a heroic part at the battle of Bothwell Brigg, he insists his duty was "to blow folk to their warm dinner, or at the warst to a decent kirkyard, no to skirl them awa to a bluidy braeside." His "irrelevancies" hit this mark repeatedly:

"Well, sir, cut all this short," said Ravenswood.
    "Short!—I had like to hae been cut short myself, in the flower of my youth, as Scripture says." (ch. 29)

It is not easy to discuss garrulity without the quotations getting out of hand. One more instance will be enough. If such a thing as "pure" or innocuous entertainment exists when the classes confront each other in the novel, it cannot be very different from the scene in *Little Dorrit* where the Meagles' housekeeper announces to Clennam, very gradually, that she has spied the long-lost Tattycoram:

"Mr. Clennam," returned Mrs. Tickit, "I was a little heavy in my eyes, being that I was waiting longer than customary for my cup of tea which was then preparing by Mary Jane. I was not sleeping, nor what a person would term correctly, dozing. I was more what a person would strictly call watching with my eyes closed."

Without entering into an inquiry into this curious abnormal condition, Clennam said, "Exactly. Well?"

"Well, sir," proceeded Mrs. Tickit. "I was thinking of one thing and thinking of another. Just as you yourself might. Just as anybody might."

"Precisely so," said Clennam. "Well?"

"And when I do think of one thing and do think of another," pursued Mrs. Tickit, "I hardly need tell you, Mr. Clennam, that I think of the family. Because, dear me! a person's thoughts," Mrs. Tickit said this with an argumentative and philosophic air, "however they may stray, will go more or less on what is uppermost in their minds. They *will* do it, sir, and a person can't prevent them."

Arthur subscribed to this discovery with a nod.

"You find it yourself, sir, I'll be so bold to say," said Mrs. Tickit, "and we all find it so. It ain't our stations in life that changes us, Mr. Clennam; thoughts is free!" (bk. 2 ch. 9)

Rich in conventional elements, this dialogue could almost serve as a gloss on the entire line. The servant's tendency to states of somnolence ("watching with my eyes closed") is both a comic surrender to the all-too-human and a prelude to special vision. Further, in a servant's mouth the phrase "the family" cannot help but resonate with the dissonance of the servant's own problematic status on its border, as we shall see further below; here this note is amplified by the gratuitously argumentative tone in which Mrs. Tickit introduces it as well as by the fact that Tattycoram had run away because to her masters she was precisely a servant and not—as the housekeeper now calls her—a "child" of the family. Most important, though, is the point that emerges where I have broken the quotation off (barely half way to the disclosure Clennam is seeking), and that the exigencies of the plot will force Mrs. Tickit to abandon again: "It ain't our stations in life that changes us, Mr. Clennam; thoughts is free!" Up to this point, Mrs. Tickit's belligerency, her desire to fight for her digressive platitudes, may have seemed a simple laughter-producing incongruity. But this digression constitutes a defense of digressiveness itself. It identifies the flood of servant volubility as a means of floating submerged perceptions of social inequality over the reefs of censorship—external and internal—and of depositing them before the common view. The free association that Mrs. Tickit abuses in the conventional manner, anticipating Virginia Woolf's Mrs. Ramsay, offers the freedom necessary to throw "our stations in life" into doubt. The entertaining *non sequitur* marks the servant's refusal to follow.

By collecting and displaying ideological nuggets like these, one can show without much difficulty that the entertainment generated by servant and master rarely contains nothing more than entertainment. Since it is in the nature of the subject that the instances are particularly dispersed and the gold of insight is mixed in with a good deal of protective dross, the simple act of accumulation is valuable. But the notion of entertainment also has to be addressed at a higher level. Weighing it against the metaphors of conflict and opposition that provide the antithetical criterion for dialogue in many discussions, including parts of this one, one is obliged to concede its relative pertinence. Dialogues of the garrulous-messenger type, for example, would be better described as entertainment than as, say, "great duels of Weltanschauung" or "the direct coming-to-grips of colliding opposites in conversation," to cite Lukács' celebratory phrases for the dialogues of Balzac and Scott.[15] The fragments of social consciousness they purvey do not add up to the totality of a world view. Ideological statement merely spins off under the centrifugal force of digression and delay, whose neutral whirl dominates the scene. Relatively speaking, the structure is peremptory while the conflict of ideas is subdued and underdeveloped. What the term "entertainment" is brought in to deal with, perhaps, is the accurate sense that the terminology of historical conflict responds awkwardly at best to what is specific in inter-class dialogue. If the affective notion of comic amusement denies even the existence of ideological engagement, the mimetic notion of a conversational clash of social forces overstates both the conceptual coherence and the directness of that engagement.

In order to arrive at a just estimate of dialogues that are neither laugh-producing mechanisms nor "great duels of Weltanschauung," it is necessary to return to an earlier point: the appeal to the reader that liberates servant voices from consideration in mimetic terms. The example of Scott is useful here precisely because his numerous and lengthy but sparsely ideological dialogues between masters and servants, which Lukács does not include in his appreciation, so clearly do not provide the "direct coming to grips of colliding opposites" that animates the world-historical conversations of Highland Jacobite and commercial Lowlander.

"Andrew, ye scoundrel!" repeated Mr. Jarvie; "here, sir! here!"

"Here is for the dog," said Andrew, coming up sulkily.

"I'll gie you dog's wages, ye rascal, if ye dinna attend to what I say t'ye— We are gaun into the Hielands a bit—"

"I judged as muckle," said Andrew.

"Haud your peace, ye knave, and hear what I have to say till ye—We are gaun a bit into the Hielands—"

"Ye tauld me sae already," replied the incorrigible Andrew.

"I'll break your head," said the Baillie, rising in wrath, "if ye dinna haud your tongue."

"A hadden tongue," replied Andrew, "makes a slabbered mouth."

It was now necessary I should intervene, which I did by commanding Andrew, with an authoritative tone, to be silent at his peril.

"I am silent," said Andrew. "I'se do a' your lawfu' bidding without a nay-say.—My puir mither used aye to tell me,

> 'Be it better, be it worse,
> Be ruled by him that has the purse.'

Sae ye may e'en speak as lang as ye like, baith the tane and the tither o' you, for Andrew." (ch. 27)

Andrew does throw out a few modest ideological tidbits: that he is ruled by their purses rather than their legitimate authority, and that servants are not to be spoken to as if they were dogs. The dialogue also acquires something in context. Jarvie is trying to get the servant's attention in order to tell him that in the Highlands it will be "as muckle as your life's worth" to use "that clavering tongue o' yours." In fact, the fate of several characters in *Rob Roy* will be determined by Andrew's verbal indiscretion.

But the battle is not joined over what Andrew says. The issue is his right to speak at all. His interlocutors do not recognize that his words contain ideas, let alone respond to them. The dialogue is brimming with conflict, but the conflict is separated from the content of the words: the first is for the master, the second is only for the reader. The servant's ideological plea is addressed outside the dialogue—not colliding with his listeners but appealing over their heads to the public. Hence the superb paradox "I am silent," which as nearly as possible satisfies both addressees, gagging itself in obedience to the master's injunction and whispering one more bit of self-conscious commentary to the reader. Hence also the prevalence of proverbs. In this brief passage, there are three. Like Mrs. Tickit's detachable, quotable exclamation "Thoughts is free!", the proverb by its very form declares the independence of servant speech from the immediate pressure to respond, obey, be silent. Proverbs are "set apart from the flow of conversation" by their "reflexive self-referencing (calling attention to their proverbial character)," and thus "one who uses proverbs out-of-context will be judged more as a performer than as a talker."[16] As communal quotations, they lift their speaker out of his personal, face-to-face dependence and remove him to the higher ground of a "common-place" where he can generalize on behalf of and to a wider audience.

In short, as suggested above, servant speech derives a peculiar power from its multidirectionality. If dialogue is imagined primarily as verbal exchange—whether as the moral ideal of mutual responsiveness or the political reflection of conflicting interests and ideologies—then the tendency of the servant voice is to project itself out of dialogue and into monologue—into a monologue, however, that is at once audience-directed and self-assertive. Nothing could be further from solipsism. The themes, the specific verbal resources, and the general aesthetic authority for the servant's self-assertion derive from the audience, a second and sovereign master. Where masters and servants confront each other, the audience introduces a crucial third term, one that is not reflected in the mirror of mimesis. Thus it might be more accurate to think of dialogue according to a secondary definition, that is, the literary genre of dialogue, in which exchange between speakers is a more or less transparent device subordinated to the overriding aim of rhetorical impact.

Within the novel, dialogue in this rhetorical sense will often look misplaced, like an interlude. Its sportive detachment from the push and pull of the plot, its urge to reach and charm the ears of a distant public, invite the descriptive vocabulary of entertainment. But a third, subsidiary sense of the word is also relevant. The compilers of the Oxford English Dictionary, whose acute consciousness of the Victorian and Edwardian "servant problem" is written into their quotations, cite certain words "betwene the lady Mary & her servant Gyles" in 1532 as the first use of "dialogue" not in the sense of a conversational event, a mere exchange of words, but as a "verbal exchange of *thought*" (my italics). This sense allows us to ask whether thought was in fact exchanged, whether the dialogue was successful. It is this connotation to which George Eliot appeals in an essay called "Servants' Logic" (*Pall Mall Gazette,* March 17, 1865). For Eliot, dialogue is tied by way of dialectic to Reason, whose kingdom is the goal toward which verbal interchange strives or ought to strive. But "servants' logic," she affirms, is only an obstacle to the inevitable dominion of truth. Her evidence is dialogues like the following:

You, sir, are perhaps a dyspeptic physiologist, with a weakness for spinach, and you wish to impress on your cook the importance of thoroughly squeezing green vegetables. You tell her the water in which they are boiled is as bad as poison. It follows that the next day they come up only a little less like a soft morass. "This will not do, Sally; the greens must be perfectly dry." "La, sir, I squeezed 'em ever so long." "But you saw there was still water left in them." "Well, sir, I'm sure it was very little for any gentleman as can eat greens at all." You are, perhaps, a little nettled, and you wish to be impressive; your mind goes in search of illustration. "I tell you, there must be no water. Suppose it was arsenic, instead of poisonous water—should you think there was no difference between little and none?" Fatal ingenuity! Sally fires up; she has heard of cooks being hanged for putting arsenic in the food; she feels herself unjustly accused. "I'm sure I never touched a bit of arsenic—no, not so much as to poison a rat, for at one place where I lived the rats ran about like mice, and the butler, as there wasn't a more respectable man anywhere, he brought some arsenic home, and he said to me, as I might be standing here—"

"Nonsense, what has that to do with the greens? Say no more, I'm in a hurry."[17]

The story of the respectable butler who brought home some arsenic unfortunately remains unfinished. Dismissing it as "nonsense" unrelated to himself, the dyspeptic master uses his authority to end the conversation. In doing so he is following George Eliot's advice. After a few more anecdotes of more or less comical misunderstanding, the essay concludes with an abrupt and surprisingly humorless endorsement of the prevailing Victorian practice: the impediment of interclass speech. "The moral of all this is, that wise masters and mistresses will not argue with their servants, will not give them reasons, will not consult them. A mild yet firm authority . . . is the best means of educating them into any improvement of their methods and habits. . . . Reason about things with your servants, consult them, give them the suffrage, and you produce no other effect in them than a sense of anarchy in the house, a suspicion of irresolute-ness in you the most opposed to that spirit of order and promptitude which can alone enable them to fill their places well and make their lives respectable" (pp. 395–396).

It is power, not reason, that is decisive here. In the discourse of the servant-keepers, the will of servants registers only as inteference, hence as aimless and unintelligible. It is quite possible that the un-completed tale of the butler and the arsenic remains closer to "nonsense" than to murder only because of the master's authority to close off speech, to frame all confrontation so as to keep his dinner rather than the independent purposes of his kitchen staff in sharpest focus. Within such a frame, there can be no "Servants' Logic," no ultimate purposefulness that would bestow rational meaning on these actions in their own right. It is remarkable, therefore, just how near Eliot's dialogues come to suggesting the existence of such a logic. The unrealized possibility that "the butler did it"—a topic about which more will be said below—is of course one example, and there are others. "In reasoning with our servants we are likely to be thwarted by discovering that our axioms are not theirs. For example, they presuppose that an effect may exist without a cause, that like causes will constantly produce unlike effects, that *all* may mean only some, that there is no difference between little and none" (p. 392). These axioms are worth considering from the viewpoint of the subordi-nated. Within the hierarchy of the household, they are right: what holds for "some" clearly does not hold for "*all*." Depending on the party concerned, it is evident that like causes will indeed produce unlike effects. Eliot's rationalism founders on an uncharted inequality, the cause of effects that seem to have no cause. In short, at the moment when the servant-keeping bourgeoisie pulls back from its commitment to the dream of enlightened Reason, the comic *non sequiturs* of servants appropriate and safeguard it. By serving as the privileged vehicle for advanced social imagery, by suspending briefly the reader's belief in the fictional status quo, the non-conflictual comedy of evasion appeals beyond today's dinners to the Reason of the future.

Since mimetic instruments register this appeal very imperfectly, it is curious that something like this argument was made by Lukács. A late essay on Lessing's *Minna von Barnhelm,* many of whose dialogues are between master or mistress and their servants, is one of the few places where Lukács can be discovered defending the procedures of comedy, and he does so by assimilating them to a vision of future Reason. In *Minna,* Lukács concedes, dialogue is not the expression of Weltanschauung, as in *Nathan der Weise,* nor does it express the interplay of concrete social forces, as in *Emilia Galotti.* But its value is no less. "The uniqueness of *Minna von Barnhelm* in the literature of the Enlightenment," he suggests, lies in Lessing's success in using dialogue so as to render "evocatively convincing" a "belief in the future" (*Zukunftsüberzeugung*), that is, a "gay conviction of the final victory of the empire of reason" (*jener heiteren Überzeugtheit vom endgültigen Sieg des Reiches der Vernunft*). Putting aside his mimetic-conflictual aesthetic, Lukács touches master-servant dialogue in its most characteristic operation: its permanent slant toward the unmirrorable endpoint of conflict.[18]

TRAJECTORIES

My discussion thus far has been synchronic, but at this point historical distinctions need to be introduced. To refer to the Enlightenment as a criterion is to raise the possibility that the broad curve of master-servant dialogue is a decline. This idea is encouraged by the most visible nineteenth-century materials. In the Victorian household, there is an impression of increased silence, of a repression of master-servant dialogue motivated, as in the Eliot passage, by fear of its subversive consequences. As Max Beerbohm was to put it, "the survival of domestic service, in its old form, depends more and more on our agreement not to mention it." "We never speak a word to the servant who waits on us for twenty years," Thackeray wrote in *Punch.* The servants interviewed by Charles Booth complained with special bitterness, on their side, of the interdiction of "free speech." As Roger Brown and Albert Gilman argue in their study "The Pronouns of Power and Solidarity," there had arisen "a distaste for the face-to-face expression of differential power," and "address between master and servant retains the greatest power loading."[19] The literary evidence substantiates these impressions. In the Victorian novel, servants tend to be less central, less distinct, more engulfed in their masters' characters and interests, in the plot machinery, in "symbolic background."[20] Titular servant protagonists like Pamela disappear or are gentrified into governesses. Verbal confrontation diminishes in length, frequency, animation, and centrality. If servants are addressed, it is often only in such mute or monosyllabic commands as Eliot requests. Harry Warrington's first words in *The Virginians* are, typically, a question not meant to be answered: "Gumbo, you idiot, why don't you fetch the baggage out of the cabin?" (ch. 3). Direct friction with the master is often explicitly disallowed. In *Adam Bede,* for instance, Arthur Donnithorne's harsh words to the groom are paraphrased: "The judicious historian abstains from narrating precisely what ensued. You understand that there was a great deal of strong language." The groom, silent in his master's presence, vents his feelings only in a choral interlude with another servant:

"The Cap'n's been ridin' the devil's own pace," said Dalton the coachman . . . when John brought up Rattler.

"An' I wish he'd get the devil to do's grooming for'n," growled John.

"Ay; he'd hev a deal haimabler groom nor what he has now," observed Dalton; and the joke appeared to him so good, that, being left alone upon the scene, he continued to take at intervals his pipe from his mouth in order to wink at an imaginary audience, and shake luxuriously with silent, ventral laughter; mentally rehearsing the dialogue from the beginning, that he might recite it with effect in the servants' hall. (ch. 12)

Despite the difficulty of making any quantitative measurement, two trends are distinguishable that diminish the amount of possible give-and-take between the classes. First, the replacement of the loquacious master-servant pair by an increasingly isolated servant chorus, and second, a reinstitution within dialogue of the earlier *Stiltrennung* that had forced the servant into some version of substandard English. In the novel of the eighteenth century this separation of styles was often abandoned. No class-based distinction of dialect infringes for example on the long confidential sessions of Roxana and her maid or the quibbling, wordy battles between Pamela and her master. Even Slipslop abruptly drops her malapropisms when it comes time to hold and (figuratively) to box Lady Booby's ears. However, a maid in Edgeworth's *The Absentee* (1812) already moans of her mistress "never talking to me confidantially,"[21] and the complaint is prophetic. A one-sided phonetic naturalism, diverting attention from ideas to "substandard" dialect while retaining the convention of correctness and fluency for the upper-class protagonist, intervenes in order to erode the common ground that genuine cross-class interaction requires. Sam Weller and Pickwick are nearly the last of the memorable novel-length couples, and it would be hard to say whether Sam is even as representative of his successors as the Fat Boy of the same novel, who never uses his mouth (in his intervals of consciousness) except to eat.

This historical curve is congruent with the one outlined in the last chapter. There, as proposed by Auerbach, we had realism as a rise away from comic tradition; here we have the falling off of the comic tradition that is left behind. The difference lies in the politics assigned to this trajectory. To the extent that the master-servant dialogues of the Enlightenment constitute a summit from which the tradition subsequently declines, it is clearly because at that moment the tradition is invested with the energies of the emergent bourgeoisie. The pragmatism, skepticism, and corporeality with which Lazarillo and Sancho set off their masters' chivalry cannot of course be attributed solely to the middle class. However, insofar as the middle class came to lead and focus all those currents in motion against the *ancien régime,* both contemporary and later readings inevitably drew these oppositional qualities into its protracted struggle. Insensibly, the servant as feudal dependent overlapped with the servant as man of talents. By the eighteenth century, the bourgeoisie had composed the subversive bits and pieces of hundreds of traditional servitors into such heroic portraits of its own servitude as Defoe's Moll and Richardson's Pamela, Lesage's Gil Blas and Beaumarchais' Figaro. "Time," as Harry Levin notes, "can revivify certain conventions. Figaro, a servant cleverer than his master, could be welcomed as a harbinger of the bourgeois revolution." Indeed, the history of this borrowed theatrical convention can be used to encapsulate the entangled histories of both the triumphant bourgeoisie and the rising novel:

Within the privacy of print, the comic spirit can be more sympathetic to the bourgeoisie and more critical of the nobility; the comic factotum, or clever servant, can rise in the world. Starting as a lackey, Lesage's Gil Blas could figure successively as a highwayman, steward, doctor, secretary to a bishop, and favorite of the king's favorite. His theatrical descendant, Hugo's Ruy Blas, could even presume to be a tragic hero, a lackey who loves a queen. But a century had passed in the meantime, and that prince of interlopers, Julien Sorel, had arrived. The bourgeois, having crept into fiction through the servant's entrance, had become the master.[22]

The symbolic *volte-face* of 1848, in which the bourgeoisie backed away from its identification with the servant figure as it achieved hegemony and began to fear the militant masses beneath it, accounts for the changes noted above. But if we follow the bourgeoisie as it creeps into fiction through the servants' entrance, then the decline of the master-servant confrontation in the novel of the nineteenth century takes on a different political significance. The decisive shift is not an abandonment of out-dated literary hierarchy in favor of literary democracy but rather the abandonment of the bourgeoisie's revolutionary self-image. Arriving in power, the bourgeoisie sheds both its popular support and the desire or possibility of conceiving itself as a meritorious but under-rewarded underling. "At length," Levin goes on, "with the arrival of Thackeray's *Newcomes,* the position of the bourgeois gentleman is so secure that the old Colonel can snub *Tom Jones* by declaring, 'I won't sit in the kitchen and boose in the servants' hall.'"[23]

If the abandonment of comic tradition was a move toward reaction, then the comic tradition itself looks a good deal less reactionary. On the contrary, the extent of its survival becomes very much worth documenting, even at the expense of the usual historical trajectories. Like the more familiar assumptions about the rise of the bourgeoisie (and of the novel) that it follows, the supposed decline or loss of comic tradition seems an instance of "progressive" thinking that may have come to interfere with political decisions about specific historical configurations and actors. There is a pertinent analogy in the revisionary reading of English history offered by writers like Perry Anderson and Tom Nairn of *New Left Review.* They argue that England's bourgeois revolution not only betrayed itself but, for fear of the forces it had unleashed below it, was never carried to completion, that the English bourgeoisie had already thrown itself into the arms of the nobility. The literary history of the servant offers some support for this substitution of confused stagnation for clear progressiveness. If we look at Pamela, Roxana, Tom Jones, or Roderick Random, it would seem that the English *picaro* (a word that once meant "kitchen boy") is always already a servant-keeper; each of these servants (or, in Tom's case, presumed son of a servant) quickly acquires a servant. Equivocation as to whether the bourgeoisie is servant or master seems coterminous with modern literature.

If we look back at the "revolutionary" uses of the comic tradition in Richardson, Fielding, and Defoe, they are compromised and constrained in much the same way as the Victorian instances given above. As far as linguistic equipment is concerned, Pamela and Mr. B fight on more equal terms than any nineteenth-century master and servant:

When I was a *little kind* to you, said he, in the summerhouse, and you carried yourself so *foolishly* upon it, as if I had intended to do you great harm, did I not tell you you should take no notice of what passed to any creature? and yet you have made common talk of the matter, not concerning either my reputation, or your own.—I made a common talk of it, sir! said I: I have nobody to talk to, hardly.

He interrupted me, and said *Hardly!* you little equivocator! what do you mean by *hardly?* Let me ask you, have you not told Mrs. Jervis for one? Pray your honor, said I, all in agitation, let me go down; for it is not for me to hold an argument with your honor. Equivocator, again! said he, and took my hand, what do you talk of an argument? (Letter 15)

Few literary servants have had every nuance of their every word scrutinized with such care, and Pamela comments on her master's discourse just as attentively, if less freely. In an artful reversal, she even uses her master's authority ("it is not for me to hold an argument with your honor") to ecape from a difficult answer. But when she goes too far, that authority interrupts to shut down the conversation: "I will not be thus spoken to!" This point holds for all such dialogue: it quickly reaches that limit where, if the servant wins, she loses. Hence, as mentioned above, the novel's deep attraction to the formula of the examining magistrate/servant defendant.

Finally, Pamela's real strength lies neither in her quick repartee (though she vies with the best of the theatrical soubrettes) nor in the coherence of her moral position, but in the indiscretion of which she is here accused. This is the servant's original sin: the making known outside the dialogue of what goes on within it. Even Pamela's under-lining suggests this function. Like an echo, it emphasizes problematic words (*foolishly*) for the reader's benefit, separating the detached writer from the engaged speaker. As Mr. B correctly observes, there is equivocation in everything Pamela says. She does not simply lie in order to save herself; she inserts a second level of meaning that salves her conscience by addressing an absent interlocutor.

I will not tell a lie for the world: I *did* tell Mrs. Jervis; for my heart was almost broken; but I opened not my mouth to any other. Very well, boldface, said he, and equivocator again! You did not open your *mouth* to any other; but did you not *write* to some other? . . . And so I am to be exposed, am I, said he, *in* my house, and *out* of my house, to the whole world, by such a sauce-box as you?

Her letters, like the proverbs of Andrew Fairservice, call upon the impersonal speech of the "whole world": "it is not I that expose you," Pamela says.

And, on the other hand, as we have already said, all this survives into the nineteenth century as well, if only in diminished forms. Eliot's soliloquizing coachman, held at arm's length by the narrator's theatrical language, is also permitted by the same language to reacti-vate some of the theatrical chorus' self-conscious complicity with the audience. Similarly, a word like "confid*an*tially" operates on two lev-els: as a revelatory slip on the level of social manners, but outside the realist illusion it is something closer to a theatrical aside in which the servant steps out of her role in order to speak its name. The Weller-ism itself is closer to such a momentary collaboration of servant with narrator than to the realistic grappling of dialogue. It has the detach-ment of the proverb. And the self-referential stinger in the tail, more detached still, is directed past Pickwick to the reader. As, for exam-ple, when Sam advises his master to "have a good night's rest": "There's nothin' so refreshin' as sleep, sir, as the servant-girl said afore she drank the egg-cupful o' laudanum" (ch. 16).

The historical perspective, in other words, has its limits. No matter how far back one goes, from Eliot to *Pickwick Papers* to Scott and beyond, the hypothetical moment of a master-servant dialogue that would be a "duel of Weltanschauung," a pure opposition of class ideologies, seems unattainable. It would be tempting to reduce this chapter of literary history to the contrast of two images: the enlightened Reason of Defoe's Friday and George Eliot's degraded "servants' logic." But one could do so only by ignoring the saving ambiguities of the latter and the comic compromises of the former. If Crusoe and Friday can be said to offer an ideal type, it involves only a restrained sparring, in which the servant assumes the role—secondary and authoritative at the same time—of commentator on his master's beliefs: that is, an inevitable bowing before the orders and errands that guard the frontier of the sayable, and on the other hand a silent explosion of utopian vocabulary that aims past the interlocutor into the world beyond.

IMPERTINENCE AS UTOPIA

One useful test for deciding between the decline and the survival of the comic tradition of master-servant dialogue is the rendering of servant speech and orthography by Thackeray. "It is difficult to take Thackeray's lower middle class or lower class characters quite seriously," as a critic remarks, "because they are always so audibly dropping their aitches."[24] Many, perhaps most of the instances are simply abusive. But as we have seen, there is a tradition that willfully confuses this sort of class humor with a much richer equivocation. As for example when a servant has the last word on the happy ending of *Humphry Clinker:* "Providinch hath been pleased to make great halteration in the pasture of our affairs.—We were yesterday three kiple chined, by the grease of God, in the holy bands of mattermoney."[25] This secularizing and materializing of divine providence, with the marriage altar as a halter in which couples are chained like kine (or conscripted into armed bands?) and matter/money is the truth of God's grace in the oiling of human affairs—this is very far from the easy ridicule of haphazard aspirates. It brings orthographic ineptitude close to the poetry of Friday's description of his deity: "All things do say O to him."

Thackeray borrows from Smollett when he describes a bride led "to the halter," but some of what passes for class abuse seems to contain lucky hits of his own, like "too retched to have any hap-pytite." Once one begins to listen or look with attention, it becomes hard to draw the line between unenlightening nonsense and faint glimmerings of surprising sense. In *Vanity Fair,* for example, a house-keeper comments on governesses: "they give themselves the hairs and hupstarts of ladies, and their wages is no better than you nor me" (ch. 6). In the servant mini-rebellion that helps close *The Newcomes,* the maid calls her place "that 'ell upon hearth," and the effect is to bring hell several spans closer to the cosy Victorian home. Ordinarily, one may note, there is little said upon this characteristic Thackerayan occasion. In "A Shabby-Genteel Story," the maid's rebellion goes no farther than "TELL HER TO FETCH IT HERSELF" in small caps. Even Morgan's revolt at the end of *Pendennis* quickly turns from words to knives and to the intervention of the police.

Malapropism is more variably and flexibly eloquent. Its themes have never been arbitrary. Mrs. Malaprop herself is primarily con-cerned with literacy, for example, and "negligible" therefore becomes "illegible" and "obliterate" becomes "illiterate." Tabitha Bramble, a Methodist, informs a prospective servant not to expect extravagant wages: "having a family of my own, I must be more occumenical than ever." Proprietary about "her" family instead of welcoming the ser-vant into it, she is too economical to be ecumenical. And Mrs. Slip-slop sees her passion "resulted and treated with ironing": for a servant, the result of failure in love is more housework.

Even at his most ponderously patronizing, Thackeray can slip sud-denly back into this tradition of deeply if not seriously self-referential speech. A footman, proclaiming the eternal fitness of upstairs and downstairs, comes up with this phrase for it: "Theirs is the first flor; hours is the basemint." As if the collective consciousness of his class spoke through his unconsciousness, the servant suggests that the masters cull the first flowers, while we spend hours in the cellar, where our labor mints their (base) money. When the orthography of the uneducated is capable of transmitting this degree of poetic com-pression, then while one must agree that Thackeray "is making no attempt to present the actual sound of an actual voice," one must go on to add that something more is involved than "a humor based on feelings of class or educational superiority."[26] Even in quantitative terms, there is an impressive number of instances that justify their existence by debunking or effecting comic reversals: "our youthful Quean," a superior's "bittiful" piano-playing (beautiful or pitiful), the "honrabble Barnet," sometimes "tolrabble" and sometimes "misrabble." In this poetic, inhuman speech "able" and "rabble" are virtual synonyms: the mob is asserting its capabilities. In an example that invites comparison with Blake's "London," Thackeray refers (via servant surrogate) to "the rainin sufferin of the French crownd"—the daily suffering of the crowd is projected into the sovereign responsible for it. "The Persecution of British Footmen," one of several works in which Thackeray filters revolutionary events (here, Paris in 1848) through a servant's voice, renders the cries of the French people as "Amore Lewy-Philip" and "Ah Bah l'Aristograt." On the transcendent level made possible by phonetic spelling, this is crying out for love and denouncing ingratitude. The comic softening diverts attention from the superficial terrors of revolution to the logic of its emotional substratum.

As Friday's description of his fellow tribesmen—"they willing love learn"—exceeds his master's translation—"He meant by this, they would be willing to learn"—so too Thackeray's bursts of turbulent, congested blunder add something of value to the message of ordinary syntax.[27] Linguistic aberration blends indistinguishably into a sort of topsy-turvy poetic diction, authoritatively remote from any actual speech community and thus able to bear suppressed insights and yearnings. Within this privileged discourse, advances by ladies to their footmen become "by no means unnatral or unusyouall"—that is, in free translation: if you would all admit it, we would find ourselves in a democratic jumble of us-you-all together. Like Friday's account of prayer, "going to say O," this is less a caricature of a class voice than a prolongation of comedy's traditional license to imagine not-yet-existent democracies.[28]

Theorists of comedy often make a distinction between conscious wordplay, like that of the servants who open *Romeo and Juliet,* and unconscious errors of pronunciation and orthography, as here. In practice, this distinction is shaky. Even C. Jeames Yellowplush, one of Thackeray's servant surrogates, adds with a wink that he has been "violetting the rules of authography." If puns are a version of pastoral, malapropism too has pastoral's power to dissolve the world of is and reveal a counter-world of might-be. Whether intentional or not, a primary effect of both is a secondary effect of the theatrical chorus: "the implication of 'other worlds'—of alternative realities."[29] And the novelistic chorus has the same effect. By their very inconsistency with the psychological realism of character and situation, servants who are exiled to the choral margins of the novel, who speak unresponsively or inconsequentially, generate images of a world of apartness and latency.

Everett Knight remarks that Dickens' dialogues do not take into account "the fact that people undergo astonishing transformations depending upon the company in which they find themselves." Thus "Susan Nipper is able to tell off Dombey exactly as she would do in imagination, as though Dombey were not there."[30] Partly paralyzed after his misfortune, Dombey is not in fact all there. But Susan's impertinence is intrinsic to the mode, in Dickens and elsewhere. Servant speech, at a disadvantage in the mimetic dimension, snubs its powerful listeners by preferring the second, rhetorical dimension, and it colors this second dimension with the servant's radical social dissatisfaction. If Susan Nipper blocks Dombey out and addresses herself instead, out of earshot, "to some and all" (ch. 44), it is because she is trying to reconcile "some" and "all"—as in George Eliot's example of "Servants' Logic"—on Florence's behalf and on her own. To flesh out her character would make this specialized but transcendent function impossible. In order to adapt it to the decorum of the novel, Dickens makes many of his servants, like Susan, partial people, constrained by varieties of Dombey's dialogue-inhibiting paralysis. Smike is an idiot, the Marchioness too small as well as too inarticulate for conversation; in *Bleak House,* Guster is an epileptic and Phil Squod a cripple who hobbles obliquely away from the object he is addressing. Such characters have a limited capacity for dialogue. But when they do speak, it's often because, like the Fat Boy in *Pickwick,* they "wants to make your flesh creep." The imagination that speaks through them runs to apocalyptic extremes.

Smike, for example, cannot muster enough vocabulary for sustained converse, and his interchanges with Nicholas Nickleby do not get much more involved than this repetitious instance, where Nicholas is trying to rehearse his "faithful hard-working servant" in the part of *Romeo and Juliet*'s Apothecary.

"Who calls so loud?" said Smike.
"Who calls so loud?" repeated Nicholas.
"Who calls so loud?" cried Smike. (ch. 25)

But the theatrical context makes up for what the dialogue itself lacks. Since Nicholas has the role of Romeo in the same performance, we are obliged to consider Smike in the character of his master's poisoner, unwilling to do him any harm but left no choice:

ROM: Contempt and beggary hangs upon the back;
    The world is not thy friend, nor the world's law,
    The world affords no law to make thee rich;
    Then be not poor, but break it, and take this.
APO: My poverty, but not my will, consents. (5.1)

Smike has been "wholly unable to get any more of that part into his head than the general idea that he was very hungry," but the part itself fills in the logic of class interest of which he remains unconscious. Another actor in the troupe, taking the role for the man, hints that Smike is "more knave than fool," and Smike does go on stage once "with another gentleman as a general rebellion," but even so melodramatic a plot as this cannot accommodate that drastic suggestion. The fragmentary traces of involuntary conflict between servant and master come closest to articulation at the end of the novel, when Smike's impossible desire to unite himself with his master's family (which is in fact his own family) through his love for Nicholas' sister leads to a mysterious death. In the event, the death too is his own, but the suggestion of the irreconcilable is the same.

An apocalyptic suggestiveness, whether of general rebellions or of the conciliations they prepare, hangs over the very impossibility of Victorian dialogue. As dialogue fades toward mutism, it seems to build. In a rather more difficult but perhaps more representative sense, this is the case for the conversation that passes between Phil Squod and his master in *Bleak House*:

"And so, Phil," says George of the Shooting Gallery . . . "you were dreaming of the country last night:" . . .
    "Yes, guv'ner."

"What was it like?"

"I hardly know what it was like, guv'ner," said Phil considering.

"How did you know it was the country?"

"On account of the grass, I think. And the swans upon it," says Phil after further consideration.

"What were the swans doing on the grass?"

"They was a-eating of it, I expect," says Phil. . . .

"The country," says Mr. George, plying his knife and fork; "why, I suppose you never clapped your eyes on the country, Phil?"

"I see the marshes once," says Phil, contentedly eating his breakfast.

"What marshes?"

"*The* marshes, commander," returns Phil.

"Where are they?"

"I don't know where they are," says Phil; "but I see 'em, guv'ner. They was flat. And miste." (ch. 26)

Here the traditional procedures of comedy touch social actuality at at least one point. Phil's "*The* marshes" seems to tally with Basil Bernstein's sociolinguistic description of working-class speech as "particularistic" or "context-bound." It is "closely tied to the context and would only be understood by others if they had access to the context which originally generated the speech."[31] The irrelevance of which marshes and where would presumably be taken for granted by someone whose experience, like Phil's, has been restricted to the poorer neighborhoods of London. To Phil's master these remain real questions, and Phil's replies miss the point; they cannot free their meaning from an immediate communal context that no longer exists and adapt to the necessary impersonality of public discourse. But this does not have the feel of abusive caricature, and the reason is perhaps a more indirect contact with social actuality. Remaining bound to a group of those who understand each other already, Phil's words activate a sort of auditory image of their lost communal context. They invite the reader to relax in the comfortable solidarity of the totally known. And in the foggy, anonymous London of Chancery and finance capital, where no one knows much of anyone, Phil's unwarranted assumption of shared prior knowledge takes on by contrast the resonance of a utopian insight.

The reader need not after all recognize himself in the straight-man interlocutor; his interests do not require acquaintance with the exact coordinates of the marshes where George's curiosity is enmired. One might say that the interests of a modern (or post-realist) reader are better served by Phil's dismissive tautology, or the one that sets the scene of *Jacques le fataliste:* "D'où venaient-ils? Du lieu le plus prochain." Knowing as he picks up the novel that it lives or dies as a communication to himself, the reader also knows that realistic details of place are only a pretext. Phil's words assume this knowledge, speak to it, and do not waste time over details. They turn themselves to a listener and respond to what is expected: "a-eating of it, I expect." What is dramatically inappropriate in his language, hence comic, is also what constitutes its extra-dramatic appeal to the reader. And this appeal coincides with Phil's vocal simulation of an absent community. Coincides with it, or even reproduces it: the communal solidarity that Phil calls to mind is doubled by that feeling of solidarity between text and audience whose most intense forms are associated with the term entertainment. Like many other comic routines, this dialogue could have appeared with a minimum of alteration in a novel by Smollett or by Beckett, but its atemporality does not deprive it of historical significance. The utopian echo in Phil's voice, borne through the centuries by comic tradition, cuts into the society of the novel with the critical edge of future reason.

3

Exposition:
The Servant as Narrator

Exposition   1. The action of putting, or the condition of being put,
out of place; expulsion.

Oxford English Dictionary

[It] was wonderful, if just a *trifle* humiliating to listen to her . . . one
got a new vision of Tevershall village from Mrs. Bolton's talk. A
terrible, seething welter of ugly life it seemed: not at all the flat
drabness it looked from outside.

Lady Chatterley's Lover

NARRATION AND AUTHORITY

In his preface to *The Turn of the Screw,* Henry James remarks that the
governess-narrator "has 'authority,' which is a good deal to have given
her."[1] The reference is secondarily to what is elsewhere called her
"supreme authority" over the children and other servants at Bly and
primarily to the authority over the reader that inevitably accrues to
her as the sole informant about the events there (p. 5). The mild pun
is a reminder that in a sense the teller of a tale is a holder of power. Of
course, the governess' credibility has not gone unquestioned. In general, contemporary criticism is inclined to challenge any author's
"unambiguous bestowal of authority"—the phrase is Wayne
Booth's—upon a narrator.[2] But this inclination only underlines the
historical fact that authority has been attributed to those characters
within a story who serve the double function of transmitting it. This
authority is confirmed by its challengers, for power can only be
disputed at a site where the disputants agree it is located. Controver-

sies over the "reliability" of narrators can be taken as proof of the aura of legitimacy that provocatively surrounds them.

There is thus a hint of paradox in the fact that the performance of narrative functions is one of the traditional prerogatives of the literary servant. "Since a novel is essentially an inside story, full of domestic atmosphere and family matters," Harry Levin writes, "the point of view has often been associated with the servant in the house."[3] "Family matters," as we shall see, have much to do with this. At a time when the majority of servants changed positions every year or two, the literary prevalence of long-serving family retainers may have stemmed both from paternalist illusions and from their peculiar usefulness as figures of family continuity.[4] They seem to be as ubiquitous as families themselves. Working down from full-time servants who narrate an entire novel, like Thady Quirk of *Castle Rackrent,* or a good deal of one, like Nelly Dean in *Wuthering Heights* and Gabriel Betteredge in *The Moonstone,* we also have a more numerous class who are both servants and narrators for a large part of a novel, like Pamela and Gil Blas, Caleb Williams and Jane Eyre. Then there are protagonists who are servant-narrators at least briefly, like Moll Flanders and Roderick Random, or are "centers of consciousness" in the employer's home, like Julien Sorel. In addition to all of these, we can count the minor servants, featureless and perhaps even nameless, to whom the author nevertheless chooses to give the floor at some strategic point, who emerge into ephemeral being in order to deliver messages, commit indiscretions, impart family secrets, administer consolations, emit prophecies, make recognitions, and so forth— through whom, in short, the business of divulging decisive information is largely carried on.

What is the significance of this odd social bias in the dispensing of expository duties? In *Rogue's Progress,* Robert Alter sets up a comparison that promises useful evidence. He places side by side two works by Lesage: *Turcaret* (1709), a play amply endowed with traditional intriguing servants, and *Gil Blas* (1715–1735), a novel in which one of those servants assumes the responsibility of narrator. The strategy is to catch the new novel when it has barely emerged from its antecedents in theatrical comedy, when the two genres still share many of their materials and conventions, and thus to isolate and describe the new phenomenon of novelistic narration. For Alter, this difference in the mode of narration is in fact decisive. "Nearly everybody in *Turcaret* is a scoundrel," he observes, while the characters of *Gil Blas* are filled with "compassion, companionship, affectionate good humor." Why? The low view of humanity in *Turcaret* is generated by theatrical distance: by "the convention of stage comedy, or a main tradition of it, where people—viewed wholly externally—are assumed to be motivated invariably by self-interest." In the novel, on the other hand, first-person narration brings reader and character into greater intimacy, and this intimacy encourages the reader to accept the "low-life, homeless, rag-clad rogue" of picaresque as "his double, his brother. One of the reasons that the picaroon always tells his own story is to close the distance between him and his reader." In effect, the "sympathy" and "identification" that result from this close, prolonged narrative contact reduplicate themselves thematically in the process of interpretation as "a sense of fellowship with humanity." Thanks to the insidious immediacy of the narrator's hold over the reader, the same "low-life" figure whom the play condemns as a "scoundrel" can disarm criticism and establish a subversive right to fellowship.[5]

Literary history, dealing with the impact of the novel's break with theatrical comedy, has tended to support this view of the social significance of its narrative technique. The relative freedom from public scrutiny and censorship inherent in it helped create, as another critic of Lesage notes, "the very different attitude of the public and of power."[6] Harry Levin gives the same innovation credit for the fairy-tale metamorphosis of the theater's auxiliary servant into an upwardly mobile protagonist of the novel: "Within the privacy of print, the comic spirit can be more sympathetic to the bourgeoisie . . . The comic factotum, or clever servant, can rise in the world."[7] Being "inherently devoid of the elements which restricted identification" in theatrical performance, Ian Watt argues, a novel like *Pamela* could wield a "more absolute power over the reader's consciousness," and thus give the old Cinderella story a hitherto impossible force.[8]

These remarks encourage the notion that there is a correspondence between power over the reader and power in, over, or against the social order—that he or she who tells the tale benefits from a

peculiar supplementary authority. But once this correspondence has
been observed in the first-person novel, it is difficult not to see
something very like it in stage comedy as well. Though theater usually
lacks a narrator, certain moments and devices in theatrical performance clearly offer statements that are, relatively to others, authoritative. And these tend to involve the theatrical servant. In opposition to
"the prevailing theoretical concept of drama as a strictly figural text
with the author 'refined out of existence, paring his fingenails,'" Paul
Hernadi stresses the intervention of the author, for example, in the
Greek chorus and in "certain types of dramatic figures (messengers,
prophets, mouthpiece characters)."[9] Into the same category we can
put prologues, epilogues, direct address, and the aside. Associated
distinctively though of course not exclusively with marginal, lower-
class characters, these techniques manifest "the playwright's concrete
ubiquity in the text of his drama."[10] The servants of comedy would
thus appear to shine with the pale fire of his reflected authority.

This is not to suggest that the authority of the servant-narrator
derives predominantly from hints of privileged access to an unseen
author. The trans-generic coincidence is noteworthy, but the very
idea of an author carries less weight in a play, whose immediate
referent is actors acting, than in a novel, which is inconceivable
without a novelist. On the other hand, figures and functions like the
prologue, chorus, messenger, and aside also share a fraternal collusion
with the audience, and it is from that source that they draw authority
in a broader sense. The aside, for example, becomes a truth convention by linking speaker and audience at the expense of the other
dramatis personae. It requires no reference to an implicit author. By
breaking "the situational frame within which the action is defined as
taking place," it takes the priority due to the world of spectators,
which precedes, surrounds, and authenticates the performance as a
whole.[11] Like the picaro's monopoly over the distribution of his
creator's words, the audience complicity of the comic servant signifies
a privileged closeness to the point of reception. Authority flows
inevitably toward the informant to whom we must either listen or put
the book down, like James' governess, and it flows as well to those
theatrical figures who actively recognize or even passively occupy the
framing endpoints of the communicative act.

Looking back now at *Turcaret,* a "hard," naturalistic comedy that does not tolerate the servant's customary violations of dramatic illusion, we can see that whenever statements are made that press up against the borders of that illusion, whenever reference to the extra-dramatic world, the creator's intentions, or the audience's reception touches the limits of the aesthetic experience, there we find the play's traditional servants. Almost half of the play's asides (21 of 47 by my count) are pronounced by three of them, who enjoy a disproportionately intimate relation with the public. In addition, it is servants who pronounce the final lines of each of the play's five acts. In two of them, moreover, the speech is a soliloquy, and Act 5 leaves the servant lovers on stage together, alone with the audience. Their presence provides defining brackets for the action. The sense of these endings is also definitive—a mixture of moral generalization and prophecy—and this adds to the authoritative finality that we are in any case eager to attribute to endings as such, as Frank Kermode has shown.[12] At the end of Act 1, for example, Frontin, who is valet to two leading characters, declares to the audience in soliloquy:

I admire the course of human life! We fleece a coquette; the coquette devours a businessman; the businessman plunders other businessmen; it makes the most amusing chain of knavery in the world.[13]

Here Frontin, still for the moment no more than a traditional comic factotum, concentrates in himself as no other character does the totalizing and generalizing of authorial vision; an unmediated, winning contact with the audience, strategic position within the structure of the play; and an outsider's detached realism about motive and consequence. His theatrical existence is too bound up with what is most authoritative in the text for us to think him, as Alter does, a "scoundrel" no better than those he cheats.

The point here is not to demonstrate that, as one would in any case expect, *Gil Blas* and *Turcaret* after all have much in common. Nor is it to blur the real generic distinctions between drama and novel. In indicating how far the social connotations of the servant's expository prerogative transcend genre, I am trying to resist a narrowly formal interpretation and to enable a broader, more historical questioning of this odd privilege. As the example of *Turcaret* suggests, not to question it is to miss a good deal. Frontin may be, as Alter says, no better or worse than those he dupes, but he, unlike them, enjoys a special relationship with the author and the audience, and this ensures that he will be taken for more, and will end better, than the deflating epilogue foresees. At the end of the play, Frontin assures his personal fortune by pretending to have been duped; he himself provides the conservative "poetic justice" for which the epilogue and the moral orthodoxy of the time cry out (*à trompeur, trompeur et demi*). In so doing he both aligns himself with the putative intentions of the author and exorcizes the possibility of his downfall. In a similar way, the power of Frontin's complicity with the audience results in his moral elevation. In this jungle of competing self-interests, only Frontin, loyal to the audience, has the loyalty of friends: Lisette, sardonic but faithful, and a seemingly inexhaustible supply of onstage and offstage accomplices for his ruses. Even his vocabulary is colored by the gregariousness of his stage habits. To Lisette he calls the stolen money "the first foundations of our community" (3.11), just as she later refers to their trickery as "the act of solidarity" (5.1). Both use the servant's quintessential, ambiguous "we," by means of which they at once include themselves impertinently in the fortunes of their masters ("It is a conquest, madam, that we made") and, more impor- tant, remember if not quite include the audience:

LISETTE (low): Who is she saying it to? Who knows it better than we do? (4.10)

It is their expository functions that enable the servants of *Turcaret* to realize a moral value beyond the competitive individualism to which so much else in the play can be reduced: the value of solidarity. It is as if the expository act of sharing knowledge with the audience and then, in a typical "entre nous," reminding us of it, automatically gave the two servants the moral sanction of the community, and with it the power to win out in the end.

THE NARRATOR AS VILLAIN

As suggested above, the inescapable authority of the narrator seems to assert itself by spilling over into a sense of the narrator's power over the world his words evoke. This thematic duplication of technique also seems to transcend genre. The servants of Medwall's *Fulgens and Lucrece* step outside the play to comment on it and thus imply, as Elizabeth Burns perceives, "some control over it." By the same logic, "double characters" like Iago, with their privileged vice-like intimacy with the public, will be "part presenter, part instigator of the action."[14] In a discussion of confidants in the tragedies of Racine, Roland Barthes puts this point incisively. The servant's odd powers over the plot, he suggests, must be seen in the light of her or his expository proximity to the world of the audience. "For the confidant, the world exists; leaving the stage, he can enter reality and then return from it. . . . The first result of this *droit de sortie* is that for him the universe ceases to be absolutely antinomic. . . . Whence the dialectical nature of his solutions"—and his continuity with "that whole line of irreverent valets who will oppose the lord and master's psychological regression by a supple and happy mastery of reality."[15]

In a sense, therefore, this line of masterful expositors could be said to give power to the people. Where the public is in fact largely popular, as in nineteenth-century melodrama, the principle is clearer still. Since its flowering at the time of the French Revolution, melodrama had revealed a distinct social bias. Michael Booth reminds us of its working-class public, its reflection of "class hatreds," its generally "anti-authoritarian" stance.[16] And this bias works through its characteristic configuration of causality and audience contact. The causality shows an "apparent discrepancy between motive and action, cause and effect."[17] That is, the action tends to be determined by such providential, off-center actors as the working-class Comic Man, "a friend or manservant" who, "in the absence or incapacity of his superior," shifts rapidly from comic relief to heroism. "His strength and energy can be astonishing . . . In many plays he is much better at coping with the villain than the hero is, and is frequently entirely responsible for the triumph of virtue."[18] This social dislocation of causality cannot be separated from the stagecraft, or rather housecraft, of the interaction between melodrama and popular audience. As Bernard Sharratt points out, the exteriority of "the people" on the stage also characterizes "the people" in the house. If they are "taken in" by the theatrical illusion, they are simultaneously full of "desire for anecdote, for 'inside knowledge' about the people behind the image": "the audience both 'knows' the actor behind the role and claims an expertise in the techniques of his art: the sense of fear is accompanied by, though not fully replaced by, an awareness of the illusory nature of its source. A perhaps related aspect of this complex of attitudes is the urge to pass comments on a performance while it is still in progress: the 'aside' and 'ad-lib' are as much a feature of the audience's contribution as of the performer's." In short, the audience of melodrama is "allowed to subvert the role *and* asked to make it live, in quite explicit ways (boos, hisses, 'Watch out behind you,' etc.)."[19]

The suggestion is that the audience seeks and takes power over the performance, both directly (in its participation) and indirectly, in the translation of its determining presence into the otherwise inexplicable powers of its representatives, like the Comic Man. This suggestion finds some support in the history of adaptations of "middle-class" novels for the working-class stage. Rewritings of *Robinson Crusoe* tend to build up the role of Friday; rewritings of *Frankenstein* often add a comc and incompetent but ultimately determining servant precisely at the crucial point where the origin of evil must be accounted for. For example, in the 1932 film version (directed by James Whale) Fritz, a hunchback assistant (played by Dwight Frye) who doesn't exist in the novel, is doubly responsible for the tragedy: first, when he "mistakenly steals a pickled criminal brain (prominently labeled 'ABNORMAL BRAIN')" to be planted in the Monster, and then when "he amuses himself by torturing the newly resurrected Monster with whips, chains, and torches until it responds by hanging him."[20] The modification of the story for a larger (and lower) audience gives a larger role to the representative of the people—a role that is extraordinarily powerful, despite its comic trappings, and also of an extraordinary moral ambiguity.

The notion that the people could or do possess power, or that power might even inhere in their very skepticism and exteriority, has never been anything other than morally suspect when it has not simply been identified with evil itself. In Racine's most famous source, Euripides' *Hippolytus,* it is the Nurse, who represents skeptical reason and who, as Bernard Knox notes, "has more lines than either Phaedra or Theseus," who also becomes "the most important link in the chain of events which Aphrodite has forged": "Her love for Phaedra is the motive for her actions from first to last. But in the end she succeeds only in destroying Phaedra's honor and her life as well."[21] The principle seems quite similar in *The Turn of the Screw*. For many readers, the governess who has all the lines becomes a sort of villain, incited by sexual fantasies and class snobbery to unwitting manslaughter. And it seems likely that here too the hypothesis of her ultimate villainous determination of the events she recounts is induced, rightly or not, by the fact that it is she who recounts them. The reader suspects that she controls as an actor the events whose presentation she manifestly controls as narrator.

It is remarkable, in fact, how often this suspicion crops up when servants have a major role in the narration. In *The Turn of the Screw* itself it has been proposed several times, with various degrees of seriousness, that the true culprit is the housekeeper-confidant through whom the governess obtains most of her scanty information, Mrs. Grose.[22] Equally revealing, if no more plausible, is the occasional argument that "The Villain in *Wuthering Heights*" is its narrator-in-chief, Ellen Dean.[23] The point to insist on in these readings is that, unconvincing as they may be, they respond to real textual impulses that are part of the way we read the words of servants. Fielding's hostile interpretation of *Pamela*—a hypocritical maid manipulating her booby master—clearly detects a real current of the novel: Pamela's use of the narrative privilege, among other weapons, to hold her own in an unequal class and sexual struggle. It is in large part her letters—which "outshine her virtue," as Ellen Moers comments, and are equally indispensable—that win her master's heart. Her power is in her pen. "Clearly Richardson was obsessed with the power of letters to change the world."[24] Yes, but no such obsession is required in order to spot an impulse to world transformation when servants seize their pens or open their mouths.

William Godwin's *Caleb Williams, or Things as They Are* offers another instance. Both characters within the novel and critics outside it fling accusations of villainy at Caleb, its protagonist and narrator. The first word his master addresses to him is "Villain!" (bk. 1, ch. 1). This is surprising, since Caleb is truly the victim of extraordinary persecution, as he claims to be. Yet by the end of the novel he is even accusing himself: "I have been his murderer" (Postscript). If murder there be, some guilt once again adheres to exposition itself. When Caleb uncovers the secret of Falkland's mysterious behavior, he is acting on behalf of the reader's shared curiosity. His personal motives, like those of Iago, remain ultimately unfathomable, perhaps because his tie with the reader, like Iago's with the audience, dispenses him from psychological diagnosis.

The knowledge he acquires will be defined in context as power for evil (the discovery is followed by a scene in a Garden) and Falkland deals with it as such, despite Caleb's "best intentions" (bk. 2, ch. 2).[25] The insurrectionary meaning of such knowledge, its translation into "authority" and "control," had been predicted by Samuel Johnson. Johnson seems almost to give a recipe for Godwinian Gothic:

> The danger of betraying our weakness to our servants, and the impossibility of concealing it from them, may be justly considered as one motive to a regular and irreproachable life. For no condition is more hateful or despicable, than his who has put himself in the power of his servant; in the power of him whom, perhaps, he has first corrupted by making him subservient to his vices, and whose fidelity he cannot enforce by any precepts of honesty or reason. It is seldom known that authority, thus acquired, is possessed without insolence . . . he is, from that fatal hour, in which he sacrificed his dignity to his passions, in perpetual dread of insolence or defamation; of a controuler at home, or an accuser abroad.[26]

Falkland takes much this view. "Base, artful wretch that you are! Learn to be more respectful! Are my passions to be wound and unwound by an insolent domestic?" (bk. 2, ch. 2). Caleb, like Pamela, is in fact neither insolent nor artful. But as soon as he steps into the servant-master relation, his "character" becomes irrelevant, or incoherent. "Caleb is introduced as a frank and open youth," Robert Kiely points out, "but from the beginning his attitude toward Falkland is ambivalent and their conversations a network of ambiguity." As is the case again and again for servant narrators, Caleb's knowledge overflows the channel of his loyal intentions, forcing unwanted suppressions and garbled disclosures that render the Godwinian doctrine of sincerity "an ideal incapable of realization."[27] He never ceases to revere his master, but his revelations lead directly to his master's death: "you have conquered!" the latter tells him, "I see that the artless and manly story you have told, has carried conviction to every hearer" (Postscript). Critics who hold him responsible for this fatal discourse miss part of the point.[28] His character is incoherent, though the violence of his discourse is not.

After Falkland's death, Caleb concludes, "I began these memoirs with the idea of vindicating my character. I have now no character that I wish to vindicate." Indeed, as a "character"—a moral, emotional being—Caleb experiences the ending without satisfaction. But as an agent of narration he is also an agent of political justice, pushing the novel to its final triumphant reversal. The same contradiction between muddled character and social coherence is basic to Maria Edgeworth's *Castle Rackrent.* Thady Quirk, the faithful family retainer who narrates it, could hardly be called a villain. However, the novel does contain a rising, unscrupulous figure who little by little takes over the Rackrent estates, dispossessing those whom Thady calls "the family." And this is none other than "my son Jason." Jason has worked his way up in the story under cover of his father's comic digressions, his harmless, irrelevant allusions to himself and "his" family. But the real story is in these asides. The garrulous messenger who obtrudes himself into his message turns out to act upon as well as transmit the story. Here its structure follows the curve of Thady's overblown first sentence: "Having, out of friendship for the family, upon whose estate, praised be Heaven! I and mine have lived rent-free time out of mind, voluntarily undertaken to publish the MEMOIRS OF THE RACKRENT FAMILY, I think it my duty to say a few words, in the first place, concerning myself."[29] "I and mine" interrupt the subordinate clause and occupy the main clause, where the sentence descends from the eulogistic capitals of the Rackrents to land solidly on "myself." By the end of the novel, the estate where he and his have lived rent-free time out of mind is theirs by a still better title.

Commenting on Thady's "muddledness and repugnance to taking one side or the other" in telling a tale to which he cannot be personally indifferent, Ernest A. Baker remarks that "he can run with the hare and hunt with the hounds."[30] Edgeworth herself shows her awareness that any narrator is liable to be suspected of being one of the hunters: "Where we see that a man has the power, we may naturally suspect that he has the will to deceive us" (ch. 8). To my knowledge, at least two critics have indulged this suspicion in print. There is clearly a good deal of material for them to go on. It is Thady who hands over Sir Condy's last guineas to be lost, and he who pours the fatal bumper from which Sir Condy will not recover. Both he and his master cry out against son Jason's sharp practice as "murder" (p. 53). This may seem like the sort of colorful Irishism the footnotes are continually smiling over (e.g. "kilt and murdered"), until Jason makes his killing, Thady fills his master's glass, and Sir Condy topples over. James Newcomer goes farther, interpreting the flip of the coin as a "ploy" to advance "a Quirk to the position of mistress of the estate" and discerning Thady's "fine finger" behind "Jason's rise to affluence and power." If this is a bit much, there is at least no mistake about Thady's comparison of his master's high-living indebtedness to the antics of a decapitated duck. "'How is it,' says I, being a little merry at the time: 'how is it but just as you see the ducks in the chicken-yard, just after their heads are cut off by the cook, running round and round faster than when alive?'"[31] What Walter Allen calls Thady's "typical Irish humor" is largely made up of such piquant specimens as this comment on the death of a previous Rackrent: "The whole country rang with his praises. Happy the man who could but get a sight of the hearse!"[32] Language of this sort seems designed to incite the most sanguinary hypotheses.

To resolve the ambivalence of this language into an indictment of the speaker is to close off prematurely the ambiguities that trans-class narration opens up. If the awarding of certificates of character to servants is a measure of social control, then the critical gesture of discovering the hidden villainy of a servant narrator is an extreme and paradigmatic example. The terms of the charge are almost formulaic. What James Newcomer says about Thady could have been taken from articles on Pamela, Caleb Williams, or Nelly Dean—perhaps even from an unfavorable certificate of character: "He is artful rather than artless, unsentimental rather than sentimental, shrewd rather than obtuse, clear-headed rather than confused, calculating rather than trusting."[33] As Robert Kiely insists in his discussion of *Wuthering Heights,* the familiar choice between two such readings of character is short-sighted: "It is pointless to argue about whether Nelly Dean is a 'good' or 'bad' character, whether she is sympathetic, genuinely close to the families she serves, or whether she is selfishly detached, even jealous, and therefore hypocritical in her protestations of loyalty."[34] To opt for "good" character is to deny the sense of dangerous, misplaced worldly power that the servant's narrative role evokes; to opt for "bad" character is to exaggerate it to the point where it can be condemned and dismissed. It is not Pamela's virtue or hypocrisy that contorts her style, but the structural ambivalence of an intermediary between two powers:

What a happy change is this! And who knows but my kind, my generous master, may put it in my power, when he shall see me not quite unworthy of it, to be a means, without injuring him, to dispense around me, to many persons, the happy influences of the condition to which I shall be, by his kind favor, exalted?[35]

If we smooth out the folds of this sentence, the nervous backward glances at the still unsecured source of her future "power," what we are left with is the Plautine slave's invitation to the audience to share the bounty of the post-nuptial, post-performance festivities. Pamela is doing her best to mediate between her master's established power and the implicit claims of the community, the "many persons" whom she vaguely addresses and who accede, through her, to a power of their own. The words of such a mediator cannot avoid duplicity. Their muddledness is structural and irreducible.

SURVEILLANCE AND THE FAMILY

The bounty that Pamela dispenses and the suspicion of her Machiavellian designs are two sides of one coin. Similarly, an outcome in which, with or without the servant's help, the master dies and his estates pass into the hands of the servant-narrator's family, as in *Castle Rackrent*, neatly realizes the "twin identity as servant and spy" that Ian Ousby finds in Caleb Williams' Christian name. "His Biblical namesake was one of 'the men which Moses sent to spy out the land' of Canaan. Upon his return, Caleb was rewarded by Moses for fidelity of service: 'But my servant Caleb, because he . . . hath followed me fully, him will I bring into the land whereinto he went; and his seed shall possess it.'"[36] The servant will occupy the Promised Land that he has surveyed and told of, while the master, like Moses, will die without entering it—the prophecy seems worth applying to other instances of servant narration as well. But to feel the full strangeness of the servant's narrative authority and the prophetic reach of its corollaries is to stand before a historical puzzle. Where can this ascribed power come from? What is it that encourages the connection between exposition, aggression, and ultimate (re)possession?

The existence of this constellation in the novel cannot be explained by the borrowed authority of theatrical convention alone. There are also several aspects of the institution of domestic service itself to consider. To begin with, as mediators between rulers and ruled domestic servants have always been among the first of the latter to lay claim to the language and cultural accomplishments of the former. Ian Watt, filling in the background of Pamela's "conspicuous literacy," points out the "literary importance" of "domestic servants, especially footmen and waiting-maids," who had leisure, light, and books for reading, and by all accounts used them.[37] Richardson's early writings for "my Fellow-servants" and the origins of *Pamela* as a letter-writing manual, along with all the caustic comments about the novel's success among unmarried chambermaids, show how visible this servant readership was.[38] The consciousness of servants as an audience would also have been forced upon Fielding in his capacity as playwright:

It was a custom among playgoers to send livery servants to keep their places until they saw fit to arrive, perhaps half-way through the show. The footmen would then move upstairs to the gallery, where they would claim free or half-price admission, while reserving the right to make noisy criticism of the play. Increasingly, managements resisted the right of free admission to the gallery, and tension mounted. Angry footmen were behind at least two of the big riots which chequered the history of Drury Lane during this century.[39]

At the reception end of the aesthetic act, servants here show their power quite literally.

Fielding refers on several occasions to the voices of "the Gentlemen at the Top of the House," and Partridge's obtrusive presence at performances of *The Provok'd Husband* and of *Hamlet*—a motif taken over by Dickens among others—can be considered both a novelistic accommodation of the theater's servant commentator and a continuation of the servants' "noisy criticism."[40] From the eighteenth century on, as Richard Altick remarks, the literacy of servants was "the constant burden of contemporary satire."[41] In Victorian periodical humor "servants below stairs sing arias from Italian opera; the butler offers his services to the duchess when she has need of a dictionary; and nursemaids compliment the paintings of their military beaux in highly technical language."[42] In trying to put servants back in their place, these jokes concede that they have left it. Because of their extraordinary numbers, they were now "a fairly important part of the reading public." Recent statistics estimate that total servant reader-ship in this period was larger than that of the intelligentsia.[43]

public." Recent statistics estimate that total servant readership in this period was larger than that of the intelligentsia.[43]

Servants were sources as well as receivers of narrative. It is from a servant that Jane Eyre learns about Pamela's adventures, and Q. D. Leavis speculates that since "the packmen took round *Pamela* in cheap parts, it being so popular with servants," Charlotte Brontë may have heard about them in the same way.[44] Of course, the stories servants

servants told to their masters' children were not limited to the re-transmission of excerpts from novels and parentally approved para-bles. The dangerous independence of their influence was acknowledged and feared. In Swift's Lilliput, children "of noble or eminent birth . . . are never suffered to converse with servants."[45] Again, this is a question of power. As one servant declared, "Their mother is their mother but it was we who had the makin' and the marrin' of them."[46] As influences over the "strong mind and vivid imagination of Charlotte Brontë, Gaskell gives the first position— before that of her father, "whose intercourse with his children ap-pears to have been considerably restrained"—to "the servants (in that simple household, almost friendly companions during the greater part of the day) retelling the traditions or the news of Haworth village." The news was that of industrial Yorkshire, and among the traditions was that "secret verbal tradition" that remained, as E. P. Thompson shows, after the suppression of the Luddites. In describing the con-versation of Tabitha Ackroyd, the servant of the Brontë family for thirty years, Gaskell makes it clear that folk superstitions and social history were inseparable parts of what servants had to narrate:

Tabitha had lived in Haworth in the days when the packhorses went through once a week . . . carrying the produce of the country from Keighley over the hills to Colne and Burnley. What is more, she had known the "bottom," or valley, in those primitive days when the fairies frequented the margin of the "beck" on moonlight nights, and had known folk who had seen them. But that was when there were no mills in the valleys; and when all the wool-spinning was done by hand in the farm-houses round. "It wur the factories as had driven 'em away," she said.[47]

In the last sentence it is difficult to avoid the suspicion of a subterranean Luddism.

A servant's sense of a primal injustice in her condition could of course enter into her narratives in other ways. Dickens' nurse, Mary Weller, terrorized him vicariously through the gory exploits of Captain Murderer, a black cat thirsty for Master Dickens' blood, and an unkillable speaking rat. As a servant's invention, the rat is especially suggestive. His anomaly is to be more eloquent than the rest of his species; he is both *familiar* with the hero and his antagonist; he ends the story sitting on the hero's corpse.[48] Or again, take the offhand remark that Thackeray's servant drops at the sight of Napoleon: "The ship that brought him to England put in at St. Helena, and his black servant took him to see a man in a garden. 'That,' he said, 'is Bonaparte! He eats three sheep every day, and all the little children he can lay his hands on.'"[49] The servant's imagination enjoys and amplifies the insatiable appetite and the evil intentions with regard to little boys like Master Thackeray, both of which might be pertinent to his own situation. The notorious role played by Napoleon in the nineteenth-century nursery could perhaps be interpreted as a domestic outbreak of the French Revolution.

Nearly every English novelist read today was raised by servants. And nearly every English novelist must have experienced the division between masters and servants in the medium of novel-writing, language. The difficulties of reconciling the politeness of smooth human intercourse with the inequalities of station and the necessity of obedience were the subjects of advice in etiquette manuals:

It is better in addressing them to use a higher key of voice and not to suffer it to fall at the end of a sentence. The best-bred man whom we ever had the pleasure of meeting always employed in addressing servants such forms as these—"I will thank you for so-and-so" or "Such a thing, if you please"—

with a gentle tone but a very elevated key. The perfection of manners in this particular is to indicate by your language that the performance is a favor and by your tone that it is a matter of course.[50]

Equivocation was thus built into the artifice of daily speech. "He hated talking to servants," Virginia Woolf says of a character in *The Years;* "it always made him feel insincere. Either one simpers, or one's hearty, he was thinking. In either case it's a lie. . . . One always lies to servants."[51]

As Thackeray saw seventy-five years earlier, this structural deceit was produced by unequal power: "Do you suppose you can expect absolute candor from a man whom you may order to powder his hair? . . . the truth as between you and Jeames or Thomas, or Mary the housemaid, or Betty the cook, is relative, and not to be demanded on one side or the other. Why, respectful civility is itself a lie . . . You get truth habitually from equals only."[52] But his response proved that the power was not exerted in only one direction. Aware of the necessary deceit between masters and servants, Thackeray was also haunted by the idea that it was precisely servants that he and other writers were addressing. In his early journalism, he obsessively invokes or impersonates the servant-as-literary-critic, as a reader, that is, with the power to make himself heard in return. In the essay cited above, he wonders "whether the servants in that house will read these remarks?" In *Pendennis* he declares, with representative self-consciousness: "If I leave this manuscript open on my table, I have not the slightest doubt that Betty will read it, and they will talk it over in the lower regions to-night."[53]

If one always lies to servants, and yet one always speaks to servants, then it would seem that one should not expect to speak much of the unvarnished truth. Thackeray himself does not draw this conclusion. The Preface to *Pendennis* is on the contrary a manifesto of realist truth-to-life: "I ask you to believe that this person writing strives to tell the truth. If there is not that, there is nothing." Speaking through the servants on the edges of his fiction, however, Thackeray can intermittently acknowledge that his language, like dialogue between unequals, is permanently off-center. Even if it is the author who comments on these servants instead of the reverse, something of the theatrical convention is preserved: an apartness from the central course and conventions of the narrative, a signal to the reader that the whole truth is not being told.

In *The Dialogic Imagination* Mikhail Bakhtin suggests that the "spying and eavesdropping" of servants represents "that distinctive, embodied point of view on the world of private life without which a literature treating private life could not manage." "The servant is the eternal 'third man' in the private life of his lords. Servants are the privileged witnesses to private life. People are as little embarrassed in a servant's presence as they are in the presence of an ass [Bakhtin has been discussing Apuleius], and at the same time the servant is called upon to participate in all intimate aspects of personal life. Thus, servants replace the ass in the . . . adventure novel of everyday life."[54] Bakhtin's survey of the extent of servant exposition can stand as is, but as indicated above, the historical basis of the peculiar powers of that exposition is in need of somewhat more interpretation. To begin with, real opportunities to become party to their masters' secrets do not seem to have given servants even local leverage. On limited but suggestive evidence, a study of preindustrial English cases of defamation concludes that indeed "gossip gave women power," whether to injure reputations or to influence household decisions. But it also demonstrates the distinct "powerlessness" of female *servants* "even to use information to damage a rival's reputation," let alone that of a master or mistress.[55] Power was not so easily rocked by anyone's verbal testimony.

Moreover, in the period of the novel, at least in England, people were no longer "as little embarrassed in a servant's presence" as Bakhtin suggests. There was in fact a sudden and well-documented new anxiety on the part of masters and mistresses about the damage that servant spies and informants could do. If they were groundless, the fears were nonetheless quite real. The statement by Samuel Johnson quoted above is one of many that are no less hyperbolic and ominous. This was the period, for example, when dumbwaiters came into vogue in order to "ease the constraint" that had apparently not existed before.[56] Edmund Burke was convinced that by means of everyday espionage, "the very servant who waits behind your chair" could become the "arbiter of [his master's] life and fortune."[57] "It

seemed to the Scotsman Alexander Carlyle that the average English-
man was so aware of being observed and had such deference for the
opinion of his servant that he regulated his conduct with him constantly in mind."[58] Deference to the power of servant observation and
rebellion against that power seem to have created a prolonged crisis in
the course of the eighteenth century, which continued into the nineteenth. "In 1818 a parliamentary committee saw in Jeremy Bentham's
idea for a Ministry of Police 'a plan which would make every servant
of every house a spy on the actions of his master.'"[59]

In order to get a handle on the novel's mobilization of the expository servant in these same years, it is this trembling in the face of
servant observation that must be accounted for. There is perhaps a
hint in Fielding's letter to the *Covent-Garden Journal* quoted above: "by
the Stories I have heard from my Friends since my own Accident, one
would imagine that half of the Masters and Mistresses of this Kingdom, by the Characters they give of their Servants, live in fear of, and
are dependent upon them." Fielding too has the impression that
masters are ruled by their servants, but he derives it from the opposite experience: not from the fact that servants observe their masters, but from the fact that masters observe their servants, and record
their observations in written "characters." The fear of being observed
emerged together with a new burden of observing. As Jean-Louis
Flandrin points out, a "new mistrust toward the traditional domestic
promiscuity" expressed itself in warnings against dressing and un-
dressing in front of the servants and against the influence of servants
on their masters' children—warnings that had figured in "none of the
manuals of the late sixteenth or early seventeenth century. And this
mistrust was accompanied by an equally intense and equally new
emphasis on "duties of surveillance."[60] These duties were taken quite
seriously. What Henry Fielding and his brother John had to say about
the writing of characters was part of a much larger effort to system-
atize the hiring and firing of servants. Crowned by the Act of 1792,
which provided fines for masters who knowingly wrote "false" characters as well as for servants who presented counterfeits, it was
carried on into the twentieth century by various private bills introduced in Parliament to make character-writing accurate and com-

pulsory.[61] What was at stake, as Victorian women were instructed, was power:

Unwittingly, you are exercising in your own families a vast social and political power; you are educating the poor under you, it may be, without your own consciousness for good or evil . . . The female servants in your household, whom you have taken and instructed in their respective du-ties—whose manners you have softened—who have learned from you how to manage a household—who have caught up from you, insensibly, lessons of vast utility, lessons of order, lessons of the management of children . . . carry into a lower and a very extended circle the influence of your teaching and your training.[62]

In short, the observation of servants was only one point of the many-pronged, long-term process of imposing a new discipline on the new industrial work force. As Foucault suggests in *Discipline and Punish,* the new surveillance was qualitatively different from the for-mer relation of master and servant, "which was a constant, total, massive, non-analytical, unlimited relation of domination, established in the form of the individual will of the master, his 'caprice.' "[63] And yet the rationale of domination for this surveillance was borrowed, along with the expository servant, from the past. The notion that supervision and correction of servants can make "good subjects" of them belongs, Flandrin continues, to a "patriarchal vision" that had in fact lapsed but was now suddenly revived.[64] It was revived not be-cause domestic servants had become more unruly or households more complicated to manage but because the rest of the work force had gone out of control. The patriarchal or paternalistic ideology that had previously taken the household as the model unit for all of society had lost its hold over an industrial working class no longer subordinated by households or under patriarchs. The need for surveillance was a sign that the "family" had broken down. But it was precisely in the name of the family that surveillance could be (re)instituted; the ideal that was thought to survive only in the institution of domestic service could be transferred to the work force outside the home. Hence ladies are urged to make philanthropic visits of inspection to work-houses, where the poor belong "mainly to a class which has never come in contact with the upper classes of society. They have not been domestic servants. . . . Upon them the more fortunate classes have no hold, and exert over them no influence."[65]

How had this anarchic situation come about? Within paternalist ideology, there was a ready answer: these were stray sheep who had been allowed to wander from the paternal fold. This perspective was becoming vestigial. From the new viewpoint of political economy, relations between the classes were ruled not by mutual rights and duties within a hierarchical family but by the impersonal workings of the market. The effects of this new ideology extend into the family itself. Lawrence Stone notes two of them: first, "the breakdown of the paternalistic practice of apprentices living in their masters' houses in the late eighteenth century," and again "at the end of the eighteenth century a new consciousness of privacy began to be stressed."[66] The latter can be seen as an effect of the former: bourgeois privacy is a domestic sphere jealously guarded as a compensatory preserve of the values that legitimate profane competition in the marketplace. What we are watching, in other words, is the birth of the modern family— not in the sense of "nuclear" versus "extended" but in the sense of blood kin tied together by certain intense emotional bonds. It helps to be reminded that the word "family" derives from the Latin *famulus,* or "servant." Before the middle of the eighteenth century, as Raymond Williams points out in *Keywords,* "family" continued to mean not a small group of immediate blood-relations but what we would now call a "household," that is, the blood relations *plus the servants.* It was only in the course of the eighteenth century that the idea of membership in the family came little by little to exclude servants.[67] What has in fact happened, in terms of the older, paternalistic ideology, is that the masters have *expelled* the working class from its proper and traditional place in the family, driving it out into the modern world of dangerous, unsupervised mobility. We who no longer want our apprentices to live under our roof, who protect our privacy from the eyes of class aliens, have abdicated our responsibility to them— such is paternalism's powerful reproach.

And to the extent that paternalism retains its powers, or has had its fading power restored by the threat of new worker unrest, residual servants share that power. When masters inexplicably hang back from writing bad characters about their servants, totting up praise and blame in impartial fashion, the inhibition does not come simply from the inconvenience of being "plagued" but from an imperfect accommodation to the impersonality of the market. The old preindustrial ideology weighed heavily on masters and mistresses whose allegiance to industrial modernity remained fragile; meanwhile, the new demand for surveillance insisted that workers were servants who had lost their masters and that order and discipline could be restored only by making them servants again. When servants look at their masters, it is the power and authority of the paternalist ideal, both old and new, that looks through them. It is the family that looks at and judges the market.

The second meaning of the word "exposition" given in the *Oxford English Dictionary* is "the action of putting (a child) out in the open; abandonment to chance; = Exposure." Through this meaning, the explusion of servants from the eighteenth-century family enters into a strange intimacy with the literary function that is so frequently taken over by servants: the "presentation of essential information, especially about what has occurred before this piece of action began."[68] Servants speak on behalf of the family, its past, its continuity over the generations; this is why Bakhtin associates them with "idyll," and why their words have such an uncanny power.[69] But what they expose in this way, as we shall see further below, is something far from idyllic: the story of their own exclusion, their own "exposition."

DEATH NOTICES

Germinie wasn't a maid for Mlle. de Varandeuil, she was the devotion that would close her eyes.

Germinie Lacerteux

"Well, friend Gerasim," said Peter Ivanovich, so as to say something. "It's a sad affair, isn't it?"

"It's God's will. We shall all come to it some day." said Gerasim, displaying his teeth—the even, white teeth of a healthy peasant—and, like a man in the thick of urgent work, he briskly opened the front door.

"The Death of Ivan Ilyitch"

In the history of the English novel, developed voices like those of Ellen Dean and Thady Quirk make up a vigorous but subordinate tradition. For the most part, the use of servants to convey information is sporadic, constrained, and functional, if not wholly silent and decorative. There are more disclosures than discourses, and more voiceless tableaux than either. As with dialogue between servants and masters, there is clearly also a decline: from the discourses of the eighteenth century toward the disclosures and tableaux of the nine-teenth and twentieth, and from the centrality and resonance of the picaresque narrator toward the marginality and muteness of servants who sometimes seem to convey no more than a whiff of the drawing room. Pamela, a figure for all those whose masters were the gentry, is both actor and observer, but by the nineteenth century the servant observer tended to separate off from the bourgeois actor, and to have less and less right to speak about an action in which he or she was less and less involved. In the Victorian novel and after, servants are often simply counters in a status game whose players, as a character says in *North and South,* "took nouns which were signs of things which gave evidence of wealth,—housekeepers, under-gardeners, extent of glass, valuable lace, diamonds, and all such things; and each one formed his speech to as to bring them all in, in the prettiest accidental manner possible" (ch. 21).

Between the minority tradition of servant storytellers and the majority tradition of intermittent tattletales there exist important continuities, however, continuities for which the career of Thackeray provides ample evidence. Thackeray's enthusiastic early use of servant personae as narrators and vehicles for literary criticism, the reporting of current politics, and other topical writings carried over into a strangely faithful attachment to the domestic's point of view. "We are not the Historic Muse," he declares in *The Four Georges* and is fond of repeating, "but her ladyship's attendant, talebearer—*valet de chambre* —for whom no man is a hero."[70] In the novels servants continue to invoke their creator's deepest convictions: the impatience with his-torical hero worship that Carlyle called "Valetism," the aesthetic self-consciousness of *Vanity Fair*'s puppet master, the critical eye for snobs. Having given up the full-length mimicry of servant voices and orthography, Thackeray continues to associate his narrative viewpoint with the ubiquitous domestic staff: "he who stands behind a fashion-able table knows more of society than the guests who sit at the board."[71] "Indeed, what more effectual plan is there to get a knowledge of London society, than to begin at the foundation—that is, at the kitchen-floor?"[72] If the omniscient narrator is felt to represent a sort of collective consciousness, it is largely because of such earthly surrogates, who whisper in the hushed voice of the community behind the backs of the guests:

Bon Dieu! it is awful, that servants' inquisition! You see a woman in a great party in a splendid saloon, surrounded by faithful admirers, distributing sparkling glances, dressed to perfection, curled, rouged, smiling and happy: Discovery walks respectfully up to her, in the shape of a huge powdered man with large calves and a tray of ices—with Calumny (which is as fatal as truth) behind him, in the shape of the hulking fellow carrying the wafer-biscuits. Madam, your secret will be talked over by those men at their club at the public-house tonight. Jeames will tell Chawle his notions about you over their pipes and pewter beer-pots. Some people ought to have mutes for servants in Vanity Fair—mutes who could not write. If you are guilty, tremble.[73]

In the mode of humorous allegory servants who are assigned no speaking part, who have a minimal existence, become almost a counterforce, spicing the narrator's own report with a soupçon of physical threat. When Thackeray declares in *Pendennis,* "Nothing is secret. Take it as a rule that John knows everything," he elevates the footman into a symbol of narration itself, giving him the disproportionate authority of an agent of the public.[74]

As occasional or "disguised" narrators—-that is, as Wayne Booth explains, "used to tell the audience what it needs to know, while seeming merely to act out their roles"—servants "often have more effect on us than on their official auditors." This is because their final loyalty is to "us," to the world outside the performance, and is another reason why they sometimes "speak with an authority as sure as God's."[75] But even where their authority is more provisional and more expressive of worldly contradictions, as in the majority of cases, it is often guaranteed by the particular nature of the news they tell. Novelists have never discouraged the mischievous tradition that associates the messenger with his message and treats him accordingly. And the typical literary servant, like Scott's Andrew Fairservice, is "one of those persons who have no objection to the sort of temporary attention and woeful importance which attaches itself to the bearer of

bad tidings."[76] The worse the tidings, the more important the messenger, and servants derive a great deal of rather peculiar importance
from their preference for announcements of death, especially the
deaths of those in authority over them.

The multitude of corpses discoverd and survivors notified in nineteenth-century fiction, suggestive in their sheer quantity, indicate
first of all that servants were usually entrusted with "the potentially
disruptive and polluting fundamentals of life: birth, infancy, illness,
old age, and death."[77] This is not to say that social prestige is accorded to those who handle life's fundamentals—Leonore Davidoff
suggests that here the opposite is true—but some appeal to their
primacy remains open. In an epoch of social and religious crisis this
briefly peremptory authority would have been reinforced by "the idea
that the death scene was a uniquely significant pointer to the quality
of the life," an idea which A. O. J. Cockshut traces through nineteenth-century biography.[78] More suggestive still is the servant's own
insinuation of complicity with his bad news. In rare cases this complicity can be gross approval:

Suddenly the manager's boy put his insolent black head in the doorway, and
said in a tone of scathing contempt:

"Mistah Kurtz—he dead."

More often it is subtler, hidden in comic reticence or hyperbole,
hinted faintly by an innocuous juxtaposition. The fourth weekly installment of *The Turn of the Screw* concludes, for example, with the
housekeeper's rapid conflation of Quint's authority and Quint's
death:

". . . then the master went, and Quint was alone." I followed, but halting a
little. "Alone?" "Alone with *us*." Then as from a deeper depth, "In charge,"
she added.

"And what became of him?"

She hung fire so long that I was still more mystified. "He went too," she
brought out at last.

"Went where?"

Her expression, at this, became extraordinary. "God knows where! He
died."

"Died?" I almost shrieked.

She seemed fairly to square herself, plant her self more firmly to express
the wonder of it. "Yes. Mr. Quint's dead."

The "Mr." remembered suddenly here, though passed over in the first sentence, is telling: Quint's death becomes his payment for the authority he exercised "alone with *us*." It remains an absurdity to suspect Mrs. Grose of manipulation and murder, but the structure of retribution is there.

Mrs. Grose can be exonerated more easily, perhaps, when we consider how widespread an aspect of the literary servant this is. Thady Quirk's ambiguous elegies have already been noted. In *Wuthering Heights* Nelly's accounts of death and dying are even more frankly tinged with satisfaction:

"She's fainted or dead," I thought: "so much the better. Far better that she should be dead than lingering a burden and a misery-maker to all about her. . . . I don't know if it be a particularity in me, but I am seldom otherwise than happy while watching in the chamber of death." (chs. 15–16)

Servants who, unlike Nelly and Mrs. Grose, have never been accused of wilful malice are continually playing variations on these themes of aggression and triumph in the vicinity of death. Mr. Merdle's Chief Butler in *Little Dorrit,* for example, takes the news of his master's suicide "exactly as he had looked on at the dinners in that very room."

"Mr. Merdle is dead."
   "I should wish," said the Chief Butler, "to give a month's notice."
   "Mr. Merdle has destroyed himself."
   "Sir," said the Chief Butler, "that is very unpleasant to the feelings of one in my position, as calculated to awaken prejudice; and I should wish to leave immediately."[79]

All those in his position are enveloped by the same prejudice, whether they announce the death or only discover, frame, or amplify it. It would be difficult to find a work of nineteenth-century fiction that did not contain some variant of this domestic *Schadenfreude*. In *Pendennis* the passing of Pendennis senior is announced by servants with a whistle and a wink: "As the chaise drove through Clavering, the ostler standing whistling under the archway of the Clavering Arms, winked to the postillion ominously, as much as to say all was over" (ch. 2). In *Middlemarch,* one page before Dorothea discovers Casaubon's corpse in the garden, her maid (who had been with her to

Rome) says to the butler, "I wish every book in that library was built into a caticom for your master" (ch. 48).

Most often, in fact, eager servants are one step ahead of fatality. The narrator of Charles Collins' "The Compensation House" is informed by the "butler, valet, factotum, what you will, of a sick gentleman" that the latter is "ebbing away fast with every passing hour. The servant already spoke of his master in the past tense."[80] Scott's *Old Mortality,* whose domestics bang away relentlessly at the title theme, illustrates several familiar enhancements of bad news, from an over-willingness to imagine that the worst has arrived (when her mistress faints, the maid cries out "Help, for God's sake! my young lady is dying") to an immunity from feeling it when it does arrive. After a gory defeat: "'Ay, ay,' said Pike composedly; 'a total scattering.'" When there is a catastrophe to be announced, servants are there to be violently untroubled.

"The Whigs about to hang Lord Evandale?" said Morton, in the greatest surprise.

"Ay, troth they are," said the housekeeper. "Yesterday night they made a sally, as they ca't, (my mother's name was Sally . . .)"[81]

Discussing "the special office of young women to watch over the dying" in Victorian fiction, Alexander Welsh calls attention to the ominous hints, even the "expressed hostility," that can surround these deathbed angels, "so supremely confident that a hero's happiness is not of this world that one scarcely trusts oneself alone with them."[82] In *Jane Eyre,* for instance, Rochester is surely right to detect a menacing callousness in Jane's simple syntax:

"I have been with my aunt, sir, who is dead."

"A true Janian reply! Good angels be my guard! She comes from the other world—from the abode of people who are dead." (ch. 22)

"Rochester," Welsh goes on, "pretends that Jane is a ghost or a bad angel. Reader, we know better—though Jane, after all, had plenty of reason to wish her aunt dead."[83] More to the point, she had reason for ill-will toward Rochester himself. And in the end, of course, only enough of Rochester is left as to permit the forms of matrimony. In fact, Jane hastens somewhat improbably to exaggerate news of

Rochester—reported with typical ambiguity by another garrulous servant—into an obituary:

> "You know Thornfield Hall, of course?" I managed to say at last.
> "Yes, ma'am; I lived there once."
> "Did you?" Not in my time, I thought; you are a stranger to me.
> "I was the late Mr. Rochester's butler," he added.
> "The late!" I gasped. "Is he dead?"
> "I mean the present Mr. Edward's father," he explained. (ch. 36)

Waiting to hear the worst about the events at Thornfield, Jane is also quick to read malicious intention into the former butler's loquacity: "What agony was this! And the man seemed resolved to protract it." As it happens, he does add, "I have often wished that Miss Eyre had been sunk in the sea before she came to Thornfield Hall." But he does not know to whom he is speaking; the malice resides in the convention. When a messenger whose very voice is enough to indicate his living, breathing presence, and whose self-referring, uninvited volubility further stresses that presence, bears tidings of a superior's death or destruction, a tension is set up that makes the slightest ambiguity or awkwardness of language vibrate with sinister potential. Even so straightforward a phrase as "I was the late Mr. Rochester's butler"—somewhat like "Mr. Quint's dead"—can then seem to imply that if he is no longer a butler it is because his master is no more. His social ascension can be identified with his master's demise. One imagines this supplementary "because" the more readily in that this is Jane's own case. Her freedom to stop calling Rochester "my master" depends on the butler's news of Bertha's death and, more obscurely, on Rochester's disfigurement. The servant's notice of death is saturated with an impersonal, explosive wishfulness.

As this example helps us to see, the Victorian religious compromise that Welsh ingeniously reconstructs, with its hopeful and fearful idealization of women as saving angels of death, does not account for all the gruesome overtones of the deathbed scene. Men feared the women whom they exalted as representatives of the beyond, but they also feared the servants, mostly women, who in fact ushered their suddenly helpless bodies into it, and this fear had no more to do with salvation than simple piety has to do with Nelly Dean's surprising joy in the company of corpses. On the other side of men's fears are women's wishes. When the mortality of the masters is so closely associated in the telling with the joy, power, and social ascension of their subordinates, then the shadow of social and sexual revenge descends over apprehension, warning, prophecy, and simple announcement, over the tender nurse as over the indifferent messenger.

It is true, as Welsh and Cockshut have shown, that the language of the death scene tends to remain more orthodox than the participants in it.[84] But the same shadow darkens the most unobjectionable sentiments. A friend speeding to rescue a Scott hero from imminent execution is met at the gate by an old retainer (who has spent the night, with the hero's enemies, toasting "much luck in raking this country clear o' whigs and roundheads") and is told, "life is short, sir; we are flowers of the field, sir—hiccup—and lilies of the valley."[85] This is the letter but not the spirit of scripture. Under the circumstances, the servant is much too willing to see our hero pay the debt of nature, and his language both protects and betrays him. The usual impertinent "we" and the repetition of "sir" remind his superior that if deference is his due, so is mortality; note that he brings the deference and the mortality suggestively close together. The hiccup, as comic punctuation, further disburdens his own insouciant shoulders of the heavy moral and unloads it onto his interlocutor. His comic preaching is social aggression; the borrowed generalizations hide an individual cutting edge.

This duplicity is typical. Lyddy, the Lyons' maid in *Felix Holt,* wields her piety to the same end: "Dear, dear, don't you be so light, miss. We may all be dead before night" (ch. 26). Again, the "we" that homes in on what is universal, hence authoritative, in cultural belief gives the servant an authority that can be used against her mistress. In *Our Mutual Friend,* the narrator who speaks *for* the servant calls upon the same characteristic language:

"Dinner is on the table!"

Thus the melancholy retainer, as who should say, "Come down and be poisoned, ye unhappy children of men!" (bk. 1, ch. 2)

Biblical language, like death itself, invests the servants who exploit it freely and loosely with the power to make themselves heard. They can strike from behind its universality and yet know their blow will be felt. This instrumentality, and not simply the facts of religious adherence among the poor, explains why the literary servant is so often a strong believer in a sect or dogma other than that of his masters. The doctrine may be esteemed dangerous in itself, like the Methodism of Humphry Clinker or the Presbyterianism of Andrew Fairservice, or it may combine, as more often happens, a caricatured backwardness with the authority of an enduring heritage. The particular authorities invoked are less important than the fact of authoritative speech itself. Proverbs, which "carry the force of appearing to embody norms and are therefore voiced by ones who appear to represent society," work as well as scriptural citation, even where they contradict both scripture and other proverbs.[86] The single aim of the servant's unrepentant quoting is an immediate impact on received opinion. Jumbles are thus the rule. As when, in a Le Fanu tale, the butler's grandson recounts to a visitor the ruin of his masters' house. First, "Food for worms, dead and rotten; God over all," and then a social modulation: "If death was a thing that money could buy, / The rich they would live, and the poor they would die."[87]

This rhetorical opportunism, ready to endorse nearly any authorities in order to undermine Authority, sets obvious limits to the coherence of servant protest. But it also gives servants' words the strength of relative anonymity. Since their opposition takes an established, even an archaic form, its claim to universality can slide by without arousing the resistance of a new, rival language. And this is something more than a means of camouflaging aggression. "Dying," Walter Benjamin writes, "was once a public process in the life of the individual and a most exemplary one; think of the medieval pictures in which the deathbed has turned into a throne toward which the people press through the wide-open doors of the death house." By their simple presence, or by the few touches they add to the telling, servant spectators might be said to restore to dying something of this lost communal significance. It is at the moment of death, the moment that definitively tests the disappearing individual's place in the surviving community, that the servant stands in for the missing medieval spectators, brings into the modern privacy of the death scene the older perspective of the public. What underlies the comic self-importance of the servant messenger, in other words, is the authoritative image of the continuity of the generations. In *One-Way Street,* Benjamin remarks: "A bearer of the news of death appears to himself as very important. His feeling—even against all reason—makes him a messenger from the realm of the dead. For the community of all the dead is so immense that even he who only reports death is aware of it. *Ad plures ire* was the Latins' expression of dying."[88] "The many," *hoi polloi,* is a category that includes servants. When their delivery of the news of death presses toward a broader, more universal communion, when the mild sting in their sententiousness makes room for them, it is this category that they update.

In the ethics of Elizabeth Gaskell, death does not strike with an arbitrariness that diminishes human effort and aspiration. In its modern, industrial context, it befalls those whose efforts are insufficient, whether because history has overwhelmed them or because they have surrendered to it. Work does not consume life, but produces life and preserves from death. The deaths that punctuate *North and South* strike those who cannot cope with the new forces of the industrial North—Mr. and Mrs. Hale and their Oxford friend Bell, as well as Bessy Higden, who has been poisoned in the mills. The fact that all of these deaths are announced by or mediated through servants, and in the course of the servants' duties, places the servants' life and work up against all this fatality. What is suggested is a sort of alliance between domestic laborers and the course of history, whose direction is marked by the domestication of productive force. For the masters, Gaskell hints, survival will require an imitation of their servants' labor. As the Hale family moves into its new northern lodgings, Mrs. Hale exclaims to her maid, "Oh Dixon, what a place is this!"

"Indeed, ma'am, I'm sure it will be your death before long, and then I'll know who—stay! Miss Hale that's far too heavy for you to lift." (ch. 8)

Mrs. Hale's prompt demise, which the maid incessantly prophesies and jealously supervises, is the fate of all who cannot, will not, or are not permitted to lift heavy weights. And the prerogative of overseeing death belongs to the holders of what Gaskell, from the viewpoint of the Victorian woman, saw as the *right* to work. In the novel's main subplot, Margaret Hale earns the right to share the knowledge of her mother's impending death with the favored servant by becoming "Peggy the laundry-maid" and "working away like any servant" (ch. 9). It is as a worker that Margaret joins the community of survivors.

Death and work are entangled again when the news of Harry Carson's murder—the act of social retribution around which *Mary Barton* revolves—is brought to his unsuspecting family. The chapter (18) begins by putting the idleness and frivolity of their evening activities in the unflattering light of the working servants around them:

Mrs. Carson was (as was usual with her, when no particular excitement was going on) very poorly, and sitting up-stairs in her dressing room, indulging in the luxury of a head-ache. She was not well, certainly. "Wind in the head," the servants called it. But it was but the natural consequence of the state of mental and bodily idleness in which she was placed. . . . It would have done her more good than all the ether and sal-volatile she was daily in the habit of swallowing, if she might have taken the work of one of her own housemaids for a week; made beds, rubbed tables, shaken carpets . . .

Her daughters, meanwhile, are "in the comfortable, elegant, well-lighted drawing-room; and like many similarly situated young ladies, they did not exactly know what to do to while away the time until the tea-hour." Into this context the servant brings the news of murder.

Helen yawned.

"Oh! do you think we may ring for tea? Sleeping after dinner makes me so feverish."

"Yes, surely. Why should not we?" said the more energetic Sophy, pulling the bell with some determination.

"Tea, directly, Parker," said she, authoritatively, as the man entered the room.

She was too little in the habit of reading expressions on the face of others to notice Parker's countenance.

Yet it was striking. It was blanched to a dead whiteness; the lips compressed as if to keep within some tale of horror; the eyes distended and unnatural. It was a terror-stricken face.

These are the signs of horror at the murder, not of readiness to commit one, but how different are they from the classic physiognomy of the murderer himself? This face is the vehicle for the pain that John Barton's violence will inflict, and it seems appropriate that the young ladies "ask for it." The indifference and authoritative tone that keep them from recognizing the news in its silent, habitual guise are also the causes of the act they report. And this silence, imposed by authoritative orders, delivers a violent answer. The mode is characteristic of the minimal but definitive being of Victorian servants: those who work, in the very muteness of their labor, bring the news of death to the idle. Gaskell repeats this gesture.

The door opened slowly again, and this time it was the nurse who entered. . . . She occasionally came into the drawing-room to look for things belonging to their father or mother, so it did not excite any surprise when she advanced into the room. . . . She wanted them to look up. She wanted them to read something in her face—her face so full of woe, of horror. But they went on without taking any notice.

Her *desire* to show them the horror she holds for them, concealed by her habitual labor and their habitual inattention, carries the industrial conflicts of Manchester into the home. When she finally releases the news, it has accumulated an overload of significance that resonates beyond the curt monosyllable, "Dead!"

FRAMING

Gleaming doorknobs and scrubbed entries have heard the songs of the housemaids at sun-up and—housemaids are wishes. Whose? Ha! . . .
WILLIAM CARLOS WILLIAMS, *Kora in Hell*

Death gives servants the unaccustomed right to be heard, along with the power to hurt. Still more convenient to the Victorian novelist was work, in that the servant need not even speak—the increasing interdiction of uninvited speech in the nineteenth-century household made the servant's conventional garrulity less easily available—in order to invoke and share its authority. The silent messenger above, with murder on his face as he takes orders for tea, is paradigmatic of many less extreme instances where the barest expository mention of a servant's existence is sufficient to place the protagonist's life in problematic relation to the laboring community. If there is an equivalent in the novel for the servant's prominent place in theatrical prologues and epilogues, his gravitation to the hinges of the performance, it is perhaps these mute expository appearances in the frame around the action.

There is a precursor of this silent framing in several of the mock-epic chapter openings of *Tom Jones,* where realities of labor and servitude introduce an action they will later intrude upon. In Book Ten,

for example, sport gives way to labor: "Now the little trembling hare
. . . sports wantonly o'er the lawns" collapses into "in plain English,
it was now midnight," and then "Susan chambermaid was now only
stirring, she being obliged to wash the kitchen, before she retired to
the arms of the fond, expectant ostler" (bk. 10, ch. 2). Even so casual
a frame turns out to have some significance. Because her work keeps
her from wantonness, Fitzpatrick will find her awake, bribe her, and
interrupt Tom's wantonness. Or again in Book Eleven:

Those members of society, who are born to furnish the blessings of life, now
began to light their candles, in order to pursue their daily labours, for those
who are born to enjoy those blessings. . . . now the bonny housemaid
begins to repair the disordered drum-room, while the riotous authors of
that disorder, in broken interrupted slumbers tumble and toss, as if the
hardness of down disquited their repose.
  In simple phrase, the clock had no sooner struck seven . . . (bk. 11, ch. 9)

It is almost as if the "authors of that disorder" had to squirm in
unconscious penance for the early morning penance they have occasioned.
  In positions like this, before or after the big scenes, servants can
allude in passing to a state of social injustice that cannot be treated
more centrally without threatening to displace or overbalance the
story of the protagonists. The novelist may feel obliged to stay close
to the manners of his epoch and his peers, but servants connect
manners to the universe. Lackeys, John Carey observes, are "standard
components of this Thackerayan mood, re-emerging again and again
in his perambulations of the London streets. These figures run, ride,
and carry torches, like figures in a dream. They are never stilled or
recognized. They simply run, ride, and carry torches, and so embody
the endless hurry of time."[89] The time they embody is also moralized.
The last line of *Mrs. Perkins' Ball* concludes the satire by noticing (not
without condescension) the only alternative to the night's frivolities
that Thackeray can find on the premises: "Betsey the maid was already up and at work, on her knees, scouring the steps, and cheerfully
beginning her honest daily labor." The satire of the party-goers that
preceded it may not succeed in making the final phrase enjoyable, but
it does suggest that the line is not solely patronizing. In *The Newcomes*
we are told that the Anglo-Indians, who bring to England both capital

and virtue, rise early. But the maid rises even earlier.[90] When Pendennis' idle pleasures lead to his failure at "Oxbridge," the first person he encounters after a sleepless night is the maid scouring the steps at dawn, like the betrayed ethic of labor personified (ch. 20). The scene in which he determines to acquire an assured income by marriage rather than by his labors again ends as he "strode forth into the air, and almost over the body of the matutinal housemaid, who was rubbing the steps at the door" (ch. 45).

I will come back to the connection between this housemaid-in-the-dawn motif and the prestige of labor. But the authority to be felt in these brief allusions, their momentary sensitivity to the pressure of the excluded, comes more from simple positioning than from thematic density. Like the news of death, they cluster around endings, and thus coincide powerfully with the author's naked intention to generate coherence. They obtrude into the text at "that limit," in Walter Benjamin's phrase, "at which he invites the reader to a divinatory realization of the meaning of life by writing 'Finis.'"[91] To bracket the action, to speak within or simply occupy the frame of a scene, chapter, or installment, confers upon the novelistic servant, as upon the theatrical prologue and epilogue, a relative but appreciable hermeneutic authority, capable of magnifying thematic hints that may be slight in themselves.

The servants who gather wordlessly in the expository openings of nineteenth-century novels may be first and foremost indicators of the good or bad fortunes of their masters, like the skeleton staff that prepares for Harold Transome's arrival on the first page of *Felix Holt* or the fat coachman and black footman who drive up to Miss Pinkerton's academy on the sunny first morning of *Vanity Fair*. In any one instance, what they contribute over and above mere signs of status is not likely to be of decisive importance. And yet it is not just the composite phenomenon that is suggestive. Consider for example the casual opening page of *Pendennis*:

One fine morning in the full London season, Major Arthur Pendennis came over from his lodgings, according to his custom, to breakfast at a certain Club in Pall Mall, of which he was a chief ornament. At a quarter past ten the Major invariably made his appearance in the best blacked boots in all London, with a checked morning cravat that never was rumpled until dinner time, a buff waistcoat which bore the crown of his sovereign on the buttons, and linen so spotless that Mr. Brummel himself asked the name of the laundress.

By mentioning the laundress, Thackeray authorizes the reader to wonder too about the blacker of "the best blacked boots in all London." And when we are introduced to "Morgan, his man," it becomes rapidly and schematically clear that Major Pendennis is in every sense the latter's creation, provided by him with teeth, hair, and information as well as well-blacked boots. The master, not the servant, is the "ornament." Again and again Thackeray's passives coyly invite the reader to supply the omitted causes: "being belted, curled, and set straight, he descended upon the dining room" (ch. 7). The prevalence of passives that mark an activity whose servant subject is assumed to be unworthy of mention imparts a ghostly, comic sense of suppressed mechanism to Thackeray's scenes. The occultation of servant actions associates servants with occult powers. And here the association is supported by the plot: at the end of the novel, Morgan and his master confront each other in a perfect Hegelian turnabout, the causal servant rising to repudiate his creation.

The literary servant is far from requiring a speaking part in order to make his existence a matter of concern to the text. Minute interruptions, ringings of the bell, orders, changes of tone that the novelist brings him onstage to provoke can become charged with an incongruously weighty thematic baggage. In *Pride and Prejudice* it is a distinguishing mark of the foolish sister, Lydia, "that she had not prudence enough to hold her tongue before the servants, while they waited at table" (bk. 3, ch. 5). We know Jane Austen has little sympathy for such indiscretion. Talking before the servants is the next thing to eloping. Even Mr. Collins knows enough to allow his marriage plans to be interrupted by the presence of servants:

"But I can assure the young ladies that I come prepared to admire them. At present I will not say more, but perhaps when we are better acquainted—"
    He was interrupted by a summons to dinner. (bk. 1, ch. 12)

Lydia and her honor are saved, however, by means of information Darcy gets from a former servant (bk. 3, ch. 10). Moreover, when the news of Lydia's upcoming marriage is announced, Austen uncharacteristically uses the Bennets' servants to introduce and frame it. The chapter (bk. 3, ch. 7) begins by placing the housekeeper and her feelings in an unaccustomed position of prominence; she is almost "out of place."

Two days after Mr. Bennet's return, as Jane and Elizabeth were walking together in the shrubbery behind the house, they saw the housekeeper coming towards them, and concluding that she came to call them to their mother, went forward to meet her; but, instead of the expected summons, when they approached her, she said to Miss Bennet, "I beg your pardon, madam, for interrupting you, but I was in hopes you might have got some good news from town, so I took the liberty of coming to ask."

"What do you mean, Hill? We have heard nothing from town."

"Dear madam," cried Mrs. Hill, in great astonishment, "don't you know there is an express come for master from Mr. Gardiner?"

After this minor reversal, the chapter ends when the news is passed back to the servants who have asked for it:

"Oh! Here comes Hill. My dear Hill, have you heard the good news? Miss Lydia is going to be married; and you shall all have a bowl of punch, to make merry at her wedding."

This obtrusive framing all but bestows Lydia's happy ending on the servants in front of whom she spoke so freely. Indiscreet speech, speech that does not suspend, moderate, or freeze itself in the presence of servants, may be only one step from elopement, but Austen's romance structure, pushing against her class-bound ethics, gives partial but cordial support to the unrestrained circulation of words between the classes. Remember that Elizabeth herself owes her marriage in part to the account of Darcy's character she receives at Pemberley from his housekeeper: "the authority of a servant . . . was not to be hastily rejected" (bk. 3, ch. 2).

The community in whose name servants suddenly appear when the conversation turns to marriage is not the local "society" of visitable neighbors. It is a principle of expansive promiscuity suggested by a few, faint traces—the promised bowl of punch and its merriment, the adjective "dear" that Mrs. Hill has spontaneously addressed to Jane and that is now returned to her by Mrs. Bennet. But the effect is to sketch out a different conception of marriage: not an exchange of property or even a meeting of minds, but collective festivity. After the news is out, as Mrs. Bennet is building airy castles for Lydia and her husband to inhabit, we are told that

Mr. Bennet allowed her to talk on without interruption, while the servants remained. But when they had withdrawn, he said to her, "Mrs. Bennet, before you take any, or all of these houses, for your son and daughter, let us come to a right understanding. Into *one* house in this neighborhood, they shall never have admittance." (bk. 3, ch. 7)

In the long run, as usual, Mr. Bennet is wrong. What he allowed to be said in front of the servants turns out to hold. The loose, wishful, socially inclusive talk in which his wife indulges gains them admittance to his house as well. And the suggestion is that the social circle that is stretched in this way in and by the servants' presence could be stretched even farther.

One might say that servants do not so much interrupt as allow themselves to be invoked, like tutelary dieties, by propitious subjects or expressions. Their presence marks, elicits, and solemnizes words that promise a community in which they might have a larger share. One final example is Charlotte Brontë's *Shirley*. Here the usual constraining arrival of a servant keeps alive the ambiguity of a vision that is half courtship, half industrial utopia. The industrialist's brother, Gérard Moore, declares:

"I wish to live, not to die: the future opens like Eden before me; and still, when I look deep into the shades of my paradise, I see a vision, that I like better than seraph or cherub, glide across remote vistas."
  "Do you? Pray, what vision?"
  "I see—"
The maid came bustling in with the tea things. (ch. 16)

The maid is precisely what must be included if Moore is to realize his utopia, and her entrance reminds us of it. And as a fitting sign that, despite the concluding gestures of conventional marriage, this utopia has not yet been realized, another servant is called in—"my old housekeeper"—to pronounce the novel's epilogue. She looks not forward but back to before the mills came:

"I can tell of it clean different again: when there was neither mill, not cot, nor hall, except Fieldhead, within two miles. . . . A lonesome spot it was— and a bonnie spot—full of oak trees and nut trees. It is altered now. (ch. 37)

The quiet disappointment of this macro-frame complements the mute hope of the earlier micro-frame, but also, postponing it, keeps it alive. This is what exposition does: in going back to what happened before the action started, it also suggests how much the action has left unresolved.

4

Agency: The Servant as Instrument of the Plot

Principal characters ought always to act. . . . The principal actors are those who carry on the theatrical plot, like a slave, a soubrette, or a knave.

FRANÇOIS D'AUBIGNAC

It is less the agent who explains the act, but rather the act which, revealing its authentic meaning after the event, returns upon the agent, illuminates his nature, discovers who he is.

JEAN-PIERRE VERNANT

THE *VALET DE CHAMBRE* AS HERO

Among servant commonplaces, the most common and most strange is the one announced in phrases like "Laissez-moi faire" and "J'en répons" and "Well, I will do the best I can for you"—the convention that makes the hero's fate depend on a servant's intervention in his affairs. This convention is so strange, first of all, because it is so common. According to one count, in the three centuries before the French Revolution the majority of French stage comedies reach their happy endings "by way of a deus ex machina" and no less than half the servants in them participate decisively in the dénouement.[1] Estimating all the sources, derivatives, and analogues of this central tradition in the other European literatures, one is tempted to redefine the *deus ex machina* as a *servus ex machina*. This figure inspires one of Northrop Frye's breathtaking demonstrations of the repetitiveness of literary function in the *Anatomy of Criticism*, and it is precisely this passage, tracing "the schemes which bring about the hero's victory" from the

tricky slave of Roman comedy through the scheming valet of Renaissance comedy to Figaro, Leporello, the characters of Scott and
Dickens, and Jeeves, that Fredric Jameson singles out in *The Political
Unconscious* when he argues that there are some apparent affronts to
historicality which a historical criticism must learn to digest.[2]

The persistence that seems to float free of literature's usual connections with social circumstance is all the stranger because it also
embodies a social reversal. Here the unexpected power that we found
hidden in the servant's expository functions is more evident.
D'Aubignac, the seventeenth-century critic who formulated the doctrine of the three unities, suggests how large an attribution of cultural
authority the convention involves. If, as he says, it is the servants
rather than the masters who in fact move the plot, then it is they who
usurp the palpable prestige attached to action, to the thing done. In
this sense the agent becomes "principal." And the society bodied
forth on stage becomes, in the words of a critic of Plautus, "a world
whose hero is the slave."[3]

It might of course be objected that when it occurs in one of the
comic genres, heroism of this sort is in effect contained and cancelled
by the generic inconsequentiality of any and all action. Richard
Levin's description of the clown adopts this viewpoint. In terms of
effect on the plot, Levin says, the clown functions as "someone who
occupies a world and embodies a level of sensibility so far below the
major plot (or plots) that his fate does not really matter to the other
characters or the audience (or ultimately, it will be shown, to himself). This is actually just another way of saying that his line of action
is 'farcical.'"[4] One might imagine, then, that the survival of this *topos*
into the novel would be confined to texts where the Aristotelian
priority of plot has given way to a playful disrespect for temporality
or historical rationality. Indeed, there is no easier way to make a farce
of history than by bequeathing it to the servants. On the face of it, for
example, the fact that the young Tristram Shandy is first misnamed
and then unmanned (while urinating out the window) by the inatten-
tions of the maid, who is also guilty of broadcasting Mrs. Wadman's
opinion of Uncle Toby's groin, is not to be interpreted as a promotion
of the servant but as a depreciation of causal logic.[5] And yet such
effects are to be found among the most seriously historical works in

the canon: in *Old Mortality* as well as *Pride and Prejudice,* in *North and South* as well as *Pendennis,* in *Wuthering Heights, Felix Holt, Little Dorrit, The Way of All Flesh.* The question is whether the admixture of farce to history does not also compose, within the limited possibilities and responsibilities of the comic mode, an alternative historical vision.

Thackeray again provides a useful illustration. His fondness for the historical viewpoint of the valet, for whom no man is a hero, has already been mentioned. But there is a corollary of this preferred perspective that is less obvious: an enlarging of the powers of Thackeray's valets at their heroic masters' expense. In "The History of the Next French Revolution"—one of his few comic pieces on contemporary history in which the narrator is *not* a servant—the army of one of the four noble pretenders to the French throne includes an English unit of "superb footmen" known as "Jenkins' Foot." Thackeray stays with this pun for the duration of the hostilities.

It was a touching sight, on the morning before the battle, to see the alacrity with which Jenkins' regiment sprung up that the first *réveille* of the bell, and engaged (the honest fellows) in offices almost menial for the benefit of their French allies. The Duke himself set the example, and blacked to a nicety the boots of Henri.[6]

Turning 1848 upside down to get his hypothetical Revolution of 1884, Thackeray, like Marx in the *Eighteenth Brumaire,* sees the repetition of French revolutions as farce. But while taking an irreverent look at the personalities of French politics, he also raises their menials to the rank of substitute heroes.

Among a bewildering array of armies, regiments, and so on, "Jenkins' Foot" proves with almost tedious regularity to be the only genuine force in this lengthy fantasy. "Down went plume and cocked-hat, down went corporal and captain, down went grocer and tailor, under the long staves of the indomitable English footmen" (ch. 6). Patriotism may have something to do with this aggrandizement, but the suggestions of domestic conflict are also unmistakable. Italics bring the valet's razors into the fray. "Knowing how irresistible a weapon is the bayonet in British hands, the intrepid Jenkins determined to carry on his advantage and charged the Saugrenue infantry with *cold steel.*"

The Footmen of England still yelled their terrific battle-cry, "Hurra, hurra!" On they went; regiment after regiment was annihilated, until, scared at the very trample of the advancing warriors, the dismayed troops of France screaming fled. Gathering his last warriors round him, Nemours determined to make a last desperate effort. 'Twas vain: the ranks met; the next moment the truncheon of the Prince of Orléans was dashed from his hand by the irresistible mace of the Duke of Jenkins; his horse's shins were broken by the same weapon. Jenkins' hand was at the Duke's collar in a moment, and had he not gasped out, "Je me rends!" he would have been throttled in that dreadful grasp! (ch. 6)

As he snickers at military glory, Thackeray replaces it with an order of violence that his readers will feel is closer to home: the household shiver of razors at the neck and hands at the collar.

Little by little, these hints of private, rebellious violence coalesce to form the only stable framework of meaning this text enjoys. As usual in farce, neither side threatens to accomplish much that will have to be taken seriously. The National Guard, loyal to a thinly disguised, niggardly Louis-Philippe and representing the bourgeoisie—"the grocers, the rich bankers, the lawyers, &c"—finds "the noise, the kick of the gun, and the smell of the powder . . . very unpleasant," and disintegrates. The Eau-de-Cologne lancers, aristocrats with whom the footmen are allied, reach the battlefield and fashionably faint. Such consequential actions as the farce allows are performed by the footmen alone. "Duke, I owe my crown to my patron saint and you," Jenkins is told. But as far as the reader can see his men needn't share the honors with anyone.

As the text draws to its conclusion, the suggestion becomes stronger that the footmen have not only taken over the main plot, but that they are aimed against the class they supposedly serve. Immediately after taking second place to the patron saint, they are further robbed of the glory of victory. Drawing the class line now that the battle is over, their Prince "treated the illustrious Duke with marked coldness, and did not even ask him to supper that night." And "the indignation of Jenkins and his brave companions may be imagined when it is stated that they were not even mentioned in the dispatch!" Thackeray's quarrel with the aristocratic bias of historiography then leads him further. The material interests of the footmen clash with their alliances. They desist from combat while "rifling the pockets of the National Guard." Proving "not so amenable to discipline as they might have been," they mutiny. The mutiny is defeated in a quick phrase, and their defeat is at once transformed into victory: allowed to leave the forts around Paris, they become the only survivors of a holocaust in which the armies of king and pretenders blow each other into nonexistence. The piece ends when the Tuileries are occupied, in the absence of other authority and with the support of Jenkins' Foot, by a contingent from the asylum at Charenton. The new rulers announce a program that ends in madness but begins well: "There shall be no more poverty; no more wars; no more avarice; no more passports; no more custom-houses; no more lying; no more physic" (ch. 9).

Like all utopias, this vacillates between *eu-topia* and *ou-topia,* a good place and no place. But it is weighty enough to anchor Thackeray's levity. Once it can be seen in the light of even so compromised a final purpose, the footmen's violence acquires some coherence; once it has the class hostility and force of the footmen behind it, the madmen's utopia becomes something more than mere whimsy. We shall see this again: images of violent confrontation and images of utopian reconciliation, which in isolation from one another seem chaotic or half-serious, come together to form a suggestive whole that invites more thoughtful attention.

Neither the instrumental servant's surprising monopoly of effective power nor his sudden swings toward rebellion are exclusive to free-wheeling farce. In the novel, servants who save their master's money may also save their lives, and this surrogacy too conceals pregnant ambiguities. The power to save a life and the power to take it are sometimes indistinguishable. In *Henry Esmond,* for example, Thackeray rather cavalierly pushes a servant-surrogate onstage just as the hero loses consciousness in the midst of the battle of Blenheim:

Beyond this moment, and of this famous victory, Mr. Esmond knows nothing; for a shot brought down his horse and our young gentleman on it, who fell crushed and stunned under the animal. . . . When he woke up, it was with a pang of extreme pain, his breast-plate was taken off, his servant was holding his head up, the good and faithful lad of Hampshire† was blubbering over his master, whom he had found and thought dead (bk. 2, ch. 9).

At the foot of the page we read:

†My mistress, before I went this campaign, sent me John Lockwood of Walcote, who has ever since remained with me.—H.E.

And raising our eyes again, we see that this quick footnote has saved Esmond's life.

But for honest Lockwood's faithful search after his master, there had no doubt been an end of Esmond here, and of this his story. The marauders were out rifling the bodies as they lay on the field, and Jack had brained one of these gentry with the club-end of his musket, who had eased Esmond of his hat and periwig, his purse, and fine silver-mounted pistols which the Dowager gave him, and was fumbling in his pockets for further treasure, when Jack Lockwood came up and put an end to the scoundrel's triumph.

"No man is a hero to his valet de chambre." The adage is here enacted in the form of its contrapositive: the valet is a hero to his master. This episode can be distinguished from, say, the parallelism of Falstaff and Hal on the battlefield of Shrewsbury. Thackeray does not so much parallel master and servant as substitute the realm of the latter for that of the former. The private realm of the all-too-human assumes a determining role in public events.

Lockwood comes into existence at the point where Thackeray turns his gaze away from military glory, and it is implied that the squalid scene we observe instead is more meaningful. What is its meaning? Late in the novel Esmond says that Lockwood "took me out of the fire on his shoulders" (bk. 3, ch. 3). But he is as forgetful here as when he has to remedy his omission of Lockwood's existence by a hasty footnote. "The battle was over at this end of the field, by this time: the village was in possession of the English." Lockwood does not rescue him from enemy fire, in fact, but from "marauders" of unspecified nationality. And three chapters later, after another English victory, Esmond numbers Lockwood himself among these marauders. As becomes clear at this point, they are Englishmen.

Honest Lockwood, Esmond's servant, no doubt wanted to be among the marauders himself and take his share of the booty; for when, the action over, and the troops got to their ground for the night, the Captain bade Lockwood get a horse, he asked, with a rueful countenance, whether his honor would have him come too; but his honor only bade him go about his business, and Jack hopped away quite delighted as soon as he saw his master mounted. (bk. 2, ch. 12)

He joins, that is, those from whom he saved his master's life, hat, periwig, and purse. If the reality of battle is sordid, it would seem it is because the real issue is less patriotism than property. The struggle between England and France has not yet given way to a struggle between masters and servants, but this is the eventuality Thackeray evokes.

In this sense, to bestow history upon the valet is not, as Hegel thought, to concentrate on "small, human particularities which have nothing to do with the historical mission of the person concerned."[7] On the contrary, the shift in point of view that brings servants closer to the center of the picture helps to refocus a history whose motion has carried it out of the traditional frame. Another, more famous instance is the Waterloo sequence in *Vanity Fair,* where the main-plot battlefield is again suppressed in favor of its lower, private parallel. Here the master's elegant possessions, which add a note of class cleavage to the national rivalry at Blenheim, are again in evidence:

Isidor, the valet, had looked on very sulkily while Osborne's servant was disposing of his master's baggage . . . for in the first place he hated Mr. Osborne, whose conduct to him, and to all inferiors, was generally over-bearing . . . and secondly, he was angry that so many valuables should be removed from under his hands, to fall into other people's possession when the English discomfiture should arrive. Of this defeat he and a vast number of other people in Brussels and Belgium did not make the slightest doubt. The almost universal belief was, that the Emperor would divide the Prussian and English armies, annihilate one after the other, and march into Brussels before three days were over: when all the moveables of his present masters, who would be killed, or fugitives, or prisoners, would lawfully become the property of M. Isidor. (ch. 31)

Here Thackeray does not resort to the awkward expedient of the protagonist's temporary unconsciousness in order to move the reader from the battle to the reality behind it. He simply turns his regard away from the front. The maneuver works, in Avrom Fleischman's opinion, because the point when Isidor shocks his masters by crying "C'est le feu!"—it is of course the servant who delivers such news— is "the moment when history impinges upon the individual life; it is the meeting-point of reality and subjective experience."[8] But there is a deeper reason. On the battlefield, the forces of the French Revolution are defeated. But within the English colony in Brussels, what we see is their victory. Becky, the French-speaking former governess, upsets the aristocracy in a triumph of brains over birth. And Isidor, lowly parallel both to her and to Bonaparte, makes an even more revolutionary gesture. His master, Jos Sedley, has been dressing the part of a military hero, with military-style coat, hat, and whiskers. When he hears his valet's news, he concludes that he will be taken for an officer and massacred:

and staggering back to his bed-chamber, he began wildly pulling the bell which summoned his valet.

Isidor answered that summons. Jos had sunk in a chair—he had torn off his neck-cloths, and turned down his collars, and was sitting with both his hands lifted to his throat.

"*Coupez-moi,* Isidor," shouted he: "*vite! Coupez-moi!*"

Isidor thought for a moment he had gone mad, and that he wished his valet to cut his throat.

"*Les moustaches,*" gasped Jos; "*les moustaches—coupy, rasy, vite!*" . . .

Isidor swept off the mustachios in no time with the razor, and heard with inexpressible delight his master's orders that he should fetch a hat and a plain coat. "*Ne porty ploo—habit militair—bonny—donny a voo, prenny dehors*" were Jos' words—the coat and cap were at last his property. (ch. 32)

What is raised here is the specter of throat-cutting. Jos, who is terrified of having his throat cut by Napoleon's armies, in blissful ignorance bares it to his domestic, a secret Bonapartist who is highly motivated to cut it for him. On the other hand, Isidor, who is contemplating the same eventuality—his master's throat being cut by Napoleon's armies and himself benefiting thereby—is innocent of any designs of his own respecting his master's person. Nothing happens except a shave. But it is a shave heavy with historical implications. It suggests that the truth of history, which has clearly decamped from the offstage battlefield, is coming to inhere in a conflict between upper and lower plot lines, a conflict which now usurps the narration. The parallels do not of course intersect. Lockwood's marauding is set apart by a few pages from that of the "scoundrel" he kills over his master's body, and though Isidor's dreams are wild and historical, his actions remain sedate and domestic. But the violent intersection between these parallels is now imaginable and indeed, in the mode of comedy, made vividly present.

Comparing the basic geometry of novel and drama, Lukács argues that "since the subject of a novel is the total span of social life, a fully carried-though collision can only be a marginal case among many others." In this more diffuse and comprehensive form, parallel plots also exercise a correspondingly more decisive influence.[9] The novel is more conducive to parallels than to collisions, but it valorizes those parallels, allows the comic fragment to deliver a cosmic implication.

Take the example of the shave-as-parallel-to-Waterloo. Geoffrey Tillotson remarks of Thackeray that "the poor come into the novels . . . mainly as they barber their patrons."[10] In itself this mode of integration of "the poor" would seem an ultimate in subsumed otherness. But my reading of the Waterloo episode is supported by the tonsorial allusions to be found in shorter forms. In "The History of the Next French Revolution," as mentioned above, the razor is likened to a bayonet. In "The Rose and the Ring," a fairy tale intermixed with domestic parody, the shaver and the executioner are conflated: a valet goes up to shave the prince as the prince descends to the guillotine. In "Cox's Diary" the barber makes the same joke: "I've cut seventeen heads off (as I say) this very day."[11] The one obvious masterpiece that embodies this morbid motif, Melville's *Benito Cereno,* is short enough for its structure to be, as Warner Berthoff observes, that of a riddle.[12] For those who might not catch the hints typical of the Victorian triple-decker, the answer is given: the servant who shaves the captain controls the ship. His "impromptu touches" evince "the hand of a master." He contemplates the supposed master before him "as, in toilet at least, the creature of his own tasteful hands." The razor at the captain's throat governs his laconic replies to the naive Yankee who has come aboard, and the latter's "vagary, that in the black he saw a headsman, and in the white a man at the block . . . one of those antic conceits, appearing and disappearing in a breath, from which, perhaps, the best regulated mind is not always free," has already been realized in blood.[13] In longer fiction, where the "antic conceits" remain unfulfilled prophecies, the reader has to learn, like Melville's Yankee, to decipher the homely traces of a hidden upheaval.

There is a long tradition of barbershop clowning. We find it in the *commedia dell'arte* and some English Renaissance plays, and it enters the English novel from Cervantes and Lesage by way of those exact contemporaries, Fielding's Partridge and Smollett's Strap. To remember this tradition is to recall the basic indignity of posture that puts the master in an interesting if not wholly reversed relation to his dependent. Even the traditional loquacity of barbers seems related to this temporary reversal of power. In Eliot's *Romola,* for example, the servant-barber's function as central clearing-house of information is activated as well as colored by the routine humiliation:

It is not a sublime attitude for a man, to sit with lathered chin thrown backward, and have his nose made a handle of; but to be shaved was a fashion of Florentine respectability. . . . It was the hour of the day, too, when yesterday's crop of gossip was freshest, and the barber's tongue was always in its glory when his razor was busy; the deft activity of those two instruments seemed to be set going by a common spring. (ch. 16)

An analogy with warfare, an association with sexuality, and a hint of danger to the master already surround the comic shaving in *Roderick Random*. Seconding his servant in a minor affair of honor, Roderick proposes razors as the dueling weapon (ch. 12). Sexuality, interfering with the instrumentality of shaving, renders Strap dangerous as well. Aroused by the sight of "a fine buxom wench," Strap admits that "my hand sh-sh-shook so much that I sliced a piece off a gentleman's nose" (ch. 16). Any emotion makes the same point. In the tempest of good news that heralds the end of the novel, Roderick declares himself "too well acquainted with Strap to trust myself in his hands while he was under such agitation" (ch. 64).

In the nineteenth century, the most pervasive symbolism of dangerous shaving is sexual and political. As E. J. Hobsbawm points out, men's hair and beards were among the "secondary sexual characteristics" that were "grotesquely overemphasized" in the period of Victorian prudery.[14] One may think of how George Osborne's whiskers "do their work" on Miss Swartz in *Vanity Fair* (ch. 21). Like Littimer, who brings young David Copperfield "that reproachful shaving water" (ch. 21), servants in Dickens and Thackeray are thus agents of sexual humiliation. The motif also evokes the master's more extreme helplessness—as in *The Newcomes,* where Sir Brian wears "the look of extra neatness, which invalids have, who have just been shaved and combed, and made ready by their attendants (bk. 2, ch. 42). This can turn to tableaux of social apocalypse (the maid making faces at the paralyzed Sir Pitt Crawley) or, later, to the erotic self-abandonment of Sir Clifford Chatterley in his nurse's skillful hands (ch. 9). There are also oblique revolutionary associations. *Little Dorrit* opens with a reference to "the national razor in its case—the guillotine shut up" and ends with Pancks carrying out his "tremendous threat" against the landlord, Casby: "I don't mean, cut his throat. But by all that's precious, I'll cut his hair!" (bk. 2, ch. 9). In Beardsley's "Ballad of a Barber," the king's daughter loses her head to a man who suddenly feels "mighty as a king's commands."[15] When one sees Thackeray's domestic version of Waterloo in this light, it comes as no surprise to learn that Wellington chose to shave himself.

The actual psychology of servant violence has been outlined by Albert Memmi, taking off from a discussion of Joseph Losey's *The Servant,* and by Lucien Goldmann in his analysis of Genêt's *Les Bonnes.* For both analysts, the key is the servant's amorous identification with his or her dominator. Since one end of the chain of dependency is within the servant, breaking it is suicidal. The crime is almost always self-destructive rather than self-interested; most often the criminal in fact makes no effort to escape. Violence against the master presumes the servant's lack of autonomy at the same time that it accords him the power of ultimate determination. The private, intimate context and the ease with which it can be committed make it seem as gratuitous as it is unavoidable. Memmi quotes Octave Mirbeau: "When I think that each day a cook, for example, holds the life of his masters in his hands . . . a pinch of arsenic instead of salt . . . a drop of strychnine instead of vinegar . . . and that's that!"[16] This combination of apparent irrationality with absolute power is perhaps a further reason why so much badinage about murder is overhung with the notion of the servant as Fate, at once avenging and arbitrary.

In the novel, the hypothesis that our lives are in our servants' hands is argued by the rhetoric of comedy. The comic avoids real pain, as Aristotle said, but it does so by first ostentatiously threatening real pain. Its inconclusiveness presupposes an initial violence, if only a violence suffused into the atmosphere by analogies and affinities. For example, in Mr. Lillyvick's fatalistic surrender to the barber in *Nicholas Nickleby:*

"I should be glad to have somebody like me, somehow," said Mr. Lillyvick, "before I die."

"You don't mean to do that yet awhile?" said Newman.

Unto which Mr. Lillyvick replied in a solemn voice, "Let me be shaved"; and again consigning himself to the hands of the journeyman, said no more. (ch. 52)

Even so miniscule a *non sequitur* gains something from the knowledge that eventually the plots of the two villains will be foiled by their two servants, who act the parts of personal fates. But between such inconsequential comic incidents and the novel's complete chain of consequences, there is a middle ground where the "absurd" perception that one's life is at stake every time one is shaved can be assimilated to the decorum of realism.

Consider the extraordinary scene toward the end of *Pendennis* in which Morgan, Major Pendennis' valet, stands up to his master's curses and orders him out of the house—which he himself, as the valet announces, now owns. In an earlier shaving scene, the Major's amusement at the expense of "pore men" is rewarded by his valet in mid-story: "Beg your pardon, did I cut you, sir?" (ch. 36). In retrospect, their final confrontation brings out the implications of this mildly comic shave. As Barbara Hardy observes, this episode "is not a turning-point in the action, though it may look like one for a little while. . . . the triumph, though real in personal-professional terms, is short-lived and deceptive."[17] The rebellion is totally spontaneous, and despite Morgan's villainous presence in the dénouement, the Major "neither yields his Money nor his Life." But outside the plot, this instant is intensely disorienting. It reveals that the Major's life is not in fact his own. "Throughout the scene," Hardy goes on, "the emphasis is on two things: on the sheer interest of the reversal and the quarrel to the bored old man; and also on the vivid revival of earlier days, of fighting, fencing, and 'affairs.'"[18] The Major's life is empty; it is propped up and fleshed out, as we have remarked, largely by his valet's gossip and petty attentions. Now, because of the conflict with the servant, interest all at once floods back into it. The ultimate self-definition that he once found in fighting and fencing expresses itself now not in confrontation between gentlemen but in confrontation between master and man. Thackeray acts out Hegel's social allegory of Herr and Knecht with overwhelming psychological conviction. At the moment when, a rentier living idly on the labor of others, the Major is thrown out of his lodgings, when the relations that determine his existence rise tumultuously to its surface, we see the man come back to life. Without taking the trouble to work the character of Morgan into anything more than a hastily sketched agent of the plot, Thackeray forces the recognition that "life" has a new center.

Thackeray's odd anachronistic interest in "fighting, fencing, and 'affairs'" also offers evidence of this social relocation of "life." His treatment of dueling, John Lester writes, is typical of Thackeray's "avoidance of violent, dramatic action." With a novelist like Dumas, whom Thackeray so much admired, the duel is the climax of the story. With Thackeray, though more than a dozen duels are fought or threatened in his novels, they are almost never presented scenically."[19] One reason, perhaps, is that the only antagonists who could render the duel meaningful cannot be faced or even characterized. An example is the near duel between Pendennis and one M. Mirobolant, a French cook with a passion for the same lady. As usual, Thackeray marches the reader to the brink of an abyss and then wanders vaguely away from it; Pendennis is not finally obliged "to go out with a servant" (ch. 27). But this is the possibility that has been raised. The protagonist has been asked to risk his life against that of a character who is perilously close to nonentity, a character who does not matter. Having given Mirobolant a utopian name ("merveilleux, trop beau pour avoir des chances de se réaliser"), along with French, the language of revolution (and a major ingredient in the revolutionary idiolect of "Servant Gal-isms"), and having made him a Chevalier de la Croix de Juillet (the reference is to the Revolution of 1830), Thackeray has by no means created a serious proletarian menace. On the other hand, he has suggested that the arbitrariness of the protagonist's potential fate can be seen as a *social* absurdity.

The effect here verges from the comic to the grotesque, defined by Wolfgang Kayser as a confrontation with "the estranged world" or its "demonic aspects."[20] But this estranged world, with its "dark, ominous, and mysterious forces that . . . defy all human explanation," is no existential abstraction, but merely a class of human antagonists which determines the hero's existence but whose humanity the hero is unable to acknowledge. As Thackeray notes: "the idea of having insulted a cook, or that such an individual should have any feeling of honor at all, did not much enter into the mind of this lofty young aristocrat, the apothecary's son" (ch. 26). If one does not recognize life where it exists, then one will label "absurd" or "grotesque" those "tools," mechanical or human, which, as Kayser says, "unfold a dangerous life of their own," those "instruments" which "are demonically destructive and overpower their makers."[21]

The double motif of the abortive duel and of the duel with a social inferior enables Thackeray to suggest that as affairs of honor between gentlemen have become peripheral and slightly ridiculous, dishonorable conflict between masters and men has crept in from the periphery toward the center of the social canvas. These too avoid a climax, but they at least show why they meander. They circle around a story that Thackeray cannot tell without ceasing to write about and for his own class.

INFECTION AND THE FAMILY

I cannot but with some wonder find some people, now the contagion is over, talk of its being an immediate stroke from Heaven, without the agency of means.

DEFOE, *A Journal of the Plague Year*

The dueling and shaving motifs make of the featureless servant Other, little more than a name and rank appended to a superior, a palpable and portentous threat to life. This threat is executed by the further motif of servant contagion. *Bleak House,* where Jo assists the metaphoric malignancy of the atmosphere in carrying plague from the slums to the homes of the rich, is perhaps the most familiar instance in the novel of infection as accidental class revenge.[22] Counter to scientific evidence, the plague in fiction is not transmitted without human carriers, without an interlocking chain of face-to-face encounters. Servants, whose substitute presence at doors and bedsides protects from danger and defilement, declare by means of contagion that they are more than buffers and proxies. It is significant that Jo passes the smallpox to Esther through her maid, Charley—a child of the slums who has induced her mistress to visit him and who strangely dominates and frames the chapter. In this literal sense servants are, as the Mayhew brothers called them, "the greatest plague of life"; they infect innocent diseases with the injustice they themselves suffer.[23]

By the logic of infection, large consequences follow from lowly causes. When Henry Esmond carries smallpox into the Castlewood home, he brings it direct from the serving-maid at the inn (who dies of it). "There would be no need to mention these trivialities," he says of his attraction to that local beauty, "but that they actually influenced many lives, as trifles will in the world" (bk. 1, ch. 9). In this case, "her Ladyship's beauty was very much injured by the smallpox," and Lord and Lady Castlewood both date the fall of the family from Henry's hours with the serving-maid. "Why did you bring the small-pox . . . from Castlewood village?" Lady Castlewood asks. "You could not help it, could you? Which of us knows whither fate leads us? But we were happy, Henry, till then" (bk. 1, ch. 12). Lord Castlewood also invokes fate. "Ever since you brought that damned small-pox into the house, there has been a fate pursuing me" (bk. 1, ch. 12). These references to fate suggest a causal logic that has been obscured or suppressed. J. Hillis Miller proposes that, like so much else in the novel, its causality follows Freud's explication of the Oedipus complex. It is true that Henry's awakening sexuality breaks up the marriage of his surrogate parents, leading to Lord Castlewood's death and indirectly enabling Henry to marry Lady Castlewood.[24] But we might say equally well that what destroys the Castlewoods is their unacknowledged debt to the people of the village. Esmond himself, the go-between, is a page, described as "little more than a menial" (bk. 1, ch. 7). He is thus an appropriate mediator for the "friends at the ale-house" to whom Lady Castlewood, miffed at his interest in the serving-maid, angrily bids him return. Disease makes the ambiguity of his position evident: "it is impossible," his "Mistress" tells him, "that you can continue to stay upon the intimate footing in which you have been in this family" (bk. 1, ch. 8). It will turn out that the family from which he is expelled is his own, along with the house and title, even before he marries its mistress. Though Thackeray makes light of this romance machinery of buried documents and long-lost heirs, it helps construct a hypothetical logic for the "fate" of the smallpox episode: the child who has been deprived of his birthright and therefore brought into his own home as a servant will bring the deadly contagion of his fellow servants along with him, destroying the family in which he and they are denied full membership.

This hypothesis, which restates the argument of the previous chapter, gains additional support from a similar constellation of servants, infection, and family in Smollett's *Humphry Clinker*. In *Esmond* the working class asserts its common humanity positively via sexual attraction and negatively via infection. The two are linked: Lady Castlewood, who is jealous of her husband, like many actual employers chooses maids who have been marked by smallpox and so are in both senses non-contagious. In *Humphry Clinker* infection and affection are fused by the malapropisms of Win Jenkins, the maid: "Yours with true infection," ". . . said a civil thing to me in the way of infection," and so on. They are also connected by the loathing of Matthew Bramble, the authoritarian and hypochondriac heavy father. Bramble's perfunctory opposition to true love is far surpassed by his obsessive terror of contagion. In his eyes, Bath is "the rendez-vous of the diseased," and London is "this center of infection." Infection, as he makes clear, is the visible sign of the breakdown of social hierarchy: "there is no distinction or subordination left—the different departments of life are jumbled together." At the same time, this breakdown is embodied in London's "extraordinary number of domestics. The ploughboys, cowherds, and lower hinds, are debauched and seduced by the appearance of those coxcombs in livery. . . . They desert their dirt and drudgery, and swarm up to London, in hopes of getting into service." One such worker-turned-domestic is Clinker himself, and it is he who carries the general infection into Bramble's family. Preaching that "at the day of judgment there will be no distinction of persons," he shows his power—in Bramble's words—"to infect others with your fanaticism." First by converting the women in the family, and then by proving to be the "love-begotten babe" of Bramble himself. The happy ending of comedy acts out Clinker's day of judgment: "the sins of my youth rise in judgment against me," Bramble says. The virus of affection, of which servants are the privileged carriers, abolishes the distinction of persons and takes over the family organism.[25]

The point of this rapid paraphrase is to bring out a pattern. Whether the mighty are humbled by the menial or happily integrate them, it would seem that they are threatened with infection—that is, with forcible interference in their destinies—when blood kin are disguised as hired servants and treated accordingly. Infection is a danger when the worlds inhabited by children and servants come too close in their parallel orbits; it is a malady of parallelism. This idea may shed some light on Angus Fletcher's proposal that infection is the type of *all* novelistic causality. Hints of fateful causality, Fletcher suggests, are inseparable from parallelism in general. Following Empson, he holds that "double plots are bound to suggest a magical relationship between the two levels on which these two plots are told." Much of what Empson calls pastoral "might better be termed the literature of class struggle," therefore, for it includes "a strong suggestion that the servants are, or could be, rulers."[26] The reader receives this suggestion by reverting to primitive or magical habits of thought. The causative role of servants, for example, can be assimilated to "contagious magic": "whatever 'goes with' the object of the spell will suffice to bring that object under control." Causality is imaged as contiguity, as a species of infection.[27]

Defoe's *Journal of the Plague Year* is thus, Fletcher says, "a story of allegory's central fable," and all its social detail is just so much veneer over a core of magic.[28] But it would seem that the detail has a strong logic of its own. As far as the immediate causes of the infection are concerned, the narrator is categorical:

The Infection generally came into the Houses of the Citizens, by the Means of their Servants, who they were obliged to send up and down the Streets for Necessaries, that is to say, for Food, or Physick, to Bake-houses, Brew-houses, Shops, &c. and who going necessarily thro' the Streets into Shops, Markets, and the like, it was impossible, but that they should one way or other, meet with distempered People, who conveyed the fatal Breath into them, and they brought it Home to the Families, to which they belonged.[29]

Again, Defoe's counterpart to what Fletcher calls the "cure" of "symbolic isolation" is socially specific: "not so many, by several

Thousands, had died," the narrator says, "had every Master of a Family, as soon as any Servant especially, had been taken sick in his House, been obliged to send them to the next Pest-House, if they were willing, as many were, and had the Examiners done the like among the poor People."[30] The word that gives pause is "especially." Defoe recognizes that the "master" or *pater familias* might feel some scruples about expelling an infected son or daughter to the dreaded "pest-house." But servants do not "belong" to the family in quite the same sense—though they still belong enough to require the awkward ambiguity of "especially," which implies that the same might be done to *anyone* under the father's authority. In Defoe's vision, the family opens itself to the city's dangerous promiscuity by means of its servants, and it can close itself off again by isolating the alien element and expulsing it.

This alternative version of Defoe's allegory can be understood without recourse to primitive thought. In Defoe's period, as was remarked in the last chapter, the sense of "family" as an extended household including both blood kin and servants had not yet been supplanted by the present restricted sense of immediate blood relations. A great deal of eighteenth-century literature negotiates between the two meanings. In *Pamela* the new definition gets the emphasis of italics when Lady Darnford's husband sees nothing wrong in a gentleman seducing his waiting-maid: "He hurts *no family* by this." This still required to be said because servants still counted as part of the family. Defoe, like Smollett, uses the word in both senses. For example: "a whole Family was shut up and lock'd in, because the Maid-Servant was taken sick."[31] The process of redefinition, visible in this sentence itself, is exacerbated by the plague. Under duress, it becomes tempting to make a (new) distinction of persons, as Defoe does elsewhere, between "Servants and Family"[32] This is what Foucault finds as well. The plague, he says, can be considered the initiating moment of those procedures of disciplinary surveillance discussed above. "Each individual is fixed in his place. . . . Against the plague, which is a mixture, discipline brings into play its power, which is one of analysis."[33] One major result of this analysis, and the surveillance within the home that accompanies it, is the recomposition of the "family."

"The one really telling difference between the family in Stuart England and the family we know in our own time," Peter Laslett writes, "is that servants were then counted as belonging to it." This aspect of the transition to modernity did not affect only a small, wealthy minority. "In the West something like one-fifth (20%) of all children were, during their earliest, impressionable years, members of domestic groups which contained servants. Of the other four-fifths, something like a half (40% of all children)—though the proportion was very variable—themselves became servants in their late teens or early twenties. At most one in five, then, of all young people escaped the experience of living with servants or of living as servants."[34] In trying to measure the moral significance of this statistic, it would of course be anachronistic to project the hothouse emotions of the modern family onto the premodern household. On the other hand, it is important to remember that kinship, as Lévi-Strauss has shown, "does not consist in the objective ties of descent or consanguinity between individuals; it is an arbitrary system of representations, not the spontaneous development of a real situation."[35] In any society where kinship is a primary relation of production, the servant might well constitute a borderline case. As, for example, in the Bible: the first angel to appear in the Old Testament does so in order to adjudicate precisely this question. When Sarah casts out Hagar, her Egyptian maid, along with Hagar's son by Abraham, Ishmael, she is transgressing a code that forbids the expulsion of offspring, and Abraham needs divine dispensation in order to comply.[36] Expulsion is an act of analysis that permits us to read a promiscuous semi-equality back into the earlier social unit.

A man "does not do his wife a very material injury," Samuel Johnson declared, "if, for instance, from mere wantonness of appetite, he steals privately to her chambermaid," because the result is not, as would be the case for her adultery, "confusion of progeny."[37] But a woman's sexual transgression, as in *Tom Jones,* is not the only cause of this "confusion of progeny." Other ways of mingling with servants produce the same effect, which is in fact one of the novel's central motifs. Hidden away in the tokens and recognitions that seem to be borrowed from literary tradition rather than imposed by social actuality, this motif cannot be separated from the eighteenth-century consciousness of a new question as to *where servants came from.* This included attention to the issues of false characters, the exodus from the countryside, the instituting of Registry Offices. And in a larger sense, where they came from was at stake in proposals to establish foundling homes. Such homes, it was argued, would become "Nurseries" where upper-class women could "pick out Servants for the meanest offices of their Houses."[38] Servants were children of unknown origin; they were the confused progeny of a society that still saw itself as the ordered progeny of a single family. It is clear that servants in the premodern household were not treated as modern children. But it is not clear how far they were from being the equals of earlier children who were not servants. "There was not so much confusion as identification between all the various sorts of service to be performed by servants and taught to children, and an identification also, therefore, between servants and children. So much so that the books (and there were vast numbers of them) specifically written to teach 'servants' manners were called 'babies' books"[39] At any rate, as Lawrence Stone notes, "in many households the relations with children were not all that much closer than the relations with domestic servants." And, more important, the obligation to have a "fatherly care over his servants as if they were his children" was a powerful factor in the father-master's self-defining allegiance to paternalism.[40] The shock that is registered in *A Journal of the Plague Year* would seem to arise from the disavowal of that obligation. Capitalism required free wage labor, and the family required freedom from traditional obligations and encumbrances as well as the purity of a private retreat from the competitive market. Streamlining itself for the coming era, the family shed its burdensome public appendages. But this long expulsion of offspring produced a lingering moral crisis. Fed by paternalist ideology, the sense of communal responsibility remains. The servant, thrust out into the cold as plague victim/wage earner, keeps a claim to the former status of family member. And some of the power to determine the fate of others rests on the family's acknowledgment of that claim.

As evidence that such terms are not foreign to the author of *A Journal of the Plague Year,* we have the striking example of *Roxana,* the story of an outcast child who becomes her mother's servant. Like

Moll Flanders, Roxana can only become a fortunate mistress by ridding herself of the children to whom she has already given birth when she has to begin the world again. This chore is handled by the maid, Amy, so that the face-to-face link with the mother will be broken. As her money collector, Amy helps make Roxana's fortune in the same manner: by breaking the face-to-face tie with those who owe Roxana money, Amy protects her mistress from the emotional appeal and communal obligations that customarily restrained the accumulation of capital. In two senses, then, Roxana's money can be said to come from a new impersonality, a breaking of traditional human ties. And it is the claim to such a tie that threatens her fortune. About two-thirds of the way through the novel, Roxana discovers that "my old Cook-Maid in the Pall-Mall . . . was neither more nor less, than my own Daughter."[41] The girl does not want to remain "but a poor Servant all my Days," and when she guesses that Roxana is her mother, she demands, as Alick West comments, "both recognition as a daughter and a better life than a kitchen-maid's. . . . She is now the moving force of the action, while Roxana waits for exposure and ruin."[42] This "moving force" is not merely the force of conventional morality, nor is it the occult causal implication supposedly thrown off by all proximate parallels. It bears the residual power of a community that included kitchen maids in the family. Its antithesis is money, which bypasses the community in order to turn family members into wage laborers.

When Amy, the daughter's servant-double, tries to buy her off, the daughter says she knows "that what she [Amy] had done, was by her Mother's orders; and who she was beholden to for it; That she could never make Instruments pass for Principals and pay the Debt to the Agent, when the Obligation was all to the Original."[43] In other words, she refuses to do precisely what has made her mother's fortune (and her own servitude): to transform human Principals into paid Instruments. The discovery of high-born parents, whether in Freud or in Smollett, Defoe, Thackeray, and Dickens, is a convention of romance, and we do not need to be told not to confuse it with a widespread sociological phenomenon. But there is a significant sense in which eighteenth-century servants were in fact newly displaced children, and might truly claim to have had and lost an illustrious

parentage. When we hear these fading after-echoes of the preindustrial family, we can perhaps understand why the convention again
and again urges the reader to identify novelistic servants as abandoned children and bestows such large and dangerous powers on
them.

THE BUTLER DID IT

A factor that complicates this reading of *Roxana* as a servant's claim to
kinship, a return of the principal who lies repressed in every instrument, is the instrumentality of Amy. In the conclusion it is suggested
that Amy has murdered Roxana's daughter, acting against Roxana's
orders but in accord with her expressed wishes, and this would seem
to make her, unlike the daughter, an all-too-willing instrument. More
generally, the issue here is whether the more common interpretation
of servant agency is not a more accurate and comprehensive one. As
disposable extensions of the master who handle his dirty work and
then disappear or suffer its consequences in his place, servants can of
course be dismissed as devices of aesthetic, psychological, or moral
escapism. "It is the business of slaves," writes a critic of Menander,
"to spare people who are so virtuous the annoyance of being compromised." In Charles Mauron's psychoanalytic view, the "dissociation of
desire and technique," by which the son-hero wants and the slave
does the necessary, "can only tend to protect the son. . . . The son
imagines himself triumphant, without risk and without injury, over
the man who possesses the woman or the treasure." As Ronald
Paulson notes, Smollett splits the picaro into a master-servant pair
partly so that "when chamber-pots are discharged, they fall on Strap,
not Roderick." *Nicholas Nickleby* divides the material of *Oliver Twist* for
what seem to be the same motives. As Steven Marcus points out, the
novel gives "Oliver's protected character and destiny" to Nicholas,
and his "terrible experiences" to Smike.[44]

There would be no problem accounting for the transhistorical
continuities of the "butler did it" theme if it were no more than a
formal variant of what John Cawelti calls the "least likely person"
convention. "No bonds have been built between him and the reader,
and consequently he can serve his role as the personification of guilt
without involving the reader's feelings. The relief that accompanies

the explanation reflects the reader's pleasure at seeing his favorites and projections clearly and finally exonerated and the guilt thrust beyond question onto a person who has remained largely outside his sphere of interest."[45] But this double evasion—the protagonist's dodging of the moral burden of the situation he or she confronts and the author's hesitation to work through the situation he or she has invented—is not all there is to the device. If it can be imagined as an artificial limb, we can conclude that its function is prosthetic: it supplies a deficiency. Amy carries the contradictions of her mistress' life not only to a point where Roxana can no longer live with them, but to a point they would not otherwise have reached. The implausible shift in emotional register that accompanies the suggestion of murder indicates that perhaps, like many other murders, this one asks to be taken as a convention of moral absoluteness, employed in order to bring contradictions to the clear crisis that real life is adept at confusing and postponing.[46]

Moreover, this prosthesis has a perverse will of its own. Like other grotesque instruments, it deviously reflects the alienated life of the servant who implements another's desires. Whatever her intention, Amy's actions do not so much end the servant-daughter's demand for recognition as extend it into an undesired vengeance. In the same way, even the "harmless" Smike is an unwitting cause of his master's vulnerability. Long after Nicholas' future has been comfortably settled by the Cheerybles, his uncle can still persecute him by injuring Smike, the "instrument" (ch. 60) who turns out to be Ralph's son. As in *Roxana,* the formal instrumentality of the servant is thematized, fleshed out, by his parallelism with the child. What the financier tries to do to Nicholas via Smike is what he has already done to Smike himself: turn his flesh-and-blood into a family-less dependent.

If the crisis of the family cannot be used to interpret quite as wide a historical expanse as the "least likely person" convention, it does constitute an "event" of sufficiently *longue durée* to cover most of the period of the novel. As one sign of its continuing hold over literary discourse, there is a minor coincidence that is perhaps worthy of further reflection. Without too much exaggeration, it is possible to affirm that three of the acknowledged masterpieces of Victorian realism, *Bleak House, Middlemarch,* and *Vanity Fair,* all turn on the murder of a character by a servant. The case is weakest for *Vanity Fair,* where it must be recalled that Becky is or was a governess (the servant parallel to the "child" Amelia), and it must be accepted without conclusive evidence that she poisoned Amelia's brother Jos. In *Bleak House,* which closes with a murder mystery and the arrest of a servant murderer, the "butler did it" pattern is clearer. All of the leading suspects have far better motives to murder Tulkinghorn than Mlle. Hortense, Lady Dedlock's French maid; we are asked to believe that she murders him out of pique at his failure to find her a new place. There is thus a strong implication that she acts out and takes responsibility for passions and interests that rightfully belong to her more virtuous superiors, but that are censored in them before they reach the level of action. It is obvious that Hortense enacts the destructive and suicidal logic of her mistress' situation; she is the other face in Lady Dedlock's mirror and more than once exchanges disguises with her. It is less obvious, perhaps, that she does the same for Esther. As one critic notes, "Hortense's attempt to offer her services to Esther as her 'domestic' is, in part, a suggestion that the energies Hortense possesses either exist in some form within Esther or that they may be conferred upon her magically through some proximity to the Frenchwoman."[47]

These energies are directed against a history in which both Lady Dedlock's spurned servant and her spurned daughter might recognize themselves. Though Esther is not technically a servant, her training as a governess and her jingling of the housekeeper's keys identify her with the novel's many young people who are or become servants because a failure of parental responsibility has denied them the status of children. One of the novel's better jokes sums up this motif. When Caddy Jellyby tells her mother that she is engaged to be married, the response is "I have engaged a boy"—that is, that the services of the daughter (as amanuensis) have already been replaced by those of a hired servant. The two forms of engagement—kinship and market—have become equivalent: all the children of this world have become servants. The chapter in which this exchange occurs (23) is framed by Esther's refusal to accept Hortense as her maid and then her acceptance of Charley as her maid, a choice of submissiveness over rebellion. But the rebellion expresses itself nonetheless. It is through Charley, as I said above, that infection passes from hovel to mansion, asserting Esther's hidden kinship with orphans like Jo, and it is through Hortense that Lady Dedlock will fall. Like Hortense, Esther has been slighted by her mother. Fulfilling the prophecy of the Ghost's Walk, she like Hortense is the indirect cause of her mother's death. As in *Roxana,* the servant kills the person who has discovered the mistress/mother's primal sin: turning children into servants. But in so doing, she lets the truth out and pushes the mistress toward destruction. She acts in unconscious complicity with the child/servant that, as we may now realize, she is herself. If the murder is considered as Hortense's revenge on her mistress, it remains mechanical and unconvincing; but the artifice justifies itself as soon as we see that Hortense is Esther's surrogate, a servant rising up violently to resent not being treated as a daughter.⁴⁸

In the context of radical melodrama, it is perhaps not surprising that parallelism gives coherence to an act that would otherwise appear to be opaquely irrational or transparently instrumental. But the same effect can also operate within a texture of smooth, tight-knit rationalism. " 'One must hire servants who will not break things,' said Lydgate. (Certainly, this was reasoning with an imperfect vision of sequences. But at that period there was no sort of reasoning which was not more or less sanctioned by men of science)" (ch. 36). For all its pretensions to more advanced science, George Eliot's vision of sequences assigns some crucial positions in the plot to the apparent arbitrariness of servants who break things. When Bulstrode wants to do away with the blackmailer who knows that he, like Roxana, Lady Dedlock, Ralph Nickleby, Mrs. Clennam, and others, has kept a child from an inheritance, the force of circumstance cooperates by whittling Raffles' hold on life to a slender thread. Technically, at least, it is the housekeeper, Mrs. Abel, who cuts it. Raffles expires after Bulstrode allows her to follow traditional medical practice, and her own charitable impulse, rather than Lydgate's advice.

"It's not a time to spare when people are at death's door, nor would you wish it, sir, I'm sure. Else I should give him our own bottle o' rum as we keep by us. But a sitter up as you've been, and doing everything as laid in your power—"

Here a key was thrust through the inch of doorway, and Mr. Bulstrode said huskily, "That is the key of the wine-cooler. You will find plenty of brandy there." (ch. 70)

This act places Mrs. Abel neither at the forefront of Victorian mur-
deresses nor at the center of the novel, but it is something more than
another extenuating circumstance in Bulstrode's favor. The point is
made when Mrs. Abel's brief existence in the novel is prolonged to
one further event. It is through her, as is carefully noted, that the
news and circumstances of Raffles' death are made public (ch. 71) and
Bulstrode's downfall begins. Carrying out the murder on Bulstrode's
behalf, she is also his nemesis. And this would appear to be one
fundamental trope of servant instrumentality in the novel: done for
us, our living turns against us.

In the mode of incidental comedy, the same structure extends
throughout Victorian fiction. *Jenues premiers* like Pip and David Copperfield have nearly as much trouble with the sudden appendages
they sprout as do heavy fathers and mothers. But one should not infer
that the servant is therefore a sign of "trouble" in the abstract, of any
and all disturbance or self-division as such. Pip produces a page, as
Bulstrode unveils a housekeeper, because each is divided against himself, but more precisely because self-division is the condition of their
prosperity. In his rise each has fractured a metaphorical family, and
the obstreperous servant is thus empowered not only to mock the
social incompetence of the *nouveaux riches,* but also to invoke those
who have been sacrificed to the acquisition of wealth. The immediate
motive for Mrs. Abel's unknowing murder is charity, the assertion of
our primordial responsibility for one another, and it is her enactment
of this intertwinedness that brings her master down.

Pip's page achieves a brief but similar significance simply by his
location. He comes into existence just in time for Joe's first visit to
London and then disappears more or less completely from the novel.
He is included, that is, mainly as a mark of exclusion: he signals Pip's
failure to sustain his connection with the family he comes from. This
is perhaps why the page is immediately dubbed the "Avenging Phantom." When he ushers Joe into Pip's lodgings, it fills up with ghosts.
Joe has just seen another fellow-townsman in *Hamlet,* and his allusion
takes in his own arrival as well: "if the ghost of a man's own father
cannot be allowed to claim his attention, what can, sir?" (ch. 27).
After Herbert's appearance causes "a ghost-seeing effect in Joe's own
countenance," the Avenging Phantom effects a further confusion as to
how many people in fact belong to the household: "here his eye fell

upon the Avenger, who was putting some toast on the table, and so plainly denoted an intention to make that young gentleman one of the family that I frowned it down." Again, a servant-ghost vengefully stands in for the absent members of a larger, former family.

There are of course instances of a servant's fatal or fateful intervention that are unaccompanied by familial parallelism or other images of broader community, where nothing more seems to be involved than a sense of the arbitrary meaninglessness of destiny. In *The Virginians,* for example, Thackeray calls on a servant to create the novel's central entanglement largely because his lifeless rentier cast, like Major Pendennis, seems incapable of creating any entanglement for itself. Harry's gambling losses and his attachment to an older woman, the twin threats that are supposed to support the plot, are expressly traced to the servant's qualities "as a romancer," that is, to "the rumors which Gumbo and his fellow-servants had set afloat" concerning the extent of Harry's wealth:

So all the little knot of people at Castlewood House, and from these the people in Castlewood village, and from thence the people in the whole country, chose to imagine that Mr. Harry Esmond Warrington was the heir of immense wealth, because his negro valet told lies about him in the servants' hall. (ch. 16)

The result is immediate: "More and more the Countess and the ladies were friendly and affectionate with him. More and more Mr. Will betted with him." But there are no particular thematics to be retained from this causality.

This use of the servant as a truly arbitrary fate seems particularly relevant to the end of the nineteenth and the early twentieth century, when the alienness and irrationality of the universe become commonplaces on much the same scale. This is Richard Hoggart's reading of *The Way of All Flesh*. Butler has made generous use of "Ellen, the servant girl" and "the family's ex-coachman John," Hoggart suggests—to the point that the hero marries the former and that the marriage ends after the latter turns up to announce that he is married to her also—simply because "it suits his determination to make the hero follow the desired evolutionary line."[49] Here in fact the parallelism of child and servant remains resonant. Ernest's flight from his parents' domination repeats the earlier expulsion of the servant, and

servant agency can thus be attached again to a critique and recon-
stitution of the family. Hoggart's argument carries more weight elsewhere. "Mark how things happen!" Kipling writes in "Watches of the
Night." "If Platte's *sais* had put the new saddle pad . . . on the mare
. . . she would not have reared, bolted, fallen into a ditch." A page
later: "Mark again how *Kismet* works. . . . the driver of the carriage
was drunk and lost his way. So the Colonel returned at an unseemly
hour and his excuses were not accepted."[50]

And yet even what seems like totally gratuitous intervention or
violence often follows a pattern like that I've been describing, if only
in dark parody. The darkest version is perhaps Evelyn Waugh's classic
short story "Mr. Loveday's Little Outing." A young woman visiting
her father in an asylum is scandalized that the harmless old man who
acts as his servant, Mr. Loveday, has never been at liberty since the
episode in his youth that led to his confinement. He "valets" the
inmates and receives "small tips for services rendered." The asylum
has been his only home. When by dint of great efforts the daughter
manages to arrange his release, the director makes a farewell speech,
declaring that he is "bound to us by ties that none will soon forget."
But "within two hours of his liberation" Mr. Loveday makes his
reappearance, having realized his dream of many years. A young
woman is found strangled next to her bicycle nearby. As an anti-
libertarian allegory, this provides a useful contrast to earlier narratives of expulsion. But the logic is familiar: the child releases the
father's servant, who then murders a young woman like herself.

The association with fatality persists, interestingly enough, even
when servants are discovered as subjects of literature in their own
right and treated in copious realistic detail. In works like Flaubert's
"Un Cœur simple" (1877), George Moore's *Esther Waters* (1894), and
Gertrude Stein's *Three Lives* (1909), the soubrette as agent of fate
becomes the maidservant as the suffering victim of a fate that seems
beyond any human power to alleviate. Servants pass from activity to
passivity, from agency to fatalism. And yet even in passivity, they
continue to suggest the existence of something like the Homeric
moira, fate conceived as the ultimate determining power of society as a
whole. This is because, as an archaic type, they revive the idea that
society *is* a whole. This odd, oblique pertinence to modern society has
been pointed out by Raymond Williams: "this situation of the servant

is crucial in our own kind of society." In something like Gramsci's distinction between rule by force and rule by consent, Williams distinguishes between the subject, who has no choice but to conform in order to survive, and the servant, who "is given the illusion of choice, and is invited to identify himself with the way of life in which his place is defined." This means that the servant "may even, consciously, think of himself as a member (indeed the old sense of 'member' allows this, for if the individual is an organ of the organism that is society, particular individuals will be higher or lower organs yet still feel themselves as true parts)."[51] In consenting to an illusory membership, servants submit to be ruled, but they also reactivate an image of membership. And membership confers the power of violent appeal against exclusion that we find in "the butler did it."

Consider Kipling's story "Mary Postgate" (1915). The English servant who sits up with a wounded German flier, refusing to treat him while he slowly dies, does not involve an actual murder. But the tableau displaces a domestic, familial murderousness onto the international hatreds of the war. The servant's existence has been sacrificed on behalf of the child of the family, whom she has raised devotedly—though not without signs of repressed hostility. He has just been killed in combat. He has in effect taken her life; now she in effect takes the life of the German who, though his enemy, has been doing no more than what he was doing. The Germans, she says, have killed children. What she tells the wounded man in his own language suggests this "confusion of progeny" in its confusion as to who does what to whom. "Ich haben der Todt Kinder gesehn." "I have seen the death of children"—she justifies her behavior by alluding to war atrocities. But "death" is in the nominative and "have" in the plural, so that "I," "death," and "children" are all simultaneously the subject of the plural verb. It is a neat condensation that identifies the servant with the child as well as with death, including death in the family from which the servant has been excluded.

THE CRACKED LOOKINGGLASS OF A SERVANT

Martha watched me in silence, lolling in her rocking-chair. Like a Fate who had run out of thread.

SAMUEL BECKETT, *Molloy*

As far as realism is concerned, one conclusion of such examples—
which could be multiplied—can be taken from a famous passage in
Middlemarch:

Your pier-glass or extensive surface of polished steel made to be rubbed by a
housemaid, will be minutely and multitudinously scratched in all directions;
but place now against it a lighted candle as a center of illumination, and lo!
the scratches will seem to arrange themselves in a fine series of concentric
circles round that little sun. It is demonstrable that the scratches are going
everywhere impartially, and it is only your candle which produces the
flattering illusion of a concentric arrangement, its light falling with an
exclusive optical selection. These things are a parable. The scratches are
events, and the candle is the egoism of any person now absent. (ch. 27)

This parable illustrates the crucial limit usually ascribed to realism by
its modernist critics: in diagnosing the perspectivism of social life, the
way the perspective of its characters is distorted by their social
situation and self-interest, it fails to apply the same lesson to itself.
The possibility of an impartial view of all this partiality is taken for
granted; the mirror of realism itself is not examined for possible
distortions. But what about that inconspicuous phrase "made to be
rubbed by a housemaid"? If this rubbing is worthy of mention at all, it
can only be because, preceding the words "minutely and multitudinously scratched in all directions," it suggests that the chaotic
methodlessness of the scratches is related to or is even an effect of
those who polish it. This, the passage hints, is where the scratches—
that is, the events—come from. The sense of causality may be only
another in the series of illusions, but it effectively brings realism's
pier-glass out of its illusory objectivity and back into play on the same
level as other illusions. Not only is the egoism of the characters
pushing toward their fates deflected by servant interference, which
revises and enlarges those fates, but more important, realism itself is
"placed" by their self-conscious exteriority. Those who polish the
mirror held up to nature, and are thus briefly reflected in it, determine in part what it will and will not reflect.

    This is to repeat that, in spite of the apparent divide between
realism and modernism, servants represent a continuity between
them, a modernist element that jars the complacency of realism's
unself-conscious focus on the here-and-now of a limited circle of

social destinies. One modernist counterpart to Eliot's pier-glass might be Joyce's bitter symbol of Irish art, "the cracked lookingglass of a servant." Joyce makes explicit what is already there in Eliot: the mirror is cracked because it is in a servant's keeping. Even as they turn away from a realist depiction of society and toward self-questioning, in other words, modern writers are making an oblique statement about their own servitude, the limits of their own social perspective, what they are forced to exclude from where they are, and what would be the price of inclusion—the sort of statement that we find in the margins of the realist novel as well.

Modernist contempt for conventions like servant inteference in the plot pervades Shaw's account of the well-made play: "the tables of consanguinity, the railway and shipping timetables, the arrivals and departures, the whole welter of Bradshaw and Baedeker, Court Guide and Post Office Directory, whirling round one incredible little stage murder and finally vanishing in a gulp of impossible stage poison."[52] This impatience with encrusted absurdities was codified, as I mentioned at the outset, in E. M. Forster's *Aspects of the Novel*. But Forster also puts absurdity in its social context. In *Abinger Harvest* he retells the story of how Hannah More, a distant relative who had written many tracts for the education of servants, was "mishandled and betrayed" in her old age by her own servants and thus forced to leave her beloved home. "'I am driven, like Eve, out of Paradise,' she said, 'but, unlike Eve, not by angels.'" Forster describes what her Edenic vision looks like while "the glass is unshattered."

The lovely provincialism of England takes shape, detaches itself from our suburbanism, smiles, says, "I like my books, I like my garden, I like elevating the lower orders," and manages not to be absurd. Presently the old mistress will ring a bell, Louisa will fail to answer it, there will be horror, disillusionment, flight, the Industrial Revolution, Tolstoy, Walt Whitman, Mr. and Mrs. Sidney Webb.[53]

What is absurd is to assume that commands will be obeyed and tracts read by the lower orders, that fate can be circumscribed by books and gardens. And yet Forster's self-mocking tone acknowledges that this is an absurdity he and his peers have not entirely learned to do without, at least on the day-to-day basis that tends to be the subject of the novel. They continue to inhabit their provincial paradise in full knowledge that the glass is shattered and the bell may not be answered. Thus there continues to be room in their novels for such absurdities of Victorian plotting as the agency of servants.

In Forster's *A Passage to India,* for example, servants are responsible for a good deal of what happens. Aziz stops at a mosque to rest, and thus meets Mrs. Moore, because his bicycle has a flat tire. The tire went flat when the labor of fetching the bicycle was divided: he "laid his hand on the bicycle's saddle, while a servant did the actual wheeling. Between them they took it over a tintack" (ch. 2). The expedition to the Marabar Caves takes place, though Aziz has forgotten his invitation and the ladies are unenthusiastic, when Adela's remark is "overheard by the servant," who "was not exactly a spy, but he kept his ears open. . . . As the story travelled, it accreted emotion, and Aziz learned with horror that the ladies were deeply offended with him, and expected an invitation daily" (ch. 13). The supposed rape attempt could not have occurred, as the English argue, if Adela's servant had not been bribed to stay away. Suspicion continues to suggest, to the end of the novel, that the real attacker was the guide. The myth of Esmiss Esmoor, friend of the Indian people, which is obscurely instrumental in changing the outcome of the trial, "only rests on servants' gossip" (ch. 27). And it only appears in court because, as Ronny says, "every servant I've got is a spy" (ch. 22). The friendship of Aziz and Fielding gets under way when Aziz's servant fails to bring Fielding's carriage, thus allowing a moment of unconventional contact. The friendship founders when Aziz believes the rumor that Adela has been Fielding's mistress—again, this is what "the servants say" (ch. 30). The friendship is reestablished for a brief moment at the end of the novel when Aziz goes to the Guest House to question the servants, and then again, in a climactic fusion of mysticism and farce, when their boats collide "helplessly with the servitor" (ch. 36) while observing the Hindu ritual on the lake. The list could probably be extended.

To my knowledge, this servant takeover of causality has not elicited any critical commentary, and the reason is clear enough. In a novel that is widely felt to be "about" the absurdity of any and all action, causal sequence would seem to be the least of Forster's concerns.

Nearly all of his commentators have remarked that, like Professor Godbole and Mrs. Moore, characters who speak on behalf of the Hindu-relativist vision but who refuse to become actors in the muddle of the plot, the novel pulls back in pronounced indifference from its presumed center, the trial. Whether this pulling back is regretted as a failure of nerve or used against political readings, the consensus is that it disengages the novel from social actuality in order to make room for the Hindu material—that it establishes, in Malcolm Bradbury's words, "an appeal beyond the social world, to the overarching sky."54

It has been my argument in this chapter that the sense of absurdity in social events that is marked by their relegation to the comic incompetence or mystic fatality of servants should not be interpreted as a disengagement from the social world but as a means of engaging it on another level. Despite its specifically Hindu coloration, the "overarching sky" of *A Passage to India* is a recognizable extension of this absurdity. As Bradbury goes on to say, the concentric arches that seem to dwarf human effort are also "a figure for the potential unity of man." The famous nothingness of this novel is not simply metaphysical. To use Forster's metaphor, it results from the threat of being obliged to "invite" everyone to the privileged feast of polite society. The feast loses it meaning because the uninvited press their faces to the window. And the answer that Forster phrases in Hindu terms is a universal invitation. In order to restore meaning to the world, one must be able, like Godbole, to send out wider and wider circles of sympathy, taking in the excluded. Here too, in other words, servants intervene in two stages. They signal a withdrawal of meaning from the novel's traditionally exclusive circle of "personal relations," but they also push toward the anticipatory constitution of a more inclusive gathering.

Both operations are visible when the narrative eye follows Adela's away from her case to focus on "a person who had no bearing officially upon the trial," the "almost naked and splendidly formed" punkah-man, with whom the chapter also ends.

Pulling the rope towards him, relaxing it rhythmically, sending swirls of air over others, receiving none himself, he seemed apart from human destinies, a male fate, a winnower of souls. . . . Something in his aloofness impressed the girl from middle-class England, and rebuked the narrowness of her sufferings. . . . . Victory on this side, defeat on that—complete for the moment was the antithesis. Then life returned to its complexities, person after person struggled out of the room to their various purposes, and before long no one remained on the scene of the fantasy but the beautiful naked god. Unaware that anything unusual had occurred, he continued to pull the cord of his punkah, to gaze at the empty dais and the overturned special chairs, and rhythmically to agitate the clouds of descending dust. (ch. 24)

Forster's emphatic symbolism authorizes the reader to treat this causal servant as central—central to a decentered vision. The externality of the figure brings the nihilism of sky and caves into the courtroom. He challenges the meaning of even the best-intentioned human activity. But at the same time, this "male fate" who "seemed to control the proceedings" himself acts upon them. The psychological source of his power over Adela is evident: her suppressed desire has impelled her to accuse a handsome Indian of sexual assault, and she confronts the truth and feels "rebuked" when her eyes stray to the "beautiful naked god." A few minutes later she withdraws the charge. I will say more about the connections between servants and sexuality in the next chapter. For now, it is sufficient to point out that this conventional figure of fate evokes an abstract, almost visionary desirability. Forster himself knew what it was to choose sexual objects among inferiors whom his class power made available. But here he retains only the utopian kernel—the specific desire that is stimulated by inequalities of class and race and seeks obscurely to abolish them in uniting with its object. By the detour of sexuality, Forster brings us back to our identification of fate with the movement toward enlarged and renovated community.

Supporting evidence is provided by a climactic scene of trans-class inclusion that goes a large step farther than earlier family reunions. In Forster's version, the Hindu ritual of Gokul Ashtami that closes the novel is above all a festival of sensual democracy. Godbole's "Come, come," at once invoking a god, caressing a lover, and inviting "the Despised and Rejected," ratifies the portentous suggestiveness of the punkah-man. The universal invitation allows meaning to flood back into the world. Every baby becomes Krishna, and masses of people lick a sweet paste from the floor, sharing it equally with each other and with the flies. The flies are a reminder that qualifications remain. This is not a social model designed for immediate implementation. Standing outside of time, the ritual of admission and embracement cannot "conclude" the linear history of the characters. The two versions of the ending—the broken private friendship, the general public festivity—exist side by side, and neither takes priority. The vagueness that allows an idealized gathering of supernumeraries to become a "song of the future" (ch. 30) prevents the reader from using it as a topography of the present. But each of these qualifications is indispensable to the mode, for the skepticism they engender defines utopia as a real goal to be striven for rather than an illusory possession.

5

Recognition:
The Servant in the Ending

Recognition, then, being between persons, it may happen that one person only is recognized by the other—when the latter is already known—or it may be necessary that the recognition should be on both sides.

ARISTOTLE, *Poetics*

Servants are continually jealous of the least thrift of a master or mistress; they are never easy but when they observe extravagance.

FIELDING, *The Grub-Street Opera*

THE SERVANTS' PLURAL

In a famous passage in *Dombey and Son,* Dickens calls for "a good spirit who would take the house-tops off, with a more potent and benignant hand than the lame demon in the tale," and would expand "contracted sympathies and estimates" so as "to make the world a better place!" (ch. 47). At this point in my argument, a fuller conviction that this passage fits the literary servant (as well as Dickens' own role as novelist) would seem to depend on some further elaboration of its second half, where it moves from a specific potency to a much cloudier benignancy, the vague bettering of the world that is offered as an ultimate moral purpose. Granted that it is servants who actually take the house-tops off—as, for example, a few chapters later, when it is Carker's servant who makes known his master's rendez-vous with Edith Dombey (ch. 52)—it remains to be seen how clearly, in Dickens or elsewhere, their actions are animated by a will to dilate "contracted sympathies" or to "make the world a better place" in any other specifiable sense. Contemplating the source of his information, Dombey wonders, "how does it happen that I can find voluntary intelligence in a hovel like this?" And the reader may also wonder what threads of volition tie such revelations and their consequences for the plot to the hovels and kitchens they emanate from.

On the surface, much servant intervention in the plot seems to be a muddle of aid and obstruction, manipulation and inadvertence. As is suggested by one of Pierrot's valet ancestors in the *commedia dell'arte*, servants are not entirely faithful even to love: "Pedrolino's role is not simply to fool those who deserve to be fooled and lend a hand to lovers in distress; if anything, he inexplicably seems to delay the lovers' reconciliation throughout the play."[1] The efficacious Jeeves will sometimes tie Bertie Wooster's love-lorn acquaintances into knots he can then unravel, while Samuel Lover's Handy Andy, a servant who works by the opposite principle of incompetence, bungles his master into a happy ending after first bungling him into perplexity. As we saw in the last chapter, even violence and the threat of violence are garbled messages, most often unintended or misdirected, that can only be deciphered by referring to a parallelism of child and servant that is visible not in the act itself but only in the conclusion. In general, the only annotation that seems capable of resolving an otherwise random catalog of instrumental actions into coherent units is one that ignores both immediate motive and immediate effect and instead concentrates on the ending. "It is only with the *dénouement* constantly in view," as Poe notes in "The Philosophy of Composition," "that we can give a plot its indispensable air of consequence, or causation."

A high valuation of the dénouement can of course work to devalue servant causality. The decorous organicism of Lukács, for example, acknowledges only such means as can be traced forward to an end that is their organic outgrowth. The "atmosphere of necessity," Lukács writes, is "neither dependent upon the flawlessness of individual causal connections, nor cancelled out by individual accidents in the plot."[2] The incursion of servants into stories that are not about them can thus be dismissed as inorganic accidents. And yet even by the same criterion, the fact that servants have traditionally been involved in the ending on a large scale becomes a weightier matter.

Placed in the terminal position, they retrospectively add to the sum of what from the preceding pages is to be taken as causal. Thus they help to introduce a certain excess or extravagance into whatever sense of "necessity" the text as a whole may possess.

The stretching of "necessity" by servants was discussed in the first chapter, where the image of the servant who holds in his hands his master's "fate" turned up in the *Odyssey*'s recognition scenes. In the other recognition to which Aristotle devotes the most attention, that of Sophocles' *Oedipus Tyrannus,* the issue again is fate and the agents of recognition again are servants. Oedipus arrives at a knowledge of his identity by his own efforts, of course; there is no depriving the play of this central irony. But one cannot overlook the ostentatious presence of the two servants who are his main sources of hard information.

As it turns out, each of them has also had as decisive an effect on the plot as any of comedy's tricky slaves. The Corinthian messenger who delivers the news that Oedipus' supposed father, King Polybus, is dead, in fact does so in a rather comic spirit, and commentators have remarked on other strangely comic elements in his presentation, like his punning, rhyming line-endings ("unparalleled elsewhere in Greek tragedy," according to Bernard Knox) and his atypical "characterization as a self-important dispenser of joyful tidings."[3] But what stands out most from the stern and rigorous logic of the tragedy is the doubling up of functions for both servants. The Corinthian messenger who announces that Polybus is dead turns out to be the same man who delivered Oedipus to Polybus as a baby and who thus knows all along that Polybus was not in fact his father. Similarly, the Theban shepherd who, ordered by Laius and Jocasta to abandon their child on a hillside, saved his life by handing him over to the Corinthian, then also a shepherd, is the same "servant, the only one to escape," who witnessed Laius' murder. It is when he confronts these two servants with each other that Oedipus arrives at his recognition.[4]

Though the Theban slave knows both the secret of Oedipus' parentage and his guilt in the murder, the recognition has been delayed all these years by two of his actions, each of which acquires some significance in the course of the play. First, the servant who took the child to the "lonely mountainside" has forsaken the household where he was raised in order to return to the country. As Jocasta explains, "when he came thence and saw that you held the royal power, and that Laius was dead, he earnestly begged me, with his hand on mine, / to send him into the country, to the sheep-pastures, so that he might be as far as possible from the sight of this city" (758–762). And second, it is this servant who has spread the story that Laius was killed by a number of bandits, not by one man—a story the community accepts. Once Oedipus has begun to suspect the truth, he tells Jocasta that he awaits the shepherd's arrival as his last hope: "You were saying that he told you that bandits killed Laius. So, if he still says the same number, I was not the killer; for one cannot be equal to many" (842–845).

This transformation of one into many, which seems to establish Oedipus' innocence, receives too much emphasis in the play to have escaped critical attention. For Voltaire, it was an "incontestable unlikelihood," for Wilamowitz-Moellendorff a breach of authorial good faith. "The whole action of *Oedipus the King* depends . . . on a plural deliberately used by the poet, ambiguously and misleadingly, instead of a singular."[5] Moreover, the multitude-of-robbers story is never explicitly denied or disproved in the play, as several critics have pointed out, including Jonathan Culler: "The only witness has publicly told a story that is incompatible with Oedipus' guilt. This possibility of innocence is never eliminated, for when the witness arrives Oedipus is interested in his relation to Laius and asks only about his birth, not about the murder. The witness is never asked whether the murderers were one or many."[6]

Given the surprisingly relevant themes we have already seen clustering around what appeared to be a mechanical, expedient recourse to servant causality, it seems appropriate to examine this strategic plural in the same light and perhaps try to relate the unlikelihood, ambiguity, and lingering innocence that have been read into it to the servant who brings it into circulation. On the level of psychological realism, the tale of many bandits could of course be accounted for, in Brian Vickers' words, as "a lie told, like Falstaff's, to save face."[7] But there is too much concern for number and equality in the play to stop there. Bernard Knox has collected ample evidence of this concern. "The numerical nature of the problem is emphasized at once with Creon's entry. 'One man of Laius' party escaped,' says Creon, 'he had only one thing to say.' 'What is it?' asks Oedipus. 'One thing might find a way to learn many.' . . . 'Even though you are tyrannos,' says [Tiresias] at the height of his anger, 'you and I must be made equal in one thing at least, the chance for an equal reply.' . . . Tiresias is blind, and Oedipus will be made equal to him in this before the play is over." This motiff is particularly pronounced in the conversation with the Corinthian messenger. He tells Oedipus, " 'Polybus is no more your father than I, but equally so.' Oedipus' question is indignant: 'How can my father be equal to a nobody, to zero?' . . . The answer— 'Polybus is not your father; neither am I.' "[8]

Equality with a servant—this is the beacon that illuminates the messenger's comic self-importance, the hint of apocalyptic democracy that emerges from all the repetitions of the "multitude" and the "many" (*hoi polloi*, as we still say), and the note of social inversion sounded by the story of how Oedipus' life was saved.[9]

MESSENGER: You were a gift, you must know, that he once received from my hands. . . .
OEDIPUS: When you gave me to him, had you bought me, or found me?
MESSENGER: Found you in the winding glens of Cithaeron.
OEDIPUS: For what purpose were you traveling in those regions?
MESSENGER: I was there in charge of mountain flocks.
OEDIPUS: Oh, you were a shepherd and wandered about finding work?
MESSENGER: And, my son, your preserver at that time. (1,022–1,030)

After hearing this story, Oedipus comforts Jocasta: "*you* will not be proved low-born, even if it be shown that my mother was a slave of the third generation—that I am three times a slave" (1,062–1,064). At the end of the play, as at the beginning of his life, Oedipus is identified with the slaves who preserve and then expose him. The paradox is realized: the one is equal to the many.

This is certainly not to make Sophocles into a democrat who could interpret this equation as an argument for social equality. On the contrary, we know that he gave "active support" to "the anti-democratic constitution which placed restrictions on the franchise in the last years of the Peloponnesian War" and that more generally he criticized Athenian events in the name of the older, aristocratic code of his class.[10] And yet here, as we have seen in so many other texts, it is precisely a residual, even anachronistic critique of contemporary reality that invites and valorizes the intercession of servants.

Anachronism is already present in the mythic materials of Oedipus' life. In *The Myth of the Birth of the Hero* Otto Rank has assembled many other instances of expulsion from the high-born family, preservation by a low-born surrogate family—the servant who saves the child from paternal wrath is a widespread folk motif; Stith Thompson calls it "the compassionate executioner"—and final recognition that combines revenge with acknowledgment.[11] So widespread and ancient a pattern would seem to demand the sort of psychoanalytic interpretation that Rank offers: that is, an interpretation on the level of the individual psyche alone, which is assumed to be historically universal and constant. Any yet the essay itself provides a clue to how this reading can be harmonized with one that sets in motion historical collectivities as well as levels of the psyche. Even more fundamental than the revolt of the ego against the father, in its view, is the "overvaluation of the earliest years of childhood" in which the fantasy indulges. "The entire endeavor to replace the real father by a more distinguished one is merely the expression of the child's longing for the vanished happy time, when his father still appeared to be the strongest and greatest man, and his mother seemed the dearest and most beautiful woman."[12] Psychic regression for the individual can be translated into a collective social regression in which the "vanished happy time" would signify not childhood alone but an earlier and simpler social state, whether mythic or not. This is the pastoral idyll, midway between Thebes and Corinth, that is insisted upon in the play's symbolic geography, the time long ago that the Corinthian shepherd evokes when he confronts his old fellow shepherd from Thebes: "when, in the neighborhood of Cithaeron, I was near to this man for three whole six-month seasons, /from spring to Arcturus, he with two flocks and I with one; then for the winter I would drive my sheep to the fold, and he would take his to Laius' farmstead" (1,132–1,140). As Philip Vellacott comments, this speech sets the tragedy "for a brief moment against the quiet eternal background symbolized by the world of flocks on a vast mountainside under the stars which mark the circle of the seasons; a world of natural fertility . . . the same now he is old as it was when he was young."[13] More to the point, Cithaeron is the place where Oedipus was passed from one shepherd to the other—a place of free gifts among equals, where the rivalry of cities like Corinth and Thebes doesn't stop shepherds from fraternizing, where there need be no conflict because the land is common and undivided. The place receives marked attention: "it is you Oedipus honors as . . . his nurse and as his mother" (1,089–1,091). And at the end of the play, when Oedipus' life has once again fallen into the gift of servants, it is to Cithaeron that he wants to return: "Let me live in the mountains, where this Cithaeron is named as mine" (1,450–1,451).

This subdued but poignant celebration of the pastoral life of long ago only takes its full value in the context of Sophocles' critique of the Athenian present. Now, as the chorus laments, "nowhere is Apollo conspicuous by honors [paid to him]; but worship of the gods is vanishing" (908–910). As Bernard Knox argues, Oedipus has far less in common with the tyrants than he does with later, imperial Athens, "the *polis tyrannos,* in all its political dynamism, its intelligence, its will to power." "Just as Oedipus, who pursues a murderer according to the processes of law, is himself a murderer, but goes unpunished, so Athens, the original home and the most advanced center of the law, rules with a power based on injustice and is beyond the reach of human law."[14] It was the horrors of empire and the wars it provoked that led in this period to a revaluation of the wilderness, which had been seen as savage and bestial. "The Peloponnesian War, with its shocking atrocities like the Corcyrean revolution and the Athenian treatment of the Mytileneans and the Meleans, did its work as a 'violent teacher.' . . . It laid bare the paradox that civilization could hold within itself all the savagery of the beast world. Hence, toward the end of the century *nomos* and *physis,* law and nature, undergo a strange reversal: *nomos,* the norm of civilization, is seen as repressive and destructive, and nature, *physis,* as liberating."[15] Interestingly, the subversive popular counter-ideologies of the time made much the same uses of the natural wilderness as the aristocrats did. Cithaeron is precisely where Euripides locates the Maenads of the Dionysiac cult. Oedipus was suckled, that is, where the Maenads suckled wild beasts at their breasts, breaking down "the boundaries between animals and men"—in Marcel Détienne's words—in order to achieve "a subversion of the order of the *polis* . . . from within."[16] It is in this way, as Charles Segal concludes, that "Oedipus' search comes to center upon figures who, like himself, occupy an ambiguous position between city and wild. At the climax of the search everything depends on 'the one from the fields' (*agroi,* 1,049, 1,051). . . . The shepherd, 'nurtured in the house,' as Oedipus was not . . . will reveal the horrible truth of Oedipus' place between house and wild. When this exiled servant comes back, literally, from the wild to the house for the interrogation, Oedipus makes the journey, metaphorically, in reverse, reenacting that ambiguous passage of his infancy from palace to Cithaeron. The servant who initially saved him from the destructive intent of that journey fulfills that intent when he himself returns from mountain to city."[17]

The point is not so much that the servants, like Oedipus, occupy an intermediate position between house and wild, but rather that they bring the wild into the house, or household (*oikos*). When their recognition corrects Oedipus' *hamartia,* or "mistake in the identity of blood kin," they are defending the family against incest and parricide.[18] But they are also intervening on behalf of the family in a more specific sense: at the historical conjuncture, exemplified by the *Antigone,* which confronts Creon and the demands of the modern state with Antigone's vestigial loyalty to kinship and the aristocratic ethos centered on it. And as with the familial ideology of paternalism, this appeal to the "natural" simplicity of former times permits the articulation of another appeal that overlaps but is not identical with it. The wilderness, where land is undivided and unalienated, where fraternity remains possible, and where war is unknown, reconstitutes the image of the family—the family that has been exploded by the exposure of a child, just as ancestral continuity has been interrupted by the alienations of the commercial, imperial polis. And it is this "extended" or "wild" family that reconciles the apparent contradiction by which servants both shield Oedipus and finally destroy him. On the one hand, the wilderness stands for the more inclusive, more accepting collectivity that takes in or forms around the innocent child who has been expelled from his family and has been reduced to the level of a slave. On the other hand, and for this very reason, now that Oedipus has come to represent the modern polis and now that his rule has led to the "plague" of the Peloponnesian War, the wilderness also stands (in) for the victims of the plague, the suffering "children" whom Oedipus addresses in the play's first words.[19] The collective consequence of Oedipus' recognition—that is, of the servants' intervention in the plot—must logically be (though the play does not say so) the removal of its immediate, collective cause: the end of the plague and the salvation of the city. And even if the city's troubles are by no means over, this vector of volition remains, giving direction to servant agency and aligning it with the interests of a collective subject. What has to be recognized in the servants as they provoke Oedipus' recognition of himself is the claim of a community that is both archaic (the tribal "childhood" of the polis) and anticipatory, making room in the imagination for a larger, more inclusive plural than is to be found in past or present.

As commentators have pointed out, the Theban servant's insistence on his fiction of "many" robbers turns out to be fateful. And the fiction of plurality that confronts Oedipus' singular also duplicates a confrontation between two notions of fate, one emergent and one residual. At the height of his power, Oedipus calls himself a "child of Chance" (1,080). The new goddess *Tyche* was not an "instrument of divine purpose" but a figure who rendered "the existence of the old gods meaningless."[20] Chance opened up the universe to individual merit and self-exertion; like Oedipus, it rises along with the juridical and commercial success of the polis.[21] At the end of the play, however, when Oedipus has fallen back to equality with "the many" and is about to set off for Cithaeron, he invokes not *Tyche* but *Moira,* the older Fate which worked "through pestilence or famine" to "punish those who transgressed the ancestral dispensations" and which had recently been remobilized and reinterpreted by "the aspirations of the dispossessed peasantry."[22] To connect *Moira,* equality with servants, and the unspoiled countryside is to compose a strangely faithful image of *isomoiria,* the agrarian egalitarianism that was a rallying cry for small farmers throughout Greek history. It is not sure that the connection would have been visible to Sophocles' audience. But as in Homer, the pun at least makes possible a two-sided recognition, a recognition in which the identity and right to ancestral property that are acknowledged are not only those of the hero.

GIFTS AND GRATUITIES

Now I am mistress of two servants—and ready to hang myself! . . .
Both these women are good servants, *as servants go.* But the *twoness* I
hate . . . with *one* servant, especially with one *Charlotte,* we were *one*
family in the house . . . Now, it is as if I had taken in lodgers for
downstairs . . . I ring my bell, this one answers, but it is the other's
business to do what I want. Then the solemn consultations about
"Your dinner" and "our dinner" . . . the ever-recurring "we" which in
little Charlotte's mouth meant Master and Mistress and self; but in
the mouth of the new tall Charlotte means, most decidedly, "I and
Sarah."

JANE WELSH CARLYLE

In this passage, as in *Oedipus Tyrannus,* the small difference between
one and more than one has unaccountably large consequences. It adds
up to the unstated sum of equality (two against two) between masters
and servants. Confusing the responsibility of each individual for any
given action, it liberates all and redistributes power in the household.
With this "twoness," the "one family" is obliged to stretch, allowing a
fluid redefinition of the social "we." As "ever-recurring" as complaints about the help, these are comic elements which the servant's
plural contributes to the recognition scene: comic friction against the
tragedy of Oedipus, comic expansion of the many "happy endings"
patterned on the recognition scenes of the *Odyssey.*

Where happy endings mean final weddings, expansion means
breaking open this rite of closure by combining the causality that
makes matches with a symbolism that mars—that is, distends—
them. The process is circular. Servant agency helps produce an ending
whose sense will return full circle to suggest a different reading of
servant agency. In *Pride and Prejudice,* for example, three separate
errors of three separate servants are enlisted (bk. 2, ch. 9; bk. 2, ch.
19; bk. 3, ch. 1) in order to bring Darcy and Elizabeth involuntarily
together. In *Middlemarch,* as it happens, servants again share responsibility for three unintended confrontations between Dorothea and
Will Ladislaw (chs. 37, 42, 77). With or without this help, both
couples are headed for conjunction. The mechanics of social encounter do not absolutely require these accidental breaches in the wall of
politeness. Why then are they there? Like the providential rain-

shower that sends lovers scurrying for the same shelter, the external agency of servants creates a sort of atmospheric doubling of pent-up desire: the breaches that let love in are made by representatives of the class that most wants the barriers of the social and moral order down. Hence episodes like these tend to collect congenial themes, such as the unaccustomed "openness" in two of the three *Middlemarch* scenes. Dorothea tells the housekeeper, "I will go into the library and write you some memoranda from my uncle's letter, if you will open the shutters for me," and she is answered, "The shutters are open, madam. . . . Mr. Ladislaw is there, looking for something" (ch. 62). And in the more significant scene when, because a servant has seized a moment of liberty, Dorothea is admitted without the bell ringing and thus glimpses Will and Rosamond in a compromising pose:

The street door was open, and the servant was taking the opportunity of looking out at the carriage which was pausing within sight when it became apparent to her that the lady who "belonged to it" was coming towards her.
    "Is Mrs. Lydgate at home?" said Dorothea.
    "I'm not sure, my lady; I'll see, if you please to walk in," said Martha. . . . They crossed the broader part of the entrance-hall, and turned up the passage which led to the garden. The drawing-room door was un-latched, and Martha, pushing it without looking into the room, waited for Mrs. Casaubon to enter and then turned away, the door having swung open . . . without noise. (ch. 77)

With such moments in mind, one can register some gratuitous expansiveness or centrifugal force even in an ending that forces the new couple into isolation from their closest neighbors. Dorothea's decision to renounce her mourning (in part a decision to overcome her private pain at having found Will and Rosamond together) is made as she looks out the window at dawn: "She felt the largeness of the world and the manifold wakings of men to labor and endurance. She was a part of that involuntary, palpitating life, and could neither look out on it from her luxurious shelter as a mere spectator, nor hide her eyes in selfish complaining" (ch. 80). After these thoughts, the maid enters—a domestic representative of that larger, laborious world. This contiguity is partly ironic; the heroic gesture that will bring Dorothea together with Ladislaw does not give her anything more to do with her life than enjoy the surrogate labor of maids. But

Dorothea's wishful identification with labor has its own weight in the final marriage. Despite the "imperfect social state" that distorts her "unhistoric acts," the termination signals a possibility beyond the novel's own frontiers. Similarly, after misinformation from two servants brings Elizabeth to Pemberley on the day of Darcy's arrival, forcing a meeting she had tried to avoid, she learns from the housekeeper that he is "affable to the poor" (bk. 3, ch. 1). The effect is to surround the predictable result of mutual attraction and compatible fortune with hints of more expansive conjunctions.

This is to say that the literary servant's assistance to love rests on a metaphoric expansion of private passion into an end in which she or he might have an investment. This might explain why the servants of *Pride and Prejudice* aid and abet false love as well as true. They are particularly intimate, as we saw in chapter three, with the promiscuous characters of Lydia and Wickham, and they prominently receive and frame the news of their marriage. This bond extends to causality. It is through another servant, a sort of background villain of the novel, that Wickham has gained access to and seduced Darcy's sister (bk. 2, ch. 12). The same servant shelters Wickham and Lydia when they elope, and it is also through her that Darcy locates them again (bk. 3, ch. 10), thus bringing his own marriage one step closer and bringing them into the circle of families with which the novel ends. All this machinery may not produce a proportionate amount of meaning, but it does produce some. Its operation is promiscuously additive: assisting the elopement, it adds Wickham to Lydia, and assisting their capture, it adds the new and subversive couple to their old circle. The one constant is the stretching of that social circle to admit uninvited and dubious outsiders who resemble the servants themselves.

Much the same process can be traced through the final marriage of *Tom Jones*. Despite Tom's many virtues, attempts to find moral or theological justification for the wife and inheritance allotted to him at the end of the novel have never been entirely convincing. Majority opinion today would probably assent to Robert Torrance's view:

The hero's triumph, unlike his troubles, is sheer romance. The kind-hearted reader will surely begrudge Tom neither his victory nor the rewards that lavishly crown it, but these are bestowed upon him, as on Cinderella, or Job, by an agency above or beyond him. In the last analysis it is only the benevolent author's vaunted capacity to manipulate events . . . that preserves his favorite from the pitfalls that surround and very nearly undo him.[23]

Yet the author-principle is not the only recourse in the face of this extravagance. If one looks with a certain naivete at the carefully operated causal machinery that leads to the ending, this "agency above or beyond" the hero would appear to work itself out for the most part through the novel's servants. A short list of interventions would include, for instance, the inn scene at Upton, where Tom is discovered thanks to the combined efforts of Partridge, Honour, and the chambermaid. Partridge in fact bears double responsibility for this decisive turn. As R. S. Crane notes, "what has really disturbed [Sophia] has not been so much his misconduct with Jenny, which she can forgive, as Partridge's free use of her name in public."[24] However, it is again thanks to his good offices that Tom will discover Sophia's whereabouts. In Book 12 Partridge prevails upon his master to stop for a puppet show, and Tom gets news of Sophia from the Merry Andrew. At the next inn Partridge urges his reluctant master to stop for food, and again they pick up Sophia's trail. In London, servants initially keep the lovers apart: Mrs. Fitzpatrick and Lady Bellaston both recognize Tom from the accounts of their maids, and set the appropriate obstacles. It is through the opportune encounter of Partridge with Black George (now a servant of the Westerns) that Tom finds her again, through Black George that he corresponds with her, through another servant that the correspondence is exposed. And so on.

In what way are these incidents more than simple tools of the benevolent author, a tightening of causality "to the point where it verges on the farcical," as Martin Price puts it, which makes us "securely aware of the novelist in control"?[25] Another small instance is to the point. In Book 14 Tom is about to be expelled from Mrs. Miller's house for his sexual misdemeanors; he is not only saved from eviction, but wins his landlady as a valuable ally (she will successfully plead his case both to Sophia and to Allworthy) because of the indiscretion of Partridge, who has let slip, among other things, the story of Tom's generosity to the highwayman. Tom's conventional

complaint registers the magnitude of the servant's conventional mo-
lestation: "How often . . . am I to suffer for your folly, or rather for
my own in keeping you? Is that tongue of yours resolved upon my
destruction?" In his defense, Partridge switches the blame to an
occult source:

"To be certain, sir, it is a wonderful thing, and I have been thinking with
myself even since, how it was she came to know it; not but I saw an old
woman here t'other day a begging at the door, who looked as like her we
saw in Warwickshire, that caused all that mischief to us. To be sure it is
never good to pass by an old woman without giving her something . . ."
(bk. 14, ch. 3)

This is not entirely incoherent. Partridge has released information
about his master's generosity to the dangerous poor (the highwayman), and now he hides his responsibility behind a superstition that
declares one should always give charity to the poor, who may be
dangerous: "they have a great power to do mischief." The novel thus
places servant intervention under the thematically central sign of
charity.

As Raymond Williams points out, the history of the word charity is
the history of the privatization of love, for which it is one biblical
translation. "Charity was then Christian love, between man and God,
and between men and their neighbors. The sense of benevolence to
neighbors, and specifically of gifts to the needy, is equally early, but
was at first directly related to the sense of Christian love, as in the
Pauline use: 'though I bestow all my goods to feed the poor . . . and
have not charity, it profiteth me nothing' (1 Corinthians 13) where the
act without the feeling is seen as null."[26] Etymological rehabilitation
of charity may not make the conclusion of *Tom Jones* ethically proportionate, but it does enrich the significance of servant involvement in
the love match by offering a vision of love that is worthy of servant
support.

There is evidence that the will behind servant interference in the
plot is precisely, in Williams' phrase, "benevolence to neighbors." The
earlier "mischief" Partridge mentions involved an old woman in
Coventry to whom Tom refused alms. Partridge rebukes him: "it is
always good to be charitable to those sort of people," he says, "for
fear what may happen" (bk. 12, ch. 11). According to Keith Thomas,

this is in fact how accusations of witchcraft came about. As "the old tradition of mutual charity and help was being eroded by such new economic developments as land hunger, the rise in prices, the development of agricultural speculation and the growth of towns and commercial values," residual belief in the obligation to the neighborly remained, even in those who began to turn neighbors from the door empty-handed. A poorer member of the community, typically an old woman, would be "denied the charity and help which was traditionally required. When shutting the door in her face, however, they were only too well aware of having departed from the accepted ethical code. They knew they had put their selfish interests before their social duty. . . . it was their own guilty conscience which indicated to them where they should look for the cause of their misfortune."27 When disaster of any kind struck, the cause was sought where charity had been refused. Witches were neighbors whose claims were recognized but not answered, and on whom guilt projected the power of retribution. They represent the principle of economic mutuality, invested with an oblique omnipotence.

The emergent novel was eager to demonstrate its rational superiority to popular superstitions like those of Partridge. And yet our modern awareness that such superstitions could conceal an alternative social theory—that ghost beliefs, for example, were extensively invoked in order to protect the poor against injustices like usury, enclosure, and false accusations of theft—is clearly mixed into Fielding's amusement.28 Consider, for example, the ghost story with which Partridge comically interrupts the Man of the Hill. "If any person was to be hanged upon my evidence," Partridge says, "I should never be able to lie alone afterwards, for fear of seeing his ghost" (bk. 8, ch. 11). Along with a fair quotient of absurdities, the story that follows offers a hard core of social logic. A man caught riding a stolen horse is hanged on the evidence of Partridge's neighbor, who is then attacked by a "spirit" that the listeners will identify as a white calf met in a dark lane. But the import of the story does not stop with the question of whether the ghost was real:

"One thing I own I thought a little hard, that the prisoner's counsel was not suffered to speak for him, though he desired to be heard one very short word; but my lord would not hearken to him, though he suffered a counselor to talk against him for above half an hour. I thought it hard, I own, that there should be so many of them; my lord, and the court, and the jury, and the counsellors, and the witnesses all upon one poor man, and he too in chains. Well, the fellow was hanged. . . ."

In Partridge's hesitant, naive account of the trial, normal criminal procedure is shown as so barbaric that the unreason of "never dipping our hands in blood" for fear of ghosts appears more reasonable than cooperating with it. Superstition, which is nearly a *sine qua non* of any extended servant characterization, is the necessary camouflage for a popular distrust of the legal order; ghosts are called in to enforce an oppositional code of justice.

There is no difficulty in documenting the social bias of magic. When Elizabeth Barrett Browning's maid, Wilson, followed her mistress into experiments in spiritualism and automatic writing, one of the "messages" she transmitted from the spirit world was "Send Wilson to bed—she is ill."[29] From a folklorist's perspective, it should come as no surprise that ghosts and servants are identified in *The Turn of the Screw* or that Pip's page becomes an "Avenging Phantom." As Jonathan Arac demonstrates in his masterly analysis of nineteenth-century Gothic discourse, ghosts "threaten the household that has left important obligations unfulfilled." "As dirt is 'matter out of place,' so the ghosts of *Bleak House* arise from displacements in social relations. . . . Injustice and secrecy make people incomprehensible even to themselves, while they appear to others as spirits of doom."[30] Esther, the child-housekeeper, haunts her mother's house, and Hortense, out of place, is discovered "hovering" around the courts of justice (ch. 40). There is no need to trace the lineage of the literary servant back to the Vice and the devil in order to see the transfer of subversive superstition from the witches and ghosts of Partridge's imagination to Partridge himself, and to the mischievous attendants who succeed him. His own mischief enacts the occult causality that he projects into the supernatural, and that we should not be too quick to attribute solely to the benevolence of the author. Benevolence also belongs to the occult oppositional code, which resists the rationality of law and property in the name of neighborliness. Fairies—a term derived from "fate"—were also known, as Walter Scott once noted, as "Good Neighbors."[31]

By means of the servants, this code of neighborliness is enforced, if only occultly. The community that gathers around Tom in the ending has made possible his release and reinstatement, it is not merely an adornment or by-product of the comic conclusion, but one of its producers. What the servants have prophesied—for example when Partridge insisted, against all evidence, that Tom was Squire Alworthy's relation and belonged at his side—is in effect their own restitution: "Partridge's memory was not in the least deficient. He recollected now many omens and presages of this happy event . . . 'I always told your honor something boded in my mind, that you would one time or other have it in your power to make my fortune" (bk. 18, ch. 11). By the detour of his master's largesse, it is Partridge's own fortune that is the goal, as it is his own power that is the vehicle. It is worth noting that, despite the prophetic mode, the suggestion that the largesse from which servants benefit can be read as their claim to their own is firmly grounded in eighteenth-century social reality. For example, vails, the customary tips to the servants of one's host, were both "a survival of the ancient form of largesse" and a demand that, over strong opposition beginning roughly with the rise of the novel, servants successfully banded together to defend. These gratuities belied the apparent gratuitousness of luck; they embodied an alternative social code. "Abundant funds over which the heads of families had no power," they were distributed according to an archaic popular custom: "as a rule all members of the household shared in the visitor's bounty. Those whose duties kept them in the background usually received a percentage of the takings of those who had access to the guests. In some households the servants themselves saw to it that each secured his proper share; in others, all vails were pooled, and the employer undertook to effect an equitable distribution."

What seemed to be luck was in fact an older, popular notion of "fate," reinvested with contemporary energy. The same holds for card-money, "another tax on visiting." As "card-playing was the favorite diversion of the age," card-money tended to put more in the servants' pockets than the cards could possibly be worth to the visitors who played them. As one visitor remarked of his host, "His butler is the only one who gains." If, though apparently uninvolved in the play, the servants are the only direction in which property is ultimately redistributed, it is because they represent "the house," the social whole.[32] Hence the sense of archaic *necessity* that accompanies largesse. "Largesses to the heralds and minstrels . . . were necessary accompaniments to the investiture of a person of rank," Walter Scott wrote of the age of chivalry (*OED*). And so too in the investitures of literary endings. Lessing's Minna *cannot* rejoice without gifts to her maid. "But rejoice with me! Oh, it's so sad to have to rejoice alone! Come, take it!"

"All were happy, but those the most who had been most unhappy before" (bk. 18, ch. 13)—this sentence takes in more than the leading couple of *Tom Jones*. The last sentence of the novel, similarly, extends the scope of the marriage outward in more than a conventional gesture. "And such is their beneficence to those below them, that there is not a neighbor, a tenant, or a servant, who doth not most gratefully bless the day when Mr. Jones was married to his Sophia." Hierarchy is evidently preserved, but there are implied blessings that shoot beyond it. As Alworthy says, Tom's desire to pardon Black George, in view of the "bitter distress" he and his family have suffered, does indeed "border . . . on injustice, and is very pernicious to society" (bk. 18, ch. 11). Fielding defines the virtue for which Tom will be rewarded as "a certain relative quality, which is always busying itself without doors, and seems as much interested in pursuing the good of others as its own" (bk. 15, ch. 1). Unlike worldly wisdom, this drive to better the conditions of all does not often lead, he says, to the end of worldly happiness. What Tom has come to signify to those around him is thus "infinitely too good to live in this world" (bk. 18, ch. 11). The ending takes place in this world, but the gathered community that shares and provokes it helps point it toward another.

LOOSE ENDS

Tom Jones ends with an image of charity so cosmic that it must be read with the wishful and distanced eye with which one reads utopian fiction. The final gatherings of other and especially later novels are rarely so extravagant. And yet once one has detected the utopian excess behind Fielding's reversal of the privatization of love, it is hard not to read it into quieter endings as well. Despite some loss of intensity, the principle is the same in Thackeray's *The Virginians:* "When a man is in love with one woman in a family, it is astonishing how fond he becomes of every person connected with it. He ingratiates himself with the maids; he is bland with the butler; he interests himself with the footman" (ch. 20). If he does not quite use "family" in the sense that had been anachronistic since Fielding's time (servants are "connected" with it, not members of it), Thackeray does, like Fielding, make servants both the sources and the recipients of extravagance. In the same chapter, he indicates that his protagonist's "usual sumptuous benefactions to . . . servants" (ch. 42) are effects of the same cause that leads him into prison, namely, his valet's "foolish imagination" and verbal promiscuity: "he scattered about his gold pieces to right and left, as if he had been as rich as Gumbo announced him to be." The suggestion is that through his master's liberality, Gumbo manages to reward his fellow servants. This logic is also illustrated in Jeeves; think of all those stories which end with Bertie sacrificing his loud clothing to "the under-gardener" or "the deserving poor."[33]

The novel, like Plautine comedy, presents "love" in large part as that passion which, by putting characters temporarily in the power of underlings, allows brief but memorable foretastes of social equality. Something less than festivity but more than neighborliness, the largesse that clinks audibly at final weddings is also detachable from them. In the endings of Scott, for example, marriage often fades into insignificance beside the servants who precipitate, surround, and join in the hero's restitution to identity and property. Ruskin noted the use of a servant to provide closure in *Rob Roy.* Andrew Fairservice, he remarks, "gradually falls into an unconscious fatality of varied blunder and provocation; and at last causes the entire catastrophe of the story by bringing in the candles when he has been ordered to stay downstairs."[34] Francis Hart finds a similar device in *Old Mortality:* "to close the narrative, an agent of fate—the disastrous messenger, Guse Gibbie—is needed. Through his intervention, the narrative closes with the catastrophe and the sad blessing of Lord Evandale's death."[35] Here, as in so many other versions of the Homeric recognition scene, fate can be taken not as an arbitrary, inscrutable agency that sets an opaque limit to the asking of causal questions, but rather as the sign of a certain voluntary archaism, the site of an unspoken contradiction between the dominant and an oppositional theory of causality. In the last episode of *Old Mortality,* Scott twice reminds the reader of Goose-Gibbie's role in the novel's first episode: "it was decreed that Goose-Gibbie's intermediation, whether as an emissary, or as a man-at-arms, should be unfortunate to the family of Tillietudlum" (ch. 44). The two scenes make a significant frame. In the first, after the ranks of his mistress' feudal retainers have been sapped by economic distress and revolutionary puritanism, Goose-Gibbie is reluctantly enlisted as man-at-arms for the local popular festival, the "wappen-shaw." Unused to such exercises, he loses control of his horse and, before the eyes of the assembled village, charges the coach of the assembled aristocracy, lance extended. In the mode of comedy, he thus enacts the threat to feudalism that the novel will expand and that he himself will help realize. And the comic gesture is also a portent, surpassing what the novel can realize by other means. In doubling the novel's social and emotional substance, the comic and melodramatic machinery also exceeds the crude central curve; it propels the conclusion beyond the point of closure where the desires of the characters are brought to fruition or laid to rest.

Within three pages of the undelivered message, another servant, who represents (as unwillingly as Goose-Gibbie) the perpetually frustrated aspirations of the Covenanters, shoots down the novel's acquisitive villain, representative of the emerging economic order. He has the effect on new money that Goose-Gibbie has on old land. Aware of the ambiguity of his killing "a grand gentleman," in whatever cause, he does not boast of "the lucky shot that repossessed his lady and himself in their original habitations" (Conclusion). If the artifice of the ending demands a restoration, it also permits a remembrance of defeated revolutionary ideals and an anticipatory overstepping of the social facts. Extended backward and forward, textually and temporally, the conclusion is both loosened and clarified. It does not shut with a click on the blind exteriority of fate, but dangles—a "loose end"—the social exteriority of those who embody fate.

As a symbol of the rich incompleteness that Goose-Gibbie helps introduce into the ending whose catastrophe he causes, we might take the obscurity of his own end. The narrator closes his account of the characters by saying, with a self-conscious glance at the audience, "I am not quite positive as to the fate of Goose-Gibbie." If such servants insinuate that endings are neither total nor final, it is perhaps because their own place in them cannot be resolved to full satisfaction. Scott paid attention to such matters. According to Pat Rogers, he was the first reader to notice that in *Robinson Crusoe* "we lose sight at once and forever of the interesting Xury."[36] Ruskin on the other hand tripped over this point in *Rob Roy*. "Fairservice is driven out at the kitchen door," he writes, "never to be heard of more."[37] On the contrary, Scott carefully notes that "his exclusion . . . led to some singular consequences" (ch. 39). It leads, in fact, to the rescue of the Vernons and the defeat of the villain by Rob Roy, whom Andrew alerts. In other words, it leads to the happy ending that follows hard on the fateful catastrophe. To bring Andrew back for one last, unnecessary intervention—as well as to pronounce the novel's last, irresolute words—is to focus on unresolved contradictions that mere marriage might otherwise paper over. Indeed, as in *Old Mortality*, the terminal marriage gets scarcely more than a subordinate clause, and Andrew might be considered a substitute for it. In *Old Mortality* the heroine remains "unconscious even of the presence" of the returning hero, while the servants, foregrounded in a series of Homeric recognition scenes, ask for a larger share in the interpretation of the ending.[38]

There is an extraordinary sentence in *Old Mortality* that discourages the reader of such scenes of acclamation from taking the fidelity of the retainers on faith. A public festivity forms around the captured Covenanters:

Behind these prisoners, thus held up to public infamy and derision, came a body of horse, brandishing their broadswords, and filling the wide street with acclamations, which were answered by the tumultuous outcries of the rabble, who, in every considerable town, are too happy in being permitted to huzza for any thing which brings them together. (ch. 35)

The general impression is that the crowd is deriding the prisoners and applauding the soldiers. But if one looks more closely, Scott has left this point equivocal. The prisoners are "held up" to infamy, but we are not told they receive it. The soldiers are "answered" by the crowd, but not necessarily in kind. As Foucault has shown in his analysis of the spectacle of public execution, huzzas cannot be interpreted as indicating support for what the spectators see. In its shouting the crowd affirms first and foremost the fact of its own precarious solidarity ("for any thing which calls them together"), and for its own reasons. In the same way, servant festivity cannot be conflated with the occasion the masters provide for it.

As I have already suggested, in the paternalist ending the relation between servants and masters is simultaneously one of part to whole and one of whole to part. If the servants participate only marginally in the masters' restitution, their moist eyes and fervent congratulations rewarded with handshakes and food, they also project a larger, collective whole of which the masters' private restitution is only a minor fragment. When they are summoned to identify, applaud, vouch for, or be confused with a returning heir, the implication is that the place in society the latter will now inherit and the goods he will now distribute belong by right to a wider field of dispossessed.

This logic reveals itself only in fragments. Even its Homeric paradigm, with its pun on *moira,* has a prophetic obscurity. But context can illuminate it, as the total structure of Scott's *Guy Mannering* illuminates its recognition scene. "Our friend Jock Jabos, the postilion, forced his way into the middle of the circle; but no sooner cast his eyes upon Bertram, than he started back in amazement, with a solemn exclamation, 'As sure as there's breath in man, it's auld Ellangowan arisen from the dead!'" (ch. 55). All of the main events of *Guy Mannering* stem from an unprovoked assault by the Laird of Ellangowan on the traditional rights of the local people. First, a band of gypsies "admitted to consider themselves as a sort of subordinate dependents of his family" is evicted from "their ancient place of refuge" on its property (ch. 8). This dispossession is followed by a crackdown on smuggling, which "was general, or rather universal, all along the south-west coast of Scotland. Almost all the common people were engaged in these practices" (ch. 9). It is strictly logical, therefore, that Jock Jabos, long before making the recognition, accidentally loses his way and deposits the missing heir in the hands of the smugglers and the representative gypsy (ch. 27), and then leads him into trouble with the nominal villain (ch. 32), who has dispossessed the hero's family. For one dispossession, another; the hero suffers by means of the servant for what his father did to the people.

The novel does not openly sanction smuggling, nor does it bring the gypsies back to their land. Still, it is by means of a servant who is a "friend to smuggling of every kind" (ch. 40) that the hero extricates himself from difficulty. And the dispossessed gypsies are evoked by the surrogate crowd that acclaims the recognition:

This public declaration of an unprejudiced witness was just the spark wanted to give fire to the popular feeling, which burst forth in three distinct shouts:—"Bertram forever!"—"Long life to the heir of Ellangowan"—"God send him his ain, to live among us as his forebears did of yore!"

"I hae been seventy years on the land," said one person.

"I and mine hae been seventy and seventy to that," said another; "I have the right to ken the glance of a Bertram."

"I and mine hae been three hundred years here," said another old man, "and I sall sell my last cow, but I'll see the young laird placed in his right."

All this incremental talk about land and right is extraneous to the dramatic situation, but it takes over Ellangowan's restitution on behalf of those who, recognizing him, use the opportunity to assert their *own* rights to the land. When the next speaker cries out, "the Bertrams were aye the wale o' the country side," the statement is clearly contrary to the facts as the novel has presented them. It defines the recognition as displaced and optative.

Evidence of the essential detachability and excess of the recognition can be found in texts where the same archaic utopianism pervades the ending even though marriage is absent entirely. In the American Western, the hero's lower-class sidekick represents both an ambivalence toward civilization and marriage and the utopian alternative of male comradeship. In Elizabeth Gaskell's *Cranford,* the same is true of women without men. As Nina Auerbach argues in *Communities of Women,* the "friendly sociability" that triumphs in Cranford not only replaces conjugal plotting and closure but makes up a piece of feminist utopia. "Destitute of the props and dimensions of the Victorian woman's life, the relationships of daughter, mother, and wife, Matty is restored as she presides over an organic community. . . .

Cranford's 'peace' is its quiet code for 'victory.'"[39] The one Victorian prop that Miss Matty jealously retains is the role of mistress of the household; she enforces the "no followers" rule without mercy. And it is around the disappearance of this authoritarian vestige that the sketches cohere into a plot and move toward a dénouement. As she comes to recognize the possibility for tenderness she herself had sacrificed to authority, Miss Matty recognizes herself in her maid and relaxes her authority. And the technical ending of these sketches—a continuation called "The Cage at Cranford," tacked on ten years later—is also an act of recognition. As the "little stupid serving-maiden" proves that she possesses "superior wisdom" (by knowing a petticoat from a parrot cage), the reader is invited to see through the comic humanizing of the bird to the real humanity of the maid. "Remember," her mistress says, ordering the parrot removed from the "dull" kitchen to the drawing room, "birds have feelings as much as we have!"[40] Once again, an open "we" marks the servant's excess.

Final identifications are more visible in the aggregate than in the subdued individual instance. But some, less displaced than in *Cranford,* can be known by their resemblance to traditional romance substitutions. When *Jane Eyre* announces to the servants that she has just been married and presents them with a five-pound note, the echo of the traditional ending seems merely ironic, a means of setting off a private, withdrawn "quiet wedding" in which servants have no reason to be involved:

"Mary, I have been married to Mr. Rochester this morning." The house-keeper and her husband were both of that decent, phlegmatic order of people, to whom one may at any time communicate a remarkable piece of news without incurring the danger of having one's ears pierced by some shrill ejaculation, and subsequently stunned by a torrent of wordy wonderment. Mary did look up, and she did stare at me; the ladle with which she was basting a pair of chickens roasting at the fire, did for some three minutes hang suspended in air, and for the same space of time John's knives also had rest from the polishing process; but Mary, bending again over her roast, said only—

"Have you, miss? Well, for sure!"

A short time after she pursued, "I seed you go out with the master, but I didn't know you were gone to church to be wed"; and she basted away. (ch. 38)

And yet through Jane the servants are involved in more than a three-minute reprieve from their duties. Jane is very anxious to distinguish herself from the servants. Arriving at Thornfield as governess, she is welcomed with these words: "John and his wife are very decent people; but then you see they are only servants, and one can't converse with them on terms of equality; one must keep them at due distance for fear of losing one's authority." After which Jane says, "My heart really warmed to the worthy lady, as I heard her talk" (ch. 11). She reacts this way because, from childhood on, she has been so closely identified with servants. When she meets Rochester for the first time, he says, "You are not a servant at the Hall, of course. You are——" (ch. 12). The distinction needs to be made, and remains incomplete. For the climax of the novel, Brontë stages a full-dress recognition scene, complete with faithful Argus, in which Jane's identification with the servants is reaffirmed. She returns, rich and independent, to find Rochester crippled and blinded by an act of arson—a revenge against the household that, as E. P. Thompson has remarked, was a characteristic servant's crime—committed by the wife she herself took for a servant. And when Jane impersonates a servant in the moment of recognizing and being recognized, she makes herself into another ghostly spirit of the "hearth":

"You are altogether human, Jane? You are certain of that?"

"I conscientiously believe so, Mr. Rochester."

"Yet how, on this dark and doleful evening, could you so suddenly rise on my lonely hearth? I stretched my hand to take a glass of water from a hireling, and it was given to me by you: I asked a question, expecting John's wife to answer me, and your voice spoke at my ear."

"Because I had come in, in Mary's stead, with the tray." (ch. 37)

The recognition scene allows Brontë to share Jane's triumph with servants she would never acknowledge to be her fellows.

THE EROTICS OF RECOGNITION

> Love oftens lords into the cellar bears,
> And bids the sturdy porter come upstairs,
> For what's too high for love, and what's too low?
> Oh! Huncamunca, Huncamunca, oh!
>
> FIELDING, *Tom Thumb*

> The homely nurse does all she can
> To make her Foster-child, her Inmate Man,
> Forget the glories he hath known,
> And that imperial palace whence he came.
>
>   WORDSWORTH, "Ode: Intimations of Immortality"

In Goncharov's *Oblomov* (1859), much of the responsibility for preventing Oblomov's marriage to Olga falls on his servant, Zahar.[41] Zahar fails to notify his master of a rendez-vous (bk. 2, ch. 8), fails to transmit a letter to his master's beloved (bk. 2, ch. 10), and finally provokes a decisive turn against the marriage that his master himself attributes to "the servants' stupid gossip" (bk. 3, ch. 5). In fact, Oblomov blames the servant for the paralysis of his entire life:

Something hindered him from flinging himself into the arena of life and using his will and intellect to go full speed forward. It was as if some secret enemy had laid a heavy hand upon him at the beginning of his journey. . . . Fruitless regrets for the past, burning reproaches of conscience went through him like stings; he struggled to throw off the burden of these reproaches, to find someone else to blame and turn the sting against. But against whom?

"It's all . . . Zahar's fault!" he whispered. (bk. 1, ch. 8)

Since this comic evasion of responsibility is seconded by the plot, which also ascribes causal powers to the servants, we should not be too quick to explain it as nothing more than a formal, arbitrary figure for Oblomov's psychological hesitation. In an important sense, Oblomov is right; his hesitations *can* be traced back to the servants. Specifically, they are traced back to Oblomov's rural upbringing, "permeated with the family principle" (bk. 1, ch. 5). Referring to Walter Scott, Goncharov suggests that what has spoiled his hero for worldly affairs (and for marriage) is the archaic, otherworldly ideal inculcated in him in childhood by his nurse. The idyll entitled "Oblomov's Dream" is in fact the nurse's dream: "she was whispering to him a tale about a far off, unknown country, where there was no night or cold, where miracles keep happening, rivers flow with milk and honey, no one does any work all the year round, and fine lads like Ilya Ilyitch, and maidens more beautiful than words can tell do nothing but enjoy themselves all day" (bk. 1, ch. 9). The servants are the authors of this utopia in two senses: they tell the story, filling it with their own yearnings, and they also do the work, realizing that utopia for their masters and thus, in a sort of Hegelian allegory, sucking away their masters' vital energies. The "restful idleness" that the masters can never seem to shake off comes of "knowing that there were in the house unsleeping eyes that watched over them and never-weary hands that sewed their clothes, gave them food and drink, dressed them, put them to bed, and closed their eyes when they were dead" (bk. 4, ch. 1). The result is a reversal: they are "enslaved" by the "make-believe" of "the nurse—or tradition" (bk. 1, ch. 9).

"Your very Utopia is that of an Oblomov," the hero is told (bk. 2, ch. 4). As with other paternalist archaisms, Oblomov's idyll is at once an exposure of existing hierarchy, a repetition of ruling ideology, and the source of a utopian excess that transcends both of these. Here this excess articulates itself on the one hand in resistance to Oblomov's first, passionate attempt to marry and, on the other, in encouragement of the bizarre, passive drift into marriage with his housekeeper/landlady. There is in fact no paradox. In effect, the only answer to ordinary marriage is extraordinary marriage—marriage with a servant. Declassing himself, Oblomov avoids the worldliness of marriage in order to realize the utopian excess that we have elsewhere seen to be implicit in it. Cutting out the intermediary of the wife, he bonds directly with the servant and dies slowly out of the world, feasting on the delicacies she has prepared in a kind of perpetual wedding banquet.

This marriage to a servant-mother who reproduces the childhood nurse invites a Freudian terminology. But here, as in Otto Rank's theory of the Oedipus myth, what appears to be psychological regression can also be interpreted in collective, historical terms. The libidinal redirection goes backwards in collective as well as individual time, to the childhood of premodernity. And this is to say that it extends outwards as well: shooting beyond his peers, the libido is invested in the representative of a looser, more inclusive social circle. In a langorous surrender of social authority, moreover, erotic choice does not assert its own power but rather submits to the greater power of a de-individualized servant who represents "tradition" itself. Keeping to the Freudian vocabulary, this revision of paternalism might be said to elide or circumvent the interference of the father, who ordinarily forces the child's desire away from the mother and into the fight for worldly success. The power of the father is replaced by that of an archaic, unworldly image of community.

To recognize the historical variability of "regression" is to take an important step toward the historicizing of Freud. It has been pointed out that in the very days when he was working out the concept of the Oedipus complex, Freud himself was remembering his own nurse. "In a letter to Fliess dated October 3, 1897, foreshadowing his announcement of the Oedipus complex twelve days later, Freud says he believes his father 'played no active part in [his] case' . . . Instead, it is his childhood nurse who appears to have played the most important part, and she receives the greatest amount of attention and energy in this period of Freud's self-analysis. 'The prime originator [of my troubles] was a woman, ugly, elderly but clever,' the old Czech Nannie who took him often to Catholic services, taught him about heaven and hell and, as he recalls, 'gave me a high opinion of my capacities.' "[42] In the next sentence, Freud speaks of his first sexual arousal—by his mother, he says, but it would seem that "his *nurse* is in fact his seductress." In the same letter, Freud refers to the nurse as his "teacher in sexual matters," shaming him "for being clumsy and not being able to do anything" (p. 18). At this point in his analysis—a point prior to the theoretical universalizing of the Oedipus complex and closer to the particular facts of his own biography—the nurse in fact combines both the roles he will go on to assign to the mother and the father. Like the mother, she arouses his desire; like the father, she punishes it. And the term he employs combines the two as well. "Prime originator" translates the German *Urheberin*. As Swan says, the word "means, literally, 'the first woman to raise up,' that is, arouse him, or in a literal bodily sense, give him an erection." But Freud also uses *Urheber* in connection with his early theory that the father actually seduces the child, and is thus the originator of neurosis; in this sense " 'my first authoress' would be a faithful if not quite accurate translation of *meine 'Urheberin'* " (p. 17).

In the fully developed theory, of course, the nurse will be ignored as a mere historical accident, disappearing into the universal mythology of Father and Mother. But to this refusal of historical contingency we can apply Freud's own view of accident: "A most important piece of information is often announced as being a redundant accessory, like an opera prince disguised as a beggar."⁴³ If history is restored, then the model family that is constituted by Freud's theory becomes a larger and more troublesome one. "The possibility that, in relation to his Nannie, Freud internalized a dialectic of shame and ambition takes on a larger significance when we consider her socioeconomic position as a Czech working-class woman in a German town in Moravian Austria. . . . From the thirteenth century on, Czech Moravia had been dominated by the German upper and middle classes who had taken over the towns and left the countryside to the Czechs" (p. 35). Severe economic crises in the area, from which Freud's own wool merchant father had suffered, had inspired Czech nationalism in that countryside. As a Czech Catholic employed by an urban, bourgeois, German-Jewish family, how much of the rural oppositional spirit did Freud's nurse carry into her nursing? How much of her ideological baggage became mixed up in his own sexuality? In addition to Freud's dream memories of humiliation at her hands, we know from his commentary on one of his own dreams that when Freud was two-and-a-half, she was caught stealing from the family, arrested, and sentenced to ten months in prison. "There is no telling how much repressed—and maybe not so repressed—envy and class hatred might have been behind what Jones calls 'the nurse's normal mixture of affection for children and severity toward their transgressions'" (p. 36).

What we see, in the dreams of the days leading up to the announcement of the Oedipus complex, is the crystallization of desire around this historical kernel. Freud does not in fact identify, as the theory predicts, with his father, but with his nursemaid: it is Freud himself who steals ten kreuzer notes and makes others the object of "bad treatment." The "father" of the Oedipus theory is built out of psychological dynamics that actually enter the family, with the nurse, from outside. "Freud's characteristic position, the confessed sexual aggressor, a position that finds its permanent intellectual expression in the theory of the Oedipus complex" cannot take into account "that his aggression against the 'good' mother (wife, patient) is based, in fantasy, on identification with a seductive, aggressive 'bad' mother and—hardest fact of all—that 'good' and 'bad' mothers are one and the same woman," the nurse (pp. 42–43). Freud is able to see that he wants to *have* the nurse, to confess to desire for her; what he cannot admit is that his desire is also a desire to *be* the nurse. It is she who has humiliated him and made him feel powerless, and it is her power with which he identifies, which defines what he wants to become.

The Oedipus complex of course takes this power away from her and bestows it on the father, and it is thanks in large part to the success of this theory that the massive intrusion of desire for servants into the lives of the servant-keeping classes in this period has not attracted more attention. In fact, Freud's early experiences with his nurse would seem to be part of a large and formative historical phenomenon. And it is not only the Freudians who have repressed it. As we know, Marx himself secretly fathered a son upon the beloved family servant, Helen Demuth, and Engels helped cover up Marx's paternal responsibility by allowing suspicion to center on himself. In society at large, however, the existence of such transgressions had become an open secret. In *The Origin of the Family, Private Property, and the State* there is perhaps a backhanded acknowledgement of the general scandal. Engels attributes the degradation of free women in ancient Athens to "the competition of female slaves." Women enjoyed a higher position and greater sexual freedom in Sparta than in Athens, he argues, because while Athenian slaves slept in their master's house, in Sparta "the helot serfs lived segregated on the estates and thus there was less temptation for the Spartiates to have intercourse with their women." "It is the existence of slavery side by side with monogamy, the existence of beautiful young slaves who belong to the *man* with all they have, that from the very beginning stamped on monogamy its specific character as monogamy *only for the woman,* but not for the man. And it retains this character to this day."[44]

However accurate with respect to Greece, this interpretation says much about modern Europe during the childhoods of Marx and Freud. The extent of what has been termed the "induced promiscuity" of domestic service can perhaps be imagined from the numbers involved. In the nineteenth century the overwhelming majority of the more than one million domestics in Britain were women. Of all single English women, 20 percent were servants.[45] "An unusually high proportion of prostitutes were initially domestic servants," all contemporary and later sources agree. Typical estimates are one-third and even one-half.[46] A survey of illegitimate pregnancy in Nantes revealed that "half of the girls were domestic servants, half of whom had been impregnated by their masters, mostly members of the Nantes bourgeoisie." As Lawrence Stone adds, "there is no reason to believe" that this figure "would not also apply to England."[47] The evidence is anecdotal and scattered, as is perhaps inevitable given the nature of the phenomenon, but it suggests the existence of sexual practices that were all but universal. An officer in the Indian Medical Service wrote to Havelock Ellis as follows: "once at a club in Burma we were some twenty-six at table and the subject of first intercourse came up. All had been led astray by servants save two, whom their sisters' governesses had initiated."[48]

If sexuality between servants and those they served could appear— to the latter—as the evil of being "led astray," it appears to us today as a brutality whose nakedness is still shocking. Nevertheless, more was involved in this enormous sexual exchange than the proximity of servants and the simple, outrageous power of class and money to extort or purchase sexual favors from them. The history that can be read back into the Oedipus complex is relevant here as well; the erotic desire for domestics has a historical genesis, and one that somewhat confuses the possession of power. The "first recollection of things sexual" by the author of *My Secret Life,* for example, involves, as for Freud, being mishandled at the age of five by his nursemaid: "I recollect that she sometimes held my little prick when I piddled; was it needful to do so? I don't know. She attempted to pull my prepuce back, when and how often I know not. But I am clear at seeing the prick tip show, of feeling pain, of yelling out, of her soothing me, and of this happening more than once." There follow "scenes of childhood seduction and masturbation in which this nursemaid occupied the chief role" and which are, Steven Marcus comments, "familiar and typical." The "one noticeable symptom of his early experience" that remains he also attributes to the servant: "I could not . . . thoroughly uncover the prick tip without pain till I was sixteen years old. . . . My nursemaid, I expect, thought this curious, and tried to remedy the error in my make, and hurt me."[49] Before he loses his virginity with a servant, like Havelock Ellis' informants, he conspic-

uously fails to lose it with another. His account of his "first intercourse" insists on the "disgrace," as a boy, of being told by this
inferior, "Lor! you ain't man enough."[50] Are these episodes the prod-
ucts of the maid's ignorance, or of her malice and a vengeful demonstration of power over her masters via their children?

None of these power reversals shakes his later ardor for servants.
Again, as for Freud, a combination of arousal and punishment issues
in a desire that is permeated by unspoken identification. The author
explains at one point why, in later life, he continues to find servants
so desirable.

I wanted a change, and began to look out for a nice fresh servant. I have
now had many servants in my time, and know no better companions in
amorous amusements. They have rarely lost all modesty, a new lover is a
treat and a fresh experience to them, even when they have had several, and
few have had that. They only get the chance of copulating once a week or
so, they are clean, well-fed, full-blooded, and when they come out to meet
their friend, or give way with a chance man on the sly, are ready, yielding,
hot-arsed, lewd, and lubricious. Their cunts throb at the first touch of a
finger, and moisten, and they spend freely and copiously. . . . No one will
take more spunk out of a man and give more herself than a lass who says, "I
couldn't get out before,—I'm sorry you had to wait,—I must really get
back by ten."[51]

One peculiarity of this statement is the author's pleasure in the fact
that servants have so little leisure for sexual activity. The special
impediments to having a servant lover, their long hours of work and
total supervision by their employers, are for him its attractions; that
their lives involve so much work and so little play increases their
value as sexual playthings. In a sense it is work, not play, that interests
him. I have already mentioned, in speaking of A. J. Munby, Steven
Marcus' demonstration that Victorian sexuality expressed itself in
metaphors of economic exchange, encouraging a melancholy identification between pleasure and outflow and thus leading to widespread
anxieties about sexual depletion or bankruptcy. Despite the complacency of the passage above, what underlies it is fear. In the imagination of the author and the age, the "universal currency" of all "vital
force" is not produced and accumulated by the body as fast as it is
expended. Overwork and sexual excess alike can therefore lead to the

Victorian "universal affliction" of "spermatorrhoea," defined by William Acton as "a state of ennervation produced, at least primarily, by the loss of semen."[52] In *My Life and Loves* Frank Harris worries over the same theme: "the most important lesson of my life" is "that absolutely complete chastity enabled me to work longer hours than I had ever worked. . . . the power was in the pent-up semen." He is afraid "that I had already seriously diminished my capital of vigor."[53]

What Marcus does not say when he quotes the passage above is that sex *with servants* breaks the rules of this sexual economy. For the author of *My Secret Life,* their excessive work on the contrary makes them symbols of sexual plenitude. Servants, who "spend freely and copiously," are uniquely able to "give" back more than they "take out" of a man, and precisely because they are obliged to work so hard. Thus sex can appear as a sort of transfer of funds into the master's account, a way of guaranteeing that he does not "spend" beyond his income. If sex is ordinarily depletion, sex with servants permits accumulation. In short, the author recognizes servants as producers of value: the value he ascribes to them as lovers, like Munby's fetishism of the "working hand," is a sexual restatement of the labor theory of value.

It would be interesting to follow out the traces of this extraordinary, obscure recognition among the gamekeepers and working-class homosexual companions of later novelists like Lawrence and Forster. They are to be found as far away as the scene in Norman Mailer's *An American Dream* where the hero sodomizes his wife's maid, seeking the smells of hunger and poverty, of the proletariat's mysterious "determination to get along in the world," in orifices that he likens to a "warehouse" and a "bank."[54] But there is a more general point here. As Foucault suggests, nineteenth-century sexuality was associated not only with productive power, but with power in its most abstract sense, that is, with causality itself. He speaks of "*the postulate of a general and diffuse causality . . .* the principle that sex is endowed with an inexhaustible and polymorphous causal power. The most discrete event of sexual conduct—accident or deviation, deficit or excess—is supposed to be capable of entailing the most diverse consequences all through life; there is no illness or physical discomfort for which the nineteenth century did not imagine at least a partial sexual etiology."⁵⁵ Desire for servants would thus testify to a projection of power, inspiring both dependence and identification. What seems to be recognized in the passive objects of desire, as in those nurses whose stories mediate the values of the rural community, is a fateful if postponed cultural authority.

One text where this reintroduction of collective social entities into the dynamics of the psyche can be tested is what has been, from Edmund Wilson to Shoshana Felman, the classical locus of Freudian exegesis: James' *The Turn of the Screw*. In the New York Preface, James states his intention not to specify the evil of the ghosts but to leave it to the reader's imagination. "I cast my lot with pure romance," he says. "There is not only from beginning to end of the matter not one inch of expatiation, but my values are positively all blanks."⁵⁶ Yet it is hard not to fill these blanks with the open secret of trans-class sexuality. Love between the classes is of course precisely what the governess discovers in the earthly paradise at Bly. The corruption she perceives has to do with the children's knowledge of sexual relations between their former governess and one of the servants, who was "dreadfully below." It is clear that her horror has as much to do with the sexual and class transgression as with their ghostly reappearing act. Even before she hears about them, each ghost provokes in her thoughts of a servant exceeding his or her station; later, each makes a carefully staged entry "below" her on the staircase, that ready-made icon of vertical social difference. In conversation with Mrs. Grose, the governess as much as admits to conflating supernatural evil with social anomaly: "'But if he isn't a gentleman—' 'What *is* he? He's a horror'" (p. 22). To occupy a gentleman's place without being a gentleman is sufficient to become a horror, without further need of supernatural props or special effects. The novella's systematic confusion of ghosts with servants—both categories impalpable, alien, and threatening, both filling the house with noises and mysteries—comes to a head in the final confrontation. Miles, accused of excessive intimacy with a "base menial," wonders about the "others" with whom they've been left "alone," or "not absolutely alone": "they don't much count, do they?'" (p. 82).

To say that for the governess the supernatural otherness of the ghosts coincides with the class otherness of the servants is not to fall back into the sort of politicized Freudianism in which the governess would be charged with projecting her class ambivalence along with her repressed sexuality. Just as Marx extracted the labor theory of value as a sort of utopian kernal from political economy's apologies for capitalism, so we can extrapolate from her otherwise sordid "romance" of sexual transgression a final recognition that puts love between the classes in a different light. In *The Political Unconscious* Fredric Jameson describes romance, the genre that James asks to carry the weight of his blank, motiveless malignity, as a

symbolic answer to the perplexing question of how my enemy can be thought of as being *evil* (that is, as other than myself and marked by some absolute difference), when what is responsible for his being so characterized is simply the *identity* of his own conduct with mine, the which—challenges, points of honor, tests of strength—he reflects as in a mirror image. Romance "solves" this conceptual dilemma by producing a new narrative, the "story" of a semic evaporation. The hostile knight, in armor, exudes that insolence which marks a fundamental refusal of recognition and stamps him as the bearer of the category of evil, up to the moment in which, defeated and unmasked, he asks for mercy and *tells his name . . .* at which point . . . he becomes one knight among others and loses all his sinister unfamiliarity. (pp. 118–119)

There is of course no moment at the end of *The Turn of the Screw* when "the antagonist *ceases* to be a villain," as Jameson says, when the mask of otherness is lifted and evil evaporates from the world. But to judge from the critical controversy surrounding this text, much of it builds toward just such a missing scene. The multiple mirror images, duplications, reenactments, and superimpositions between the governess and the servant-ghosts have been assembled as evidence, mainly by the anti-ghost party, in order to undermine the governess' narrative authority. Yet these parallels can also be interpreted as continual, unanswered beckonings to a recognition that would convert these threatening aliens into mere versions of herself.

Here it is helpful to remember, as my discussion of Freud and *My Secret Life* was intended to bring out, that the collapse of class otherness is erotically charged with pleasure as well as negatively charged with threat. What the governess herself desires is of course nothing but the erotic transgression of class. Her love for the Master requires

that at some future point she herself must repeat the ghosts' transgression and indulge a love prohibited by the social hierarchy. Though
the text does not follow her romance script, its unrealized happy
end—victory over the ghosts and union with the Master—develops a
utopian motif that is present from the outset. On her arrival at Bly,
the governess describes it as a "castle of romance" (p. 10). As the pro-
ghost party has observed, much emphasis is given to the aspect of a
fallen Eden, an earthly paradise. Her terms for the innocence of the
children are borrowed from the golden age. Miles, the governess says,
has an "indescribable little air of knowing nothing in the world but
love" (p. 13). In a sense, all the evil she later finds in this paradise does
not dislodge this initial view. Miles *has* known love, the governess
decides—the love between governess and valet. The hypothesis can
thus be formulated that if his innocence seems not of this world, it is
precisely *because* he, unlike most earthly children, has known love that
triumphs over class in a house without a master. And this hypothesis
returns upon the governess herself. One reviewer called *The Turn of the
Screw* "a study of infernal human debauchery."[57] But this debauchery
could better be seen as a sort of deconstruction of the human, as its
etymology (perhaps fancifully) suggests: "ébaucher" is to lay the
foundation, construct the skeleton; to debauch is to remove it, to
deconstruct. In expressing its desire, the self exposes an identity or an
identification—not upon which it is built, but toward which it is
projected. Whether the governess loves the children's innocence or
participates in their debauchery, her desire projects her toward the
servant-ghosts.

Recall how far the text goes not only to show that evil is defined in
class terms but also to remind us that the governess herself is a
servant. As one example among many, there is her cross-examination
of Mrs. Grose concerning Miles and his intimacy with Quint:

"If Quint—on your remonstrance at the time you speak of—was a base
menial, one of the things Miles said to you, I find myself guessing, was that
you were another." Again her admission was so adequate that I continued:
"And you forgave him that?"

"Wouldn't *you?*"

"Oh yes!" And we exchanged there, in the stillness, a sound of the oddest
amusement. (p. 37)

Mrs. Grose's "Wouldn't *you*?" suggests to the governess, in a mode approaching that of stage comedy, what so many critics of *The Turn of the Screw* have suggested in the mode of scholarly irony: her resemblance to the servant-ghosts, from which we can deduce the fragility of an "evil" that depends for its existence on nothing more than the illusion of otherness. In this sense it can be maintained that *The Turn of the Screw* projects an unrealized "happy end": the return of Bly to the (classless) Edenic state in which the governess first found it, the evaporation from her world of the "evil" that she added to it, which would result from her recognition of what so many voices are trying to tell her—her identity with "the others."

Conclusion:
Commonplace and Utopia

Human beings are not slaves, but neither are they masters, not serfs, but not feudal lords either, not proletarians, but certainly not capitalists. What they are has not yet become clear . . .

ERNST BLOCH

The kind of society I want is one in which my cook and I can eat in the dining room together.

G. D. H. COLE

George Eliot's *Felix Holt* describes "Utopia" as "delightful results, independent of processes" (ch. 38). The reading of *The Turn of the Screw* offered in the last chapter can be described as utopian in a more positive sense: it tries to register delightful results which are implied or projected, though not realized, when the text's causal processes are given to its servants. Like the hero's mother in the epilogue to *Felix Holt,* it infers that "justice certainly had much more in reserve" from the evidence of what justice has done already.

Still, as that which is both uncovered within the text and, more adventurously, is constructed out of it, the utopian excess of such a reading is only partly susceptible to what is usually called historical critique. The rough and reductive approximations of historical context can lend credibility to statements about what is central or essential, but they cannot take it away from a literary presence that claims to be only marginal and suggestive, achieving coherence and even visibility more in the aggregate than in the individual instance. If narratives about the organic unity of a given text, about an authorial career, or about a historical period can all be categorized as "close readings," then this narrative might be thought of as a distant reading. To be distant is to be peripheral, but distance also confers certain advantages. It permits self-consciousness about its own limited reach. It is a strength of this interpretation, for example, that the unequal power it assumes (the dominated could not speak fully or freely in the texts of their dominators) accounts for its own relatively thin and dispersed textual evidence. Distance also obviates the tempting confusion of interpreter with object of interpretation, forcing the interpreter to expose his or her separate, chosen standpoint. Unable to hide behind the authority of its object, my narrative must acknowledge that it *is* a narrative, and that however adequate it may be as an account of that object, it ultimately stands or falls as a historical narrative in its own right.

And yet if the readings I have offered seem to circumvent historical judgment entirely, then they fall disappointingly short of the intention of this book, which is precisely to sketch a working relationship between history and a set of literary materials that defy simple historical differentiation. The first and most fundamental challenge has been to read canonical texts with enough sensitivity to their minor, fragmentary, provisional, and inorganic margins so as to allow the historical pressure of subalternity to be felt at all. Having established that the pressure of contct between subaltern and dominant took the shape of a utopian "no place," I faced the second challenge that this "no place" was also a commonplace, repeated in diverse times and places, integrated or implicated in *too much* history. If the marginal readings in a sense stand by themselves, my argument as a whole depends on a satisfactory formulation of this second excess, the overshooting of what usually passes for historical source, context, or background.

This excess is of course inscribed in the book's eccentric topical organization. Its center is the novel of the nineteenth century, yet it is precisely the impossibility of restraining the *topos* within the genre and period of realism—that is, the impossibility of treating it as a manageable "theme"—that sends the argument shuttling back and forth between realist novels and other genres and periods, and perhaps also constitutes its interest. Uncharacteristic in discussions of realism, this interpretive rhythm helps to relativize both the usual association between realism and historical difference and the usual dissociation of realism from the utopian. George Eliot, whose skepticism about utopias is quoted above, provides a useful example. While writing *Felix Holt,* Eliot was reading P. W. Buckham's *The Theater of the Greeks* (1830), which includes A. W. Schlegel's "Lectures on the Drama."[1] Schlegel is particularly interested in recognition scenes. As it happens, he offers an extended comparison of three in which servants participate (though without commenting on their participation): Aeschylus' *Choephoroi,* Sophocles' *Electra,* and Euripides' *Electra* (pp. 323–333). As far as servants are concerned, what Schlegel stresses is the absolute historical difference between ancient and modern versions:

The knavish servant is generally also the merry-maker, who avows, with agreeable exaggeration, his own sensuality, and unprincipled maxims, and makes a joke of the other persons, perhaps, also, with side-speeches to the audience. Hence the comic servants of the Moderns; but I doubt whether, as our manners are, there is propriety and truth in borrowing such characters from the ancients. The Greek servant was a slave, given up for life to the sovereign will of his master, and often exposed to the severest treatment. A person, thus deprived by the constitution of society of all his natural rights, may be pardoned if he makes cunning his business: he is in a state of warfare with his oppressor, and artifice is his natural weapon. A modern servant, who is free to choose his situation and his master, is evidently a worthless rascal, if he helps the son to play off a deceit upon the father. As to the self-avowed sensuality, which gives a comic cast of expression to servants, and other persons of mean rank, this motive may still be followed without hesitation: he to whom life grants few privileges, has also less required of him, and may boldly avow vulgar sentiments, without giving offense to our moral feelings. The better servants are off in. real life, the less suitable are they to Comedy; it redounds, perhaps, to the glory of this soft age of ours, that in our family-picture works, we see downright virtuous servants, who are better suited to excite tears than laughter. (p. 384)

This assertion of historical difference has given the cue to many subsequent dismissals of literary servants who present the anomaly of being both socially unsettling and literarily traditional. But it does not quite manage to protect the present against its unsettling heritage, or against the unsettlingness *of* a heritage. On the modern stage, Schlegal declares, a servant *should* be virtuous, for he lives in a "soft age," and if he does not "excite tears" rather than laughter, he is "a worthless rogue." On the other hand, in trying to draw a safe line of distinction between the servants of the ancients and the moderns, Schlegal only posits its transgression. His prescriptions acknowledge implicitly that the ancient types have persisted, in spite of their apparent inappropriateness to modern society. And since there still *are* rogues who, ungrateful for the many benefits of modern society, persist in "unprincipled maxims," "side-speeches to the audience," jokes at the expense of others and deceits at the expense of the father, it is clear that the "freedom to choose" of modern society does not in fact exempt it from a critique that to Schlegel seemed no longer necessary. The effort to keep ancient servants out of modern literature is an effort to defend the "glory of this soft age of ours," and the failure of the first entails the failure of the second. Modern society remains paradoxically and unpleasantly vulnerable to criticism.

In this light, the fact that Eliot went on to stock *Felix Holt* with so many ancient servant types suggests that she had moved beyond Schlegel's piously progressive belief in historical differentiation to a more complex replaying of the past. When Eliot began work on *Felix Holt,* she was reading Greek tragedy intensively.[2] In *The Victorians and Ancient Greece,* Richard Jenkyns points out close parallels between the novel and several plays. "The relationship between Mrs. Transome and Denner is remarkably similar to that between Medea and her *trophos,*" for example, while her son Harold "has very nearly found himself in the position of an Orestes or an Oedipus; he has just threatened to kill a man who is, though he does not realize it, his parent."[3] More important, among these parallels there are several instances of servant causality that provocatively exceed their intelligible context. In *Choephoroi,* for example, which begins with a chorus of slaves presiding over the recognition of Orestes and Electra and in which Clytemnestra is destroyed by her long-lost son much as Mrs. Transome is destroyed by Harold, it is the intentionally distorted message delivered by Orestes' old nurse that separates Aegisthus from his bodyguard and thus permits the murders to occur. As the slave chorus tells this fellow slave, "It is the messenger who makes the bent word straight."[4]

As if in answer to Schlegel, *Felix Holt* offers a recapitulation of the full range of servant commonplaces. Like *Jane Eyre,* it reaches its conclusion by means of a recognition scene in which the heroine chooses the place and role of the housemaid for her reunion with her lover:

"Mr. Lyon at home?" said Felix in his firm tones.

"No, sir," said Esther from behind her screen; "but Miss Lyon is, if you'll please to walk in."

"Esther!" exclaimed Felix, amazed. (ch. 50)

As in other instances we have observed, parallelism saturates the novel with a sense that fate has not spoken its last word when the story closes. Last words, or words about last things, seem to be spoken largely by the two expository servants with whom Esther and Harold Transome are respectively paralleled. Lyddy and Denner are choral rather than causal, and each reflects the ideas of her master or mistress (evangelical and aristocratic). And yet this secondariness does not prevent them from offering a vision of the future that, as in *The Turn of the Screw,* suggests purposes and possibilities only temporarily left unrealized. Lyddy is a Christian millenarian. Though in a comic mode (in anticipation of the end, she cries into Esther's broth), her insistence on imminent apocalypse manages to threaten her superiors—she displays "an edifying despair as to the future lot of gentlement callers" (ch. 15)—and to remind them of an eventual social equality: "Dear, dear, don't you be so light, Miss. We may all be dead before night" (ch. 26). If Lyddy, like Marx, wields the coming end of (pre)history as a weapon, the "godless" Denner, like Nietzsche, refuses this predetermination in favor of an amoral contingency— "There's good chances and bad chances, and nobody's luck is pulled only by one string"—and in favor of the present power it allows: "I like to play my cards well, and see what will be the end of it" (ch. 1).

Most of the novel's cards are in fact played by servants. Once again, one finds the logic that links chapters three, four, and five of this book: exposition seems to imply agency, which in turn demands recognition. Eliot's description of the passive and quiescent colliers, set in motion only by the "visible cause of beer" (ch. 30) and forged into an Election Day crowd that is "animated by no real political passion or fury against social distinctions" (ch. 33), suggests that political change does not come from below. Yet the Radical candidate complains, with some justice, that he is "very much at the mercy of his agents" (ch. 16), who have of course provided the beer. The responsibility for change, appearing to issue from the vertical breach between principals and agents, resolves itself into something like the "butler did it" formula. The novel's servants, who accept "social distinctions" even more thoroughly than the miners, embody and further the cause of Radicalism by their trivial, unconscious actions. The shocking news of Harold Transome's political conversion strikes the Tories like a blow when one servant passes it on to another (ch. 7). More important, it is the servants gathered in the butler's room whose unfounded gossip is presented as the exemplary cause of his candidature for Parliament, and who thus assume the fateful omnipotence of the expository goddess "Rumor":

> When Mr. Scales' strong need to make an impressive figure in conversation, together with his very slight need of any other premise than his own sense of his wide general knowledge and probable infallibility, led him to specify five hundred thousand as the lowest admissible amount of Harold Tran- some's commercially-acquired fortune, it was not fair to put this down to poor old Miss Rumor, who had only told Scales that the fortune was considerable. And again, when the curt Mr. Sircome found occasion at Treby to mention the five hundred thousand as a fact that folks seemed pretty sure about, this expansion of the butler into "folks" was entirely due to Mr. Sircome's habitual preference for words which could not be laid hold of or give people a handle on him. It was in this simple way that the report of Harold Transome's fortune spread and was magnified, adding much luster to his opinions in the eyes of the Liberals, and compelling even men of the opposite party to admit that it increased his eligibility as a member for North Loamshire. (ch. 8)

Eliot debunks one myth in order to replace it with another. If "Rumor," demystified, amounts to no more than a chain of individual interests and evasions which are assumed to have no collective pur- pose or coherence of their own, these interests and evasions are nonetheless assigned here, as in so many other novels of the period, to social subordinates, and are colored by their uneasy subordination. The butlers who propel news into the public domain, translating private affairs into historical causes, are not an innocent figure for "folks."

The same association operates on the inheritance side of the plot. Again it is the butler who, in the course of a practical joke at the expense of another servant, unwittingly exposes the set of tokens that establish Esther's identity and her right to the Transome estate:

Mr. Scales, in pursuit of a slight flirtation with the younger lady's-maid, had preferred a more sequestered walk in the company of that agreeable nymph. And it happened to be this pair, of all others, who alighted on the sleeping Christian—a sight which at the very first moment caused Mr. Scales a vague pleasure as at an incident that must lead to something clever on his part. To play a trick, and make some one or other look foolish, was held the most pointed form of wit throughout the back regions of the Manor, and served as a constant substitute for theatrical entertainment. . . . Putting his finger up in warning to Mrs. Cherry, and saying, "Hush—be quiet—I see a fine bit of fun"—he took a knife from his pocket, stepped behind the unconscious Christian, and quickly cut off the pendant coat-tail. Scales knew nothing of the errand to the Rectory; and as he noticed that there was something in the pocket, thought it was probably a large cigar-case. . . . He threw the coat-tail as far as he could. (ch. 12)

Though it derives from theater, like so much else that servants in the novel do and say, this gesture is something more than a "substitute for theatrical entertainment." Throughout the novel, the news that "property doesn't always get into the right hands," as the coachman of the introduction puts it, is specifically and almost obsessively placed in the hands of propertyless servants. Twenty years before the story opens, the heroine's father has exchanged identities with a man who is now a servant. This servant's connection with the lost estate emerges from the "shapeless and insignificant" expository chatter in the butler's room (ch. 7). His scheming completes the chain of causes that carries the truth to Transome Court (ch. 36), thus precipitating the arrival there of a heroine who was once a governess.

The identification between the servants and the male and female leads, Harold and Esther, also emerges from Eliot's revisions of traditional comic dialogue. The unusually lengthy and philosophical dialogues between Mrs. Transome and her maid twice begin with a reversal in which it is the mistress, not the maid, who is distracted: "she could now hear the gentle knocking to which she had been deaf before" (ch. 1). One of the first things Denner says when her presence in the room is finally acknowledged is "There's a fine presence about Mr. Harold. I remember you used to say, madam, there were some people you would always know were in the room though they stood round a corner and others you might never see till you ran against them. That's as true as truth." We do not need to be told, much later, that "the sensations produced by Denner's presence were as little disturbing as those of a favorite cat" (ch. 39) in order to feel the weight of comparison carried in her praise of her mistress' son.

According to one reading, this comparison determines the moral structure of the novel. The most obvious interpretation of servant agency in *Felix Holt,* as of Eliot's "special attention to trivial causes" and "unhistoric acts" in general, is that it is there in order to demonstrate the web-like interdependence of social life and, in so doing, to teach the main characters (and the reader) how little they determine their own lives. So for example the Radical crowd, which teaches the Radical candidate that he cannot trust "in his own skill to shape the success of his own morrows" (ch. 16), becomes "an image of the day's fatalities, in which the multitudinous small wickednesses of small selfish ends, really undirected towards any larger result, had issued in a widely shared mischief" (ch. 33). In other words, the social redistribution of agency would figure as a moral negation of agency: "Living? the servants will do that for us." In the course of the book both Harold and Esther are in a sense enjoined to let drop their worldly ambitions and instead to reinstall themselves in the private nurture (the function and etymology of the *trophos*) of their aging parents, a role which had been filled by Lyddy and Denner respectively. In this positive revaluation of unheroic "valetism," Eliot suggests that the children, renouncing a higher place in the public domain, will return to full moral stature only when they leave action to the servants and take over the place of the servants in the home.

This reading inserts the survival of the *servus ex machina* into a relatively precise historical context: the notion that in order to avoid mischief, characters should refrain from action can be situated at the juncture of Eliot's scientific rationalism (what she calls "the great conception of universal regular sequence, without partiality and without caprice") and of her rural organicism, which squelches self-interested and conflict-producing action in the name of the organic community.⁵ It also accords well with Eliot's apparent intentions. "News," she writes in *Middlemarch,*" is often dispersed as thoughtlessly and effectively as the pollen which the bees carry off (having no idea how powdery they are) when they are buzzing in search of their particular nectar" (ch. 59). As a moralist Eliot is interested (to take up her simile) in flowers. Her minute attention to mouth-to-mouth chains (the passage cited above, for example, traces the powerful news of Casaubon's codicil back to Dorothea's maid) shows upper-class characters that their lives depend on the wills of indifferent outsiders, that character is not fate, that in the interest of pure character the shared domain of fate must be abandoned. On the other hand, both Eliot's simile and the cumulative social bias of the commonplaces she borrowed urge us to consider that bees too have their purposes. In order to frame another historical perspective on the unconscious efforts of unfree agents, we would have only to adjust our view of pollination so as to include the missing endpoint of honey.

A second historical reading, which would be concerned with honey, or with the hypothetical ends of Eliot's visible means, would of course focus once again on a restitution larger than any the novel actually offers. But this utopian excess does not lie beyond what might be predicted or projected from the known coordinates of its historical context. There is no final restitution in *Felix Holt;* when Esther chooses Felix over the estate, all the servant-operated machinery proves ultimately irrelevant to the plot. Yet her renunciation parallels another that is not as freely chosen. Her right to the estate comes into effect only with the death of her proletarian double, a bill-sticker distantly allied to the Transome's by blood. When he speaks of "an old family kep' out o' my rights," the confusion of singular and plural suggests that his right too is representative of wider rights. And this suggestion is amplified when he defends himself against the imagined attacks of lawyer Jermyn: "If Old Nick tries to lay hold on me for poaching, I'll say, 'You be hanged for a lawyer, Old Nick; every hare and pheasant on the Trounsem's land is mine'" (ch. 28). In his phrasing, the claim that he lays down and that passes from him to Esther becomes a restatement of those general and customary rights to the land that were in fact being attacked and defended during the lifetimes of *Felix Holt*'s characters, the period of the Industrial Revolution.

In short, we have here another historical context for the servant agency of *Felix Holt*. For Eliot, servants are both identified and contin-

uous with the old-fashioned peasants who interest her Tory imagination. We are told for example that Mrs. Transome "objects to
changes; she will not have a new style of tenants; she likes the old
stock of farmers who milk their own cows, and send their daughters
out to service" (ch. 2). In Eliot's essay "The Natural History of
German Life," this continuity between farmers and servants also
looks back to the intimacy of the eighteenth-century "family" that
did not make servants its equals, but shared both work and leisure
with them: "we must remember what the tenant-farmers and small
proprietors were in England half a century ago, when the master
helped to milk his own cows, and the daughters got up at one o'clock
in the morning to brew,—when the family dined in the kitchen with
the servants, and sat with them round the kitchen-fire in the evening." If hierarchy is maintained in this image, as in the uninten-
tionally comic epigraph from G. D. H. Cole, it is equally clear that
there are idealizing energies at work in it. Along with Eliot's moral
ideal of the "subordination of egoism" and her reverence for "hoary
archaisms 'familiar with forgotten years,'" these energies include a
loyalty to the customary rights of peasants. Thus the idealized image
of an organic community, which Eliot prized in part because it
worked to thwart self-interested action, also defines an alternative
collective *telos* for action. In same essay quoted above, she writes of
peasants:

The wide spread among them of communistic doctrines, the eagerness with
which they listened to a plan for the partition of property, seemed to
countenance the notion, that it was a delusion to suppose the peasant
would be secured from his intoxication by his love of secure possession and
peaceful earnings. But, in fact, the peasant contemplated 'partition' by the
light of an historical reminiscence rather than of novel theory. The golden
age, in the imagination of the peasant, was the time when every member of
the commune had a right to as much wood from the forest as would enable
him to sell some, after using what he wanted in firing,—in which the
communal possessions were so profitable that, instead of having to pay his
rates at the end of the year, each member of the commun was something in
pocket.[6]

Eliot seems grateful that peasants are guided by "historical reminiscence" rather than by "novel theory," but she also seems disappointed

that "love of secure possession" and being "something in pocket" are the egoistic reality, that the altruism which she values so highly cannot be securely located in this particular class, time, and place. For something like "communistic doctrines" remains her own moral standard. As Joseph Butwin has shown, among Eliot's most cherished ideals are the same cooperative action and neighborly reciprocity that she refused to see in the crowds of *Felix Holt*.[7] There is the same ambivalence when she ridicules the "idealized proletaires" of Dickens and Sue, who suggest "that the working-classes are in a condition to enter at once into a millenial state of *altruism*, wherein everyone is caring for everyone else, and no one for himself" (p. 272). She does not doubt the ideal of altruism, but rather the "realism" of a premature historical specificity which would locate it fully realized in a dominant position within the present movement—and, one might add, would ignore it if it is not to be observed in this position. While celebrating the ideal, Eliot deferred its realization by locating it in the marginal (and "unrealistic") figure of Felix Holt.[8] For what is Felix, who finds the pocketbook that the butler has thrown into the bushes and hands it unopened to the minister, but another example of a figure she ridicules in the "German Life" essay, the "conventional countryman of the stage, who picks up pocket-books and never looks into them" (p. 269)?

Though its realization is pushed back out of sight, this connection between an archaic ideal and contemporary action has visible historical sources in what E. P. Thompson calls the "moral economy." In the early years of the Industrial Revolution, "direct popular action" against such measures as rises in the price of bread and enclosure of common land was inspired and legitimized, as Thompson shows, by "a consistent traditional view of social norms and obligations, of the proper economic functions of several parties within the community, which, taken together, can be said to constitute the moral economy of the poor. An outrage to these moral assumptions, quite as much as actual deprivation, was the usual occasion for direct action."[9] This moral economy could generate significant activity, Thompson emphasizes, only because it "found some support in the paternalist tradition of the authorities" (p. 79). It seems to have found support in Eliot's paternalism as well. Felix Holt enunciates it explicitly when he defines his brand of Radicalism as "going shares with the unlucky" (ch. 27) and giving "every man a man's share" (ch. 30). And the novel's servants embody it implicitly when they labor to get Esther her fair share.

This reading is much more successful that the previous one in mediating between the modernity of *Felix Holt* and its distant Greek sources and analogues. If the notion of "going shares" fed directly into the Radicalism of the new working class, it also sounds an unknowing echo of much earlier attitudes toward the luck of the community. "Share" goes back to "ploughshare," which is to say to the division of the community's land. This is how each receives his "lot," another term for luck in *Felix Holt* which returns questions of fate to questions of land: "one must sometimes accommodate oneself to a small share. That is the lot of the majority" (ch. 27). Felix's vision of the kind of living he will offer Esther after she renounces the estate once again shares the ending with the poor who have helped bring it about. From Victorian and Elizabethan England back to Periclean Athens, the intervention of the poor in the plot seems to have brought together terms that sustain a similar moral resonance. In the word "plot" itself, the sinister connotations of contriving and devising may well go back to the laying out and dividing up of previously undivided common land. When Falstaff, in an appropriate atmosphere of archaic festivity, tells his fellow thieves, "Now, my masters, happy man be his dole, say I" (*Henry IV,* Pt. 1, 2.2), the modern term for public charity again goes back to a more generous and more authoritative standard of the public good. Dole, from deal or division, was "a portion of a common or undivided field" (dole-land, dole-meadow, and dole-moor are common lands), hence "a part allotted or apportioned to one by right; share, portion, lot." Thus dole becomes, in Falstaff's usage, "portion or lot (in life); fate, destiny." Lexical continuities like these lead all the way back to the Greek dramatists of whom Schlegel spoke. In their society, when "the mass of the Athenians had in one way or another placed itself in debt with the wealthy and had been reduced to the status of *hectemoroi,* that is to say 'sixth-parters' who were compelled to pay to their creditors one sixth of their produce," some of those who escaped into the overseas colonies "were called *gamoroi,* that is to say 'those who shared the land.'"[10]

After all, there seems to be little reason to worry that the rapidity of social progress has deprived the *Odyssey*'s buried pun on *moira* of its pertinence.

George Eliot used the evidence of Greek tragedy to argue that "the nature of human experience is unchanging."[11] The continuity sketched out above cannot lead to such a universal conclusion, for it is only a thin thread of sameness in the large tapestry of historical difference. And yet it is clear that my argument runs the risk of surrendering too much to Eliot's universalizing, ahistorical rhetoric. To claim that any system of values is so general that it extends with only minor variations the full length of the materials collected in this book, from Homer to Virginia Woolf, is apparently to retreat from history into an anthropological universal, a timeless moral essence. In defense of this procedure, there are a number of possible responses. To begin with, one might suggest for example that the opposite extreme is no better; identifying history too exclusively with historical variation has kept us from finding any value whatever in the simple, repetitive annals of the poor. On the other hand, they too are history. As argued in the first chapter, certain features of village economies and communities and of the ideologies that sought to accommodate them *do* repeat themselves at points widely separated in time and space. Though the particular forms of hierarchical modernity of course vary, the friction produced when vestigial notions of just entitlement rub up against them seems to vary less. The triumphs of the dominators and of those who challenged them successfully produce a trajectory; perhaps differentiation is one of the rewards of victory. At any rate, the story of those losers who did without the consolation of belonging to a universal dialectic does not show the same dramatic decisiveness of change. In short, this narrative repeats the confrontations of class conflict, which had been told in the Christian teleological mode, without the implicit happy end that we sometimes confuse with history itself. It would be a limited sense of history that had no room for defense of the lost cause, the minor, and the marginal against a centrality that is always defined by the victors.

In tracing a series of disturbances produced within dominant ideology, a "secret pressure" whose source is indeterminate but whose location is fixed as the point of contact between the rulers and ruled,

I could maintain that I have not been retrieving noble ancestors in order to flatten history into eternal values, but only exploring the historical twists and ironies that result from uneven literary development. To do so would not be inaccurate, but it would be somewhat disingenuous. With reference to the present state of society, if not to an eternal scheme of values, my argument has indeed had a moral bent. The vision of unsatisfied community that is pieced together here out of fragmentary servant commonplaces is offered less as a historical curiosity than as an image of the desirable that still deserves a place on today's agendas. There are extenuating circumstances: above all, I would argue, the fact that on the whole the discourse of modern literary criticism, even at its most dispassionately historical, has consisted of nothing other than an advocacy of various ethical and political preferences, never too well disguised by the need to pass through the analysis of a certain body of texts. But perhaps there is less reason to apologize for this moralizing than, acknowledging the awkwardness of its textual detour, to perform it self-consciously. The end of the guaranteed historical transcendence provided by the dialectic does not mean an end to the struggle for its aims. It only means that we have been thrown back on our own authority to construct narratives or continuities, like this one, that by striving in the mode of moral exhortation help bring those aims closer, while at the same time avowing their constructedness and frailty. As for the content of this exhortation, I am ready to grant that I have not been talking about what is necessarily most complex, sophisticated, profound, or even interesting in the English novel. But I cannot help but wonder about the cost of ignoring, in our sophistication and profundity, the claim of these lost causes hidden away in the margins of our canonical texts. It would be easier to argue that this claim has been superseded if it could be shown that it has been satisfied.

At any rate, this argument is not a case of special pleading for literature as a privileged carrier of trans-historical moral truth. By salvaging and valorizing literary vestiges, it might be taken to support an ahistorical notion of the literary canon. But its emphasis on the marginal and the overlooked must in any case give it a critical rather than a respectful posture toward the canon. According to this account, moreover, it is not just the literary servant that is provocatively sluggish in its development, persistently out of sync with the central movements and ideas of modern society. The same holds for "the people." "The 'people' or 'popular sectors,'" Ernesto Laclau writes, "are not, as some conceptions suppose, rhetorical abstractions or a liberal or idealist conception smuggled into Marxist political discourse."[12] Though expressions like "'the secular struggle of the people against oppression'" and "'popular traditions of struggle'" offer a "principle of identity" to groups that are in fact divergent, this does not mean their rhetoric is "crass opportunism" or "of merely emotional value" (p. 166). As rhetoric, language engaged in specific practice, belongs to the concrete reality of struggle, which cannot be reduced to the prior and more authentic reality of its participants, so the rhetoric of "the people" is a relative term of slowly shifting, semiautonomous contents, never reducible to the interests of a single group at a given time and place—an objective entity at the level of confrontation. And this accounts for "the *relative continuity* of popular traditions in contrast to the historical discontinuities which characterize class structures" (p. 166). To the extent that such traditions "represent the ideological crystallization of resistance to oppression in general . . . they will be longer lasting than class ideologies and constitute a structural frame of reference of greater stability" (p. 167).

Laclau's description of this "relative continuity" does not posit the popular once again as an essence, thus falling into the very trap that the servant, of all popular representatives, seemed best able to avoid. Like the Bloch epigraph, which evokes a "human being" waiting to take shape out of the fragmentary and unsatisfying masters and servants that we have been up to now, it raises the image of an entity that has not come into existence, insisting above all on what we are not, or not yet. This focus on nonrealization or negativity is self-evidently built into utopian discourse, whose name acknowledges that what it indicates is strictly "no place." It is less evident that this focus is also characteristic of those utopian commonplaces generated by the secret pressure between the people and its masters. The skepticism of popular culture has always been underestimated. It was by and large not until the modernists that popular archaism could be seen to possess its own modernity. As chapter two took pains to point out, indeterminacy begins with the first theatrical self-consciousness, the "self-avowal" of which Schlegel speaks. When one of the pair of slaves at the center of Aristophanes' *The Wasps* warns the audience that it is not to expect "a couple of slaves with baskets full of nuts to throw to you," the convention already contains a pragmatic refusal of that desire that it also prophetically evokes. Even at its most repetitive, the servant figures the people not as essential content but as appeal, as a beckoning toward something which is visibly unrealized.

Putting the negative and the positive of utopianism together, one might say that servants read into the record the stipulations that must be complied with before the keys to utopia are handed over; they make extra conditions. An example is the ending of *Nicholas Nickleby.* "Nicholas was one of those whose joy is incomplete unless it is shared by the friends of adverse and less fortunate days" (ch. 64). If a necessary condition of the final banquet's prophetic joy is a complete circle of the less fortunate, then *Nicholas Nickleby* ends with a joy that is incomplete. Its last gesture is a gratuitous glance at the tomb of Smike, the servant-cousin who could not be included in paternalism's metaphorical family. As a "somewhat naive glimpse" of Dickens' "intensely paternalistic" social ideal, Northrop Frye singles out the earlier party in the same novel "where the faithful servitors are brought in at the end for a drink of champagne, expressing undying loyalty and enthusiasm for the patronizing social arrangements."[13] But even here servants raise the price of admission to the ending's earthly paradise. The thanksgiving speaker ends with the wish that his masters may "die happy!" (ch. 37). The reminder of death is just suggestive enough to check the flow of sentiment. *Et in Arcadia ego. . . .* If I am not included in your paradise, the speaker suggests, then death. Applying this inscription to the novel's final trans-class recognitions, we must put the accent on each of the last two words: on the strong Arcadian impulse that carries the ending beyond a mere affirmation of hierarchy, and at the same time on the dissonance introduced by the servants, whose persistent "I" (or "we") will either help constitute the millenium or drag their masters back into the mortal broil of secular history.

The concept of utopia contains the detachment with which it should be received. By all accounts, Thomas More was what can only be called a good man. In his last letter to his daughter Meg, written from prison with a coal, he takes the time for attention to her maidservants: "I like speciall well Dorothy Colley, I pray you be good to her. I would wit whether this be she that you wrote me of. If not, I pray you be good to the other as you may in her affliction, and to my good daughter Joan Alleyn too."[14] (The ambiguity about the servant's identity can be consigned to a parenthesis, for it is no more than the general rule.) What is more important is that there are servants even in More's *Utopia:* "all the rough and dirty work" in the kitchen is done by slaves. In Orwell's *Nineteen Eighty-Four,* the Inner Party chief whom Winston mistakes for a democratic enemy of the regime likewise has a servant, and the master's persistent authority along with the servant's persistent servility are unheeded signs that Winston has been overhasty in taking the scene for a foretaste of true socialism:

"Martin is one of us," said O'Brien impassively. "Bring the drinks over here, Martin. Put them on the round table. Have we enough chairs? Then we may as well sit down and talk in comfort. Bring a chair for yourself, Martin. This is business. You can stop being a servant for the next ten minutes." (ch. 8)

Orwell, like most modern novelists, is usually seen as less utopian than dystopian. Yet this inability to complete the imaginary abolition of hierarchy is closer to the skeptical spirit of utopia than, for example, the self-congratulatory claim of the founder of B. F. Skinner's *Walden Two* that he has done away with servitude:

"That's the virtue of Walden Two which pleases me most. I was never happy in being waited on. I could never enjoy the fleshpots for thinking of what might be going on below stairs. . . . Here a man can hold up his head and say, 'I've done my share!'"

Like Schlegel, Skinner indulges in a premature complacency about the modern; in its light, the most archaic insistence that shares and fates have not yet been equally allotted finds a justification. As long as this is the case, as long as people are held to their place, it seems likely that there will be room on the margins of literature for some version of the utopian displacement.

Another possible defense against the charge of ignoring change in favor of repetition would be that in essence I have been describing a single moment in world history—an exceptionally long moment, perhaps, but one that is circumscribed by a unique constellation of factors and that is visible as such because it has now finally ended. There are reasons for believing that the marshalling of communal values and memories based on rural economy, and (for that reason) sanctioned by a residual, backward-looking ruling ideology, against a modernity that presented itself in the dominant form of capitalist exchange ended with the modernism of Woolf, Forster, and their generation. Perry Anderson has recently noted, paradoxically, that modernism itself depended upon the presence of servants: "the persistence of the 'ancien régimes' . . . provided a critical range of cultural values *against which* insurgent forms of art could measure themselves, but also *in terms of which* they could partly articulate themselves . . . the old order, precisely in its still partly aristocratic coloration, afforded a set of available codes and resources from which the ravages of the market as an organizing principle of culture and society—uniformly detested by every species of modernism—could also be resisted." The "hallmark" of this "old order," Anderson goes on, "setting it off completely from the existence of the rich after the Second World War," was "the normalcy of servants."¹⁵ This suggestion that a peculiar blend of apocalypse could be expressed only within the old edifice of class—another version of Schlegel's distinction between ancient and modern—can easily be illustrated from the modernist canon. Intensity of catastrophe, as in the Master-Slave dialectics of Beckett's *Endgame;* symmetry of reversal, as in *Lady Chatterley's Lover,* where Connie and her husband both, like Munby and the author of *My Secret Life,* go to servants for what they are lacking. Both works offer a luxurious sense of the good old days when it was possible to condense the imaginative negation of society into encounters between upstairs and downstairs.

By bringing out both the importance of social residues to modernism and the modernity of what seems so dumbly residual, Anderson conveniently offers a summary of my argument. But there are still reasons for resisting his strict line of demarcation. In an insidiously negative form of Schlegel's complacency, the postmodern present can be seen as having passed beyond the crudity of class confrontation on the private staircase. Yet our own confrontations are of course the hardest to recognize as such. Even supposing class to have become less visible in the home than in the days of domestic service, the old conventions still have contemporary material to feed on. In the so-called "two career" couple, or more generally for wage-earning mothers without the support of the family or the state, there is a new dependence on paid female help in the care of children. It is hard to predict the literary effects of the recent *au pair* phenomenon, especially when it is doubled, as it so often is, with a juxtaposition of First and Third Worlds. Both of these contexts bring back the servant as visible figure for much larger confrontations. Both majorities have been speaking for themselves, and what they have said has often echoed the claims to unrealized community discussed above. In the light of the stubborn centrality of peasant rebellion to global politics and of the chastened political goals of avoiding ecological or nuclear extinction, it may even be necessary to ask whether a moral resistance like the one I have associated with servants' nostalgic and utopian visions has become a more active agent today than more grandiose historical dialectics.

It is no surprise, then, that the political renovation of utopian discourse has both fallen largely to women writers and at its most successful, as in Ursula LeGuin's *The Left Hand of Darkness* and Marge Piercy's *Woman on the Edge of Time,* has brought gender together with an anthropological consciousness of global or North/South irresolution. That the servant can still combine the novel's privacy with that negative, global figuration of society that I have been calling utopianism is proved by another remarkable work in the same line, Nadine Gordimer's *July's People* (1981).[16] The time is the future; war between black and white has broken out in South Africa; a progressive white couple finds itself in hiding in the tribal village, in the mud hut, of their loyal servant, now their host. Once again, the novel's first words are spoken by a servant:

You like to have some cup of tea?—
  July bent at the doorway and began that day for them as his kind has always done for their kind.

Everything has changed, and nothing has changed. As July begins that day for them, the power over the masters that had always been waiting in the language that describes servants is still there. All that has happened is that the micro-reversal has issued in the macro-reversal this language had always promised. July's masters have now become "July's people," dependent on him for their survival. Yet this is not the end of history. New conflicts and new negotiations follow; they all move together into an unimaginable future. And these negotiations renew the value of the old, conventional confusions. "The present was his" (p. 96), Maureen knows, but she also knows the rich confusion of times and tenses that underlies his "sub-standard" English. "—I'm getting worried.—She knew his use of tenses. He meant 'am worried.'" (p. 95) Will the future be like the present, or like the past? Confusion of time is also confusion of "place," another traditional master-servant term that finds itself renovated here. Maureen wants to gain her own and her family's independence by working alongside the other women; July tells her "You don't need work for them in their place." "He might mean 'place' in the sense of role, or might be implying she must remember she had no claim to the earth—'place' as territory" (p. 97). Gender and race, like class, cannot claim secure possession of a place in the dialectic of history; no one can say where the general displacement will lead. Even the language of the servant remains enigmatic, for even as it points into the future, it responds to the secret pressure of years of orders. Gordimer sums up a great deal of what this book has been about when she defines "the servant's formula, attuned to catch the echo of the master's concern, to remove combat and conflict tactfully, fatalistically, in mission-classroom phrases, to the neutrality of divine will" (pp. 94–95). "We can only hope," July tells his former mistress, "everything will come back all right.

—Back?—
   She saw he did not want to talk to her in any other way.
   —Back?—
   His closed lips widened downwards at each corner and his lids lowered as they did when she gave him, back there, an instruction he didn't like but wouldn't challenge. —I don't want to hear about killing. This one is killing or that one. No killing.—
   —But you don't mean the way it was, you don't mean that. Do you? You don't mean that.—

If the novel itself takes away the final question mark, showing how the language of the past leads irrevocably away from "the way it was,"

July himself does not answer, and we can see why. It is because of the instructions received "back there" that the servant is not prepared to make explicit whether the intent of his desire is to go "back" or to go forward. Here again is the ambiguity of the "secret pressure" of the servant's hand. There is no place outside the power of the masters and of their language where the truth of "the people" could be known in its purity, where the future would disengage itself from past burdens and make an unprecedented announcement. And this is why servant precedents remain so valuable.

Notes

INTRODUCTION: THE SECRET PRESSURE OF A WORKING HAND

1. Derek Hudson, *Munby: Man of Two Worlds: The Life and Diaries of Arthur J. Munby 1828–1910*, pp. 83–84. Further page references are given in the text.

2. Orwell, "Charles Dickens," *The Decline of the English Murder and Other Essays*, pp. 81–82, 100.

3. Frank Lentricchia, *Criticism and Social Change*. Page references are given in the text.

4. Georg Lukács, *The Historical Novel*, p. 94.

5. Michel Foucault, *The Order of Things: An Archaeology of the Human Sciences*, p. 209.

6. Raymond Williams, *Keywords: A Vocabulary of Culture and Society*.

7. Edward Said, *Orientalism*, p. 21.

8. Said, p. 21.

9. Karl Marx, *Capital*, 1:574–575.

10. Louis Althusser, *Lenin and Philosophy and Other Essays*, pp. 116–117.

11. Stuart Hall, "Notes on Deconstructing 'the Popular," pp. 238–239.

12. Theresa McBride, *The Domestic Revolution: The Modernization of Household Service in England and France 1820–1920*, p. 11.

13. Daniel Defoe, "Everybody's Business Is Nobody's Business," *The Novels and Miscellaneous Works*, 19:13. See also the Appendix to *Religious Courtship* (vol. 14) and *The Family Instructor* (vols. 15–16).

14. Maximillian E. Novak, *Economics and the Fiction of Daniel Defoe*, p. 85. Novak notes that Defoe may also be the author of pamphlets defending servants.

15. Malvin R. Zirker, *Fielding's Social Pamphlets*, p. 30.

16. Henry Fielding, *The True Patriot: And a History of Our Own Times*, p. 225.

17. Sigmund Freud, *Jokes and Their Relation to the Unconscious*, pp. 42–45.

18. Orwell, "Charles Dickins," p. 115.

19. Wilkie Collins, "Laid Up in Lodgings," *My Miscellanies, Works*, vol. 20.

20. Cited in Robert Escarpit, *Rudyard Kipling: Servitudes et grandeurs imperiales*, p. 91.

21. Elizabeth Gaskell, *Mary Barton*, ch. 3. Since I will be quoting a large number of novels that are available in many editions, further references will be by book and chapter and will be given in the text unless otherwise specified.

22. E. J. Hobsbawm, *Industry and Empire*, p. 85.

23. Marx, pp. 576–577, and Harry Braverman, *Labor and Monopoly Capital: The Degradation of Work in the Twentieth Century*, p. 411.

24. Thorstein Veblen, *The Theory of the Leisure Class,* pp. 62–63.

25. Veblen, pp. 65–66.

26. William Hazlitt, "Footmen," *The English Comic Writers and Miscellaneous Essays,* pp. 288–289.

27. Hazlitt, "Why the Heroes of Romance Are Insipid," *The English Comic Writers,* p. 223.

28. Hazlitt, "Footmen," p. 289.

29. Antonio Gramsci, *Selections from the Prison Notebooks,* p. 59. See also Raymond Williams, *Marxism and Literature,* pp. 108–114.

30. Said, *Orientalism,* pp. 28, 12, 94–95.

31. Eugene Genovese, *Roll, Jordan, Roll: The World the Slaves Made,* p. 7.

32. Steven Marcus, *The Other Victorians: A Study of Sexuality and Pornography in Mid-Nineteenth Century England,* "Introduction: 1974," p. xiii.

33. Thomas Carlyle, *Sartor Resartus,* vol. 2, ch. 9. In G. B. Tennyson, ed., *A Carlyle Reader.*

34. Charles Dickens, *Hard Times,* bk. 1, ch. 12.

35. E. P. Thompson, *The Making of the English Working Class,* p. 99.

36. John Ruskin, *Fors Clavigera,* "Charitas," Letter 7 in John D. Rosenberg, ed., *The Genius of John Ruskin,* p. 377.

37. William Morris, "Useful Work versus Useless Toil," p. 86.

38. Karl Löwith, *From Hegel to Nietzsche: The Revolution in Nineteenth Century Thought,* p. 285.

I. FROM ODYSSEUS' SCAR TO THE BROWN STOCKING: A TRADITION

1. Erich Auerbach, *Mimesis: The Representation of Reality in Western Literature,* p. 3. Further page references will be given in the text.

2. On the real as the random in connection with Auerbach's exile, see David Carroll, "*Mimesis* Reconsidered: Literature, History, Ideology," pp. 5–12. See also Edward W. Said, *The World, the Text, and the Critic,* pp. 5–9.

3. See Carroll, pp. 8–9.

4. Georg Autenrieth, *A Homeric Dictionary.*

5. Borivoj Borecky, *Survivals of Some Tribal Ideas in Classical Greek,* pp. 10–12.

6. George Thomson, *Aeschylus and Athens,* pp. 35–51, 147–148. Gregory Vlastos discusses *Ananke* in "Slavery in Plato's Thought," in M. I. Finley, ed., *Slavery in Classical Antiquity: Views and Controversies,* On *moira* see also William Chase Greene, *Moira: Fate, Good, and Evil in Greek Thought,* and on tribal democracy see Elman Service, *Origins of the State and Civilization: The Progress of Cultural Evolution.*

7. M. M. Austin and P. Vidal-Nacquet, *Economic and Social History of Ancient Greece: An Introduction,* p. 38.

8. Gregory Nagy, *The Best of the Achaeans: Concepts of the Hero in Archaic Greek Poetry,* pp. 127–134, 215–219, 314.

9. W. B. Stanford, "The Untypical Hero," p. 125.

10. *The Odyssey of Homer,* Richmond Lattimore, tr., 14:412–417. Further line references will be given in the text.

11. Vladimir Propp, *The Morphology of the Folktale,* pp. 60, 39; Fredric Jameson, *The Prison-House of Language,* p. 67. On folktales see also Dieter Richter and Johannes Merkel, *Märchen, Phantasie, und Soziales Lernen,* and August Nitschke, *Soziale Ordnungen im Spiegel der Märchen.*

12. Michael N. Nagler, *Spontaneity and Tradition: A Study in the Oral Art of Homer,* pp. 104–109.

13. M. I. Finley, *The World of Odysseus,* p. 106.

14. M. I. Finley, *Land, Debt, and the Man of Property in Classical Athens,* p. 249–250; Austin and Vidal-Nacquet, p. 212.

15. Finley, "Was Greek Civilization Based on Slave Labor?" ed. in Finley, *Slavery in Classical Antiquity,* p. 63.

16. Louis Gernet, *Anthropologie de la Grèce antique,* pp. 366–368.

17. Ernst Bloch, *A Philosophy of the Future,* p. 94.

18. Mikhail Bakhtin, *The Dialogic Imagination: Four Essays,* p. 147.

19. Said, *The World, The Text, and the Critic,* p. 113.

20. Elliot Krieger, *A Marxist Study of Shakespeare's Comedies.*

21. Paul Stigant and Peter Widdowson, "*Barnaby Rudge*—A Historical Novel?" p. 38.

22. Fielding, *Covent-Garden Journal,* 2:103–104. Quoted in J.-Jean Hecht, *The Domestic Servant in Eighteenth-Century England,* p. 83. See also Hecht, pp. 92–94.

23. Jean Emelina, *Les Valets et les servantes dans le théâtre comique en France de 1610 à 1700,* p. 187; Charles Mauron, *Psychocritique du genre comique,* pp. 84–88. See also Bernard Knox, *Word and Action: Essays in the Ancient Theater,* p. 361.

24. Victor Bourgy, *Le Bouffon sur la scène anglaise au XVIe siècle,* p. 87; George E. Duckworth, *The Nature of Roman Comedy,* pp. 174–175.

25. Duckworth, p. 251.

26. Bourgy, pp. 168, 170.

27. K. M. Lea, *Italian Popular Comedy: A Study in the Commedia dell'Arte,* 1:63–64, and 2:398–399.

28. Claudio Guillén, *Literature as System: Essays Toward the Theory of Literary History,* pp. 81–82, 93.

29. Richard Bjornson, *The Picaresque Hero in European Fiction,* pp. 36–37.

30. Empson, *Some Versions of Pastoral,* pp. 214–215.

31. Bourgy, *Le Bouffon sur la scène anglaise,* p. 95.

32. Empson, pp. 27–86.

33. Leo Spitzer, "Linguistic Perspectivism in *Don Quijote,*" *Linguistics and Literary History,* pp. 41–87.

34. Robert Alter, *Rogue's Progress;* Milan Kundera, "The Story of a Variation."

35. John W. Draper, "Shakespeare's Rustic Servants." *Stratford to Dogberry: Studies in Shakespeare's Earlier Plays.*

36. N. N. Feltes, "'The Greatest Plague of Life': Dickens, Masters, and Servants."

37. Feltes, p. 209.

38. Harry Levin, *The Gates of Horn: A Study of Five French Realists,* pp. 38, 36.

39. Coleridge is quoted in Claude Rawson, ed., *Henry Fielding: A Critical Anthology,* p. 205.

40. E. J. Hobsbawm, *Industry and Empire*, p. 85.

41. E. P. Thompson, *The Poverty of Theory and Other Essays*, p. 44.

42. McBride, *The Domestic Revolution*, p. 30.

43. Joan W. Scott and Louise Tilly, "Women's Work and the Family in Nineteenth-Century Europe." On the massively rural origins of domestic servants, see also Jean-Pierre Gutton, *Domestiques et serviteurs dans la France de l'ancien régime*, pp. 78–81, and John R. Gillis, "Servants, Sexual Relations and the Risks of Illegitimacy in London, 1801–1900," p. 118.

44. Raymond Williams, *The Country and the City*, pp. 20–21. Further page references will be given in the text.

45. E. P. Thompson, "The Moral Economy of the English Crowd in the Eighteenth Century."

46. Bakhtin, *The Dialogic Imagination*, p. 235.

47. Charles Dickens, *Our Mutual Friend*, bk. 1, ch. v.

48. For this term and its pertinence to "backward" social types, see Ernst Bloch, "Nonsynchronism and the Obligation to its Dialectics"—an extract from *Erbschaft dieser Zeit*, which remains untranslated—in *New German Critique*.

49. Virginia Woolf, *The Captain's Deathbed and Other Essays*, p. 96.

50. Woolf, *The Years*, p. 204. On Woolf and the "servant problem," see Jane Marcus, "Liberty, Sorority, Misogyny," pp. 74–75.

51. Note that of the four "novels of the 1840s" discussed by Kathleen Tillotson in her classic treatment of the epoch of Chartism—*Dombey and Son, Mary Barton, Vanity Fair,* and *Jane Eyre*—three of the four have more to do with servants than with proletarians, and if *North and South* were substituted for *Mary Barton,* it might be a clean sweep.

52. Auguste Villiers de l'Isle-Adam, *Axel.*

53. In Rawson, *Henry Fielding*, p. 259.

54. W. M. Thackeray, "On a Peal of Bells," in *Denis Duval, etc., Works,* 12:384.

55. E. M. Forster, *Aspects of the Novel*, pp. 37, 85.

56. Woolf, *The Years*, p. 159.

2. IMPERTINENCE: THE SERVANT IN DIALOGUE

1. Robert Weimann, *Shakespeare and the Popular Tradition in the Theater*, p. 73.

2. Weimann, pp. 30, 152, passim.

3. Plautus, *Amphitryo, The Rope and Other Plays*, p. 270.

4. Terence, *The Eunuch, The Comedies*, p. 169.

5. Emelina, *Les Valets et les servantes*, p. 107.

6. Cited in Spitzer, "Linguistic Perspectivism in *Don Quijote,*" p. 70.

7. Henry Fielding, *The Grub-Street Opera, Works,* vol. 9, act 2, scene 4.

8. Christopher Marlowe, *Doctor Faustus,* 1:4.

9. Robert Greene, *The Honorable History of Friar Bacon and Friar Bungay*, p. xi.

10. Henry Fielding, *The Intriguing Chambermaid, Works,* vol. 9, act 1, scene 4.

11. Daniel Defoe, *Religious Courtship*, p. 276.

12. Daniel Defoe, *Robinson Crusoe*, p. 220.

13. *Robinson Crusoe*, p. 231.

14. Elizabeth Gaskell, *The Life of Charlotte Brontë*, p. 110.

15. Georg Lukács, *Studies in European Realism*, p. 180; *The Historical Novel*, p. 40.

16. Roger D. Abrahams and Barbara A. Babcock, "The Literary Use of Proverbs," pp. 416–417.

17. In Thomas Pinney, ed., *The Essays of George Eliot*. For more discussion of this essay, see my "The Butler Did It: On Agency in the Novel," *Representations* (Spring 1984), 6:85–97.

18. George Lukács, "*Minna Von Barnhelm*," *Werke*, 7:35–37.

19. Max Beerbohm, "Servants," *And Even Now*, p. 100; *Punch* (1850), 18:93; Charles Booth, *Life and Labour of the People of London*, 4:224–225; Roger Brown and Albert Gilman, "The Pronouns of Power and Solidarity," pp. 266, 260.

20. Mary D. Smith, "Downstairs from the Upstairs: A Study of Servants' Hall in the Victorian Novel."

21. Cited in Joanne Altieri, "Style and Purpose in Maria Edgeworth's Fiction," p. 275.

22. Levin, *The Gates of Horn*, pp. 38, 36.

23. Levin, p. 37.

24. Richard Faber, *Proper Stations: Class in Victorian Fiction*, p. 101.

25. Tobias Smollett, *The Expedition of Humphry Clinker*, p. 329.

26. P. J. Keating, *The Working Classes in Victorian Fiction*, p. 254.

27. *Robinson Crusoe*, p. 226.

28. It is of course pertinent that many of these are not from novels. The earlier journalistic pieces using a servant narrator seem free to take more liberties than is usually convenient in novelistic dialogue. Aside from those already indicated, the sources are: *The Memoirs of Mr. Charles J. Yellowplush* (*Works*, vol. 3) for "to the halter" (p. 246), "too retched" (p. 242), "our youthful Quean" and "authography" (p. 338), "honrabble" (p. 367), "raining sufferin" (p. 290), "unusyouall" (p. 283); *Vanity Fair* for "bittiful" (ch. 39); *Contributions to Punch* (*Works*, vol. 6) for "first flor" (p. 175).

29. Burns, *Theatricality*, p. 63.

30. Everett Knight, *A Theory of the Classical Novel*, pp. 126–127.

31. Basil Bernstein, "Social Class, Language, and Socialization," *Context*, p. 168.

3. EXPOSITION: THE SERVANT AS NARRATOR

1. Henry James, *The Turn of the Screw*, Robert Kimbrough, ed., p. 121.

2. Wayne Booth, *The Rhetoric of Fiction*, p. 18.

3. Levin, *The Gates of Horn*, p. 37.

4. McBride, *The Domestic Revolution*, pp. 74–75.

5. Alter, *Rogue's Progress*, pp. 24–26.

6. Roger Laufer, *Lesage ou le métier de romancier*, p. 8.

7. Levin, *The Gates of Horn*, p. 36.

8. Watt, *The Rise of the Novel*, p. 209.

9. Paul Hernadi, *Beyond Genre: New Directions in Literary Classification*, p. 159.

10. Hernadi, p. 76.

11. Elizabeth Burns, *Theatricality,* pp. 64–65.

12. Burns, p. 64; Frank Kermode, *The Sense of an Ending.*

13. Alain René Lesage, *Turcaret,* vol. 2.

14. Burns, pp. 42–43, 52.

15. Roland Barthes, *On Racine,* pp. 53–55.

16. Michael Booth, *English Melodrama,* pp. 52, 62–64.

17. Peter Brooks, *The Melodramatic Imagination: Balzac, Henry James, Melodrama, and the Mode of Excess,* pp. 170–171.

18. M. Booth, *English Melodrama,* pp. 33–35.

19. Bernard Sharratt, "The Politics of the Popular—From Melodrama to Television," p. 282.

20. Martin Tropp, *Mary Shelley's Monster,* pp. 87–91.

21. Knox, *Word and Action,* pp. 205, 220, 217–218.

22. See Eric Solomon, "The Return of the Screw," reprinted in James, *The Turn of the Screw,* Kimbrough, ed.; Thomas M. Cranfill and Robert R. Clark, Jr., "Caste in James' *The Turn of the Screw,"* John A. Clair, *The Ironic Dimension in the Fiction of Henry James,* pp. 37–58.

23. The extreme case is James Hafley, "The Villain in *Wuthering Heights."* More recently Nelly has been accused in David Musselwhite, "Wuthering Heights: The Unacceptable Text."

24. Ellen Moers, *Literary Women,* p. 115.

25. William Godwin, *The Adventures of Caleb Williams, or Things As They Are,* George Sherburn, ed., p. 8. For the garden scene, see Alex Gold, Jr., "It's Only Love: The Politics of Passion in Godwin's *Caleb Williams."*

26. *The Rambler,* No. 68.

27. Robert Kiely, *The Romantic Novel in England,* p. 91.

28. For example, Sherburn writes in his introduction: "He was ingenuous and innocent until he tried to justify himself at useless cost. His final project of doing 'justice' was conceived in self-love" (p. xii).

29. Maria Edgeworth, *Castle Rackrent,* p. 1.

30. Ernest A. Baker, *The History of the English Novel,* 6:31.

31. James Newcomer, *Maria Edgeworth the Novelist,* esp. ch. 9, "The Disingenuous Thady Quirk"; Duane Edwards, "The Narrator of *Castle Rackrent."*

32. Walter Allen, *The English Novel,* p. 109.

33. Newcomer, p. 151.

34. Kiely, *The Romantic Novel in England,* pp. 36–37.

35. Samuel Richardson, *Pamela,* p. 285.

36. Ian Ousby, *Bloodhounds of Heaven: The Detective in English Fiction from Godwin to Doyle,* pp. 19–42.

37. Ian Watt, *The Rise of the Novel,* pp. 46–47; see also Gutton, *Domestiques et serviteurs,* pp. 180–182.

38. T. C. Duncan Eaves and Ben D. Kempel, *Samuel Richardson: A Biography,* pp. 9–11.

39. E. S. Turner, *What the Butler Saw: 250 Years of the Servant Problem,* p. 42.

40. Henry Fielding, *Covent-Garden Journal,* Gerard Edward Jensen, ed. New Haven: Yale University Press, 1915 1:293–298 (No. 27, April 4, 1752).

41. Richard Altick, *The English Common Reader: A Social History of the Mass Reading Public 1800–1900,* pp. 63–64.

42. H. J. Dyos and Michael Wolff, eds., *The Victorian City,* 2:570.

43. Watt, *The Rise of the Novel,* p. 154; Darko Suvin, "The Social Addressees of Victorian Fiction: A Preliminary Inquiry," pp. 29–30.

44. Charlotte Brontë, *Jane Eyre,* Q. D. Leavis, ed., p. 485.

45. Jonathan Swift, *Gulliver's Travels,* 1:vi.

46. Quoted in Leonore Davidoff, "Above and Below Stairs."

47. Elizabeth Gaskell, *The Life of Charlotte Brontë,* pp. 80, 110–111; E. P. Thompson, *The Making of the English Working Class,* p. 496.

48. See Christopher Hibbert, *The Making of Charles Dickens,* pp. 16–19.

49. John Carey, *Thackeray: Prodigal Genius,* p. 12.

50. Cited in Turner, *What the Butler Saw,* p. 218.

51. Virginia Woolf, *The Years,* p. 171.

52. Thackeray, "On a Chalk Mark on the Door," *Roundabout Papers,* p. 283.

53. Thackeray, *Pendennis,* ch. 36.

54. Mikhail Bakhtin, *The Dialogical Imagination,* pp. 124–125.

55. Miranda Chaytor, "Household and Kinship: Ryton in the Late Sixteenth and Early Seventeenth Centuries," 10:48–49.

56. J. Jean Hecht, *The Domestic Servant in Eighteenth-Century England,* p. 208.

57. Ousby, *Bloodhounds of Heaven,* pp. 32, 36.

58. Hecht, p. 207.

59. Ousby, p. 181n.

60. Jean-Louis Flandrin, *Familles: parenté, maison, sexualité dans l'ancienne societé,* pp. 138–144; see also Gutton, p. 63.

61. Pamela Horn, *The Rise and Fall of the Victorian Servant,* pp. 45–46.

62. Quoted in Anne Summers, "A Home from Home—Women's Philanthropic Work in the 19th Century," pp. 39–40.

63. Michel Foucault, *Discipline and Punish: The Birth of the Prison,* p. 137.

64. Flandrin, *Familles,* pp. 142, 138.

65. Summers, pp. 40–41.

66. Lawrence Stone, *The Family, Sex, and Marriage in England 1500–1800,* pp., 28,

67. Along with Williams, *Keywords,* see Flandrin, pp. 11–14, and E. Anthony Wrigley, "Reflections on the History of the Family," p. 72.

68. Sylvan Barnet et. al., *A Dictionary of Literary Terms,* p. 69.

69. Bakhtin, *The Dialogic Imagination,* p. 224.

70. Thackeray, *The English Humorists,* (Dent: London, 1912) p. 316.

71. Thackeray, "Fashnable Fax and Polite Annygoats," *Works,* 13:260.

72. *Pendennis,* p. 386.

73. *Vanity Fair,* pp. 522–523.

74. *Pendennis,* p. 386.

75. Booth, *The Rhetoric of Fiction,* p. 152.

76. Scott, *Rob Roy,* p. 365.

77. Leonore Davidoff, "Mastered for Life: Servant and Wife in Victorian and Edwardian England," p. 413.

78. A. O. J. Cockshut, *Truth to Life: The Art of Biography in the Nineteenth Century*, p. 45.

79. *Little Dorrit*, p. 774.

80. Charles Collins, "The Compensation House," pp. 39–40.

81. Walter Scott, *Old Mortality*, pp. 194, 246, 317.

82. Alexander Welsh, *The City of Dickens*, pp. 183–184.

83. Welsh, p. 183.

84. Welsh, chs. 11–13; Cockshut, ch. 3.

85. Scott, *Old Mortality*, p. 167.

86. Roger D. Abrahams and Barbara A. Babcock, "The Literary Use of Proverbs," p. 415.

87. J. Sheridan Le Fanu, "Sir Dominick's Bargain," pp. 117–118.

88. Walter Benjamin, *Illuminations*, p. 93; *Reflections*, p. 90.

89. Carey, *Thackeray*, p. 129.

90. *The Newcomes*, 1:92.

91. Benjamin, *Illuminations*, p. 56.

4. AGENCY: THE SERVANT AS INSTRUMENT OF THE PLOT

1. Rolf Franzbecker, *Die Weibliche Bedienstete in der französischen Komödie des 16. bis 18. Jahrhunderts*, pp. 198–200.

2. Northrop Frye, *Anatomy of Criticism*, p. 173; Fredric Jameson, *The Political Unconscious*, pp. 136–137.

3. C. W. Amarasinghe, "The Part of the Slave in Terence's Drama, p. 62.

4. Richard Levin, *The Multiple Plot in English Renaissance Drama*," p. 110.

5. Laurence Sterne, *Tristram Shandy*, bk. 4, ch. 14; bk. 5, ch. 17; bk. 9, ch. 32. "It is not actions, but opinions concerning actions, which disturb men," the epigraph says. However, Trim's management of Shandy affairs is only one explosive reading away in literary history from the pre-hegemonic authority of Diderot's Jacques le Fataliste, and a line of direct influence passes from him to Hegel's dialectic of Master and Slave.

6. Thackeray, *Works*, vol. 6. Chapter references are given in the text. Thackeray also expressed other views about the valet's perspective. See for example "Carlyle's *French Revolution*" in *Works*, 13:240 and Robert Kiely, "Victorian Harlequin: The Function of Humor in Thackeray's Critical and Miscellaneous Prose," p. 159.

7. Lukács, *Historical Novel*, p. 47.

8. Avrom Fleischman, *The English Historical Novel: Walter Scott to Virginia Woolf*, p. 148.

9. Lukács, *Historical Novel*, p. 142.

10. Geoffrey Tillotson, *Thackeray the Novelist*, p. 188.

11. Thackeray, "Cox's Diary," *Works*, 3:234.

12. Warner Berthoff, ed., *Great Short Works of Herman Melville*, p. 238n.

13. *Benito Cereno* in Berthoff, ed., pp. 280–284.

14. E. J. Hobsbawm, *The Age of Capital,* p. 275.

15. Aubrey Beardsley, "The Ballad of a Barber," pp. 195–197.

16. Albert Memmi, *Dominated Man,* ch. 13; Lucien Goldmann, "Le Théâtre de Genêt—Essai d'étude sociologique,"pp. 275–276.

17. Barbara Hardy, *The Exposure of Luxury: Radical Themes in Thackeray,* p. 43.

18. Hardy, p. 41.

19. John A. Lester, Jr., "Thackeray's Narrative Technique," p. 73.

20. Wolfgang Kayser, *The Grotesque in Art and Literature,* pp. 184, 188.

21. Kayser, pp. 91, 183.

22. For the infection motif in *Bleak House,* see Jonathan Arac, *Commissioned Spirits: The Shaping of Social Motion in Dickens, Carlyle, Melville, and Hawthorne,* ch. 6.

23. Henry and Augustus Mayhew, *The Greatest Plague of Life: Or, The Adventures of a Lady in Search of a Good Servant.*

24. J. Hillis Miller, *The Form of Victorian Fiction,* pp. 97–104.

25. *Humphry Clinker,* letters of June 3, October 4, April 23, April 28, June 8.

26. Angus Fletcher, *Allegory: The Theory of a Symbolic Mode,* pp. 182, 183, 186.

27. Fletcher, p. 196.

28. Fletcher, p. 201n.

29. Daniel Defoe, *A Journal of the Plague Year,* pp. 73–74.

30. *Plague Year,* p. 74.

31. *Plague Year,* p. 51.

32. *Plague Year,* p. 169.

33. Foucault, *Discipline and Punish,* pp. 195, 197.

34. Peter Laslett, *Family Life and Illicit Love in Earlier Generations,* pp. 61, 13–15, 34–35.

35. Claude Lévi-Strauss, *Structural Anthropology,* p. 50.

36. See "Hagar" entry in James Hastings, ed., *A Dictionary of the Bible.*

37. Hill and Powell, eds., *Boswell's Life of Johnson,* 2:55–56.

38. Hecht, *The Domestic Servant,* p. 24.

39. Jonathan Gathorne-Hardy, *The Rise and Fall of the British Nanny,* p. 34.

40. Stone, *The Family, Sex, and Marriage in England,* p. 27. Stone's critique does not affect Laslett's assertions about the crucial place of servants in the household; Stone distinguishes "family" from "household" and restricts his discussion to the former.

41. Daniel Defoe, *Roxana, Or, The Fortunate Mistress,* p. 276.

42. Alick West, *Crisis and Criticism and Literary Essays,* p. 226.

43. *Roxana,* p. 312.

44. Ph.-E. Legrand, *The New Greek Comedy;* Mauron, *Psychocritique du genre comique,* p. 98; Ronald Paulson, *Satire and the Novel in the Eighteenth Century,* p. 167; Steven Marcus, *Dickens: From Pickwick to Dombey,* pp. 121–122.

45. John G. Cawelti, *Adventure, Mystery, Romance,* p. 90.

46. For murder as convention, see Levin, *Gates of Horn,* p. 17, and Frye, *Anatomy,* pp. 47–48.

47. Lawrence Frank, "'Through a Glass Darkly': Esther Summerson and *Bleak House,*" p. 98.

48. On this point see also D. A. Miller, "Discipline in Different Voices: Bureaucracy, Police, Family, and *Bleak House.*"

49. Richard Hoggart, *Speaking To Each Other,* vol. 2, *About Literature,* pp. 142–143.

50. Rudyard Kipling, "Watches of the Night," *Plain Tales from the Hills* (Leipzig: Tauschnitz, 1890), pp. 90–91.

51. Raymond Williams, *The Long Revolution,* pp. 104–106.

52. Quoted in Martin Meisel, *Shaw and the Nineteenth-Century Theater,* pp. 69–79.

53. Forster, *Abinger Harvest,* pp. 273–275.

54. Malcolm Bradbury, "Two Passages to India: Forster as Victorian and Modern," p. 237.

5. RECOGNITION: THE SERVANT IN THE ENDING

1. Robert F. Storey, *Pierrot: A Critical History of a Mask,* p. 13.

2. Lukács, *Historical Novel,* pp. 120–121.

3. Bernard Knox, "Sophocles' Oedipus," p. 13; G. H. Gellie, *Sophocles: A Reading,* pp. 96–97; George Thomson, *Aeschylus and Athens,* pp. 168–169. Quotations are from the literal translation of the play by Philip Vellacott, *Sophocles and Oedipus.*

4. Knox calls this the only exception in the play to the organic plotting in which "what follows is the necessary or probable result of the preceeding action." *Oedipus at Thebes,* p. 13.

5. Voltaire, *Oeuvres complètes,* 2:20; T. von Wilamowitz—Moellendorff, *Die Dramatische Technik des Sophokles,* p. 79.

6. Jonathan Culler, *The Pursuit of Signs,* pp. 173–174. See also Sandor Goodheart, "Ληστὰς Εφασκε: Oedipus and Laius' Many Murderers."

7. Brian Vickers, *Towards Greek Tragedy: Drama, Myth, Society,* p. 511.

8. Knox, "Sophocles' Oedipus," pp. 15–20.

9. On the political implications of "the many," see Padraic M. O'Cleirigh, "Political Anachronism in the Pattern of Power in Sophoclean Drama," pp. 116–118.

10. George Thomson, *Aeschylus and Athens,* p. 341.

11. Stith Thompson, *The Folktale,* p. 112; Otto Rank, *The Myth of the Birth of the Hero and Other Writings.*

12. Rank, p. 71.

13. Vellacott, *Sophocles and Oedipus,* p. 233.

14. Knox, *Oedipus at Thebes,* pp. 78, 102.

15. Charles Segal, *Tragedy and Civilization: An Interpretation of Sophocles,* p. 5.

16. Marcel Détienne, "Between Beasts and Gods," pp. 223–224.

17. Segal, p. 221.

18. Vickers, *Towards Greek Tragedy,* p. 61.

19. On the plague as the Peloponnesian War, see Knox, *Word and Action,* pp. 112–124.

20. Knox, *Oedipus at Thebes,* p. 166.

21. Knox, *Oedipus at Thebes,* p. 166, and J.-P. Vernant, "Oedipe sans complexe," pp. 79–80.

22. George Thomson, *The First Philosophers,* pp. 232–235.

23. Robert Torrance, *The Comic Hero,* p. 196.

24. R. S. Crane, "The Concept of Plot and the Plot of Tom Jones," p. 74.

25. Martin Price, "Fielding: The Comedy of Forms," p. 414. In "*Tom Jones*: The 'Bastard' of History," Homer Obed Brown suggests that the "contemporary invasion of accident" had to do with "landownership and inheritance" (p. 226).

26. Raymond Williams, *Keywords,* p. 45.

27. Keith Thomas, *Religion and the Decline of Magic: Studies in Popular Beliefs in Sixteenth and Seventeenth Century England,* pp. 563, 555.

28. Thomas, pp. 597–600.

29. Stuart, *The English Abigail,* p. 202.

30. Arac, *Commissioned Spirits,* pp. 10, 126–127.

31. Quoted in Richard Dorson, *Peasant Customs,* 1:28.

32. Hecht, *The Domestic Servant,* pp. 158–162.

33. See "Jeeves Takes Charge" and "Aunt Agatha Takes the Count," in P. G. Wodehouse, *The World of Jeeves,* pp. 18, 66.

34. John Ruskin, "The Two Servants," *Fiction Fair and Foul,* 34:385.

35. Francis R. Hart, "Scott's Endings: The Fictions of Authority," p. 58.

36. Pat Rogers, ed., *Defoe: The Critical Heritage,* p. 80.

37. Ruskin, "The Two Servants," p. 386.

38. Walter Scott, *Old Mortality.*

39. Nina Auerbach, *Communities of Women,* p. 88.

40. Elizabeth Gaskell, *Cranford and Cousin Phillis,* p. 218.

41. Ivan Goncharov, *Oblomov.*

42. Jim Swan, "*Mater* and Nannie: Freud's Two Mothers and the Discovery of the Oedipus Complex," pp. 16–17; see also Kenneth A. Grigg, " 'All Roads Lead to Rome': The Role of the Nursemaid in Freud's Dreams."

43. Sigmund Freud and Josef Breuer, *Studies on Hysteria,* 2:279.

44. Friedrich Engels, *The Origin of the Family, Private Property, and the State,* pp. 72–73. On Marx's relations with Helene Demuth and his illegitimate son, Freddy Demuth, see Yvonne Kapp, *Eleanor Marx,* especially the appendix to vol. 1, pp. 289–297. Marx played chess with Helene Demuth and said she "could have managed the universe" (2:430). When she died in 1890 she was buried in a common grave with Marx and his wife. An unsigned obituary in the *People's Press* called her "An Old Friend of Labour."

45. McBride, *The Domestic Revolution,* p. 102.

46. George Rosen, "Disease, Debility, and Death," 2:657. The figure of one-third is Michael Ryan's, quoted in Françoise Basch, *Relative Creatures: Victorian Women in Society and the Novel 1837–1867,* p. 199.

47. Stone, *The Family, Sex, and Marriage,* p. 642.

48. Smith, "Downstairs from the Upstairs," pp. 49–50.

49. Marcus, *Other Victorians,* p. 168.

50. Anon., *My Secret Life,* pp. 69, 105.

51. Marcus, *Other Victorians,* p. 133.

52. Marcus, p. 27.

53. Frank Harris, _My Life and Loves,_ pp. 268, 548. Stephen Heath, _The Sexual Fix,_ pp. 14–23, argues that sex as expenditure was not exclusively Victorian, but intensifies in that period.

54. Norman Mailer, _An American Dream,_ pp. 43–49. See also Kate Millet, _Sexual Politics,_ pp. 12–21.

55. Michel Foucault, _La Volonté de savoir,_ pp. 87–88.

56. James, _The Turn of the Screw,_ Kimbrough, ed., pp. 121, 123. Further page numbers will be given in the text.

57. Kimbrough, ed., p. 178.

CONCLUSION: COMMONPLACE AND UTOPIA

1. P. W. Buckham, _The Theater of the Greeks;_ page numbers are given in the text. See also Fred C. Thomson, "The Genesis of _Felix Holt,_" and "_Felix Holt_ as Classical Tragedy."

2. Gordon S. Haight, _George Eliot: A Biography,_ p. 383.

3. Richard Jenkyns, _The Victorians and Ancient Greece,_ pp. 123–127.

4. Aeschylus, _Oresteia,_ Richmond Lattimore, tr., p. 120.

5. George Eliot, "The Influence of Rationalism: Lecky's History," in Pinney, _The Essays of George Eliot,_ p. 413. On "rural organicism" see Terry Eagleton, _Criticism and Ideology,_ pp. 110–125.

6. Pinney, p. 284. Further page references are given in the text.

7. Joseph Butwin, "The Pacification of the Crowd: From 'Janet's Repentance' to _Felix Holt,_" p. 374.

8. Catherine Gallagher, "The Failure of Realism: _Felix Holt,_" pp. 372–384.

9. Thompson, "Moral Economy," pp. 78–79. For an extension of this concept see James C. Scott, _The Moral Economy of the Peasant: Rebellion and Subsistence in Southeast Asia._

10. Austin and Vidal-Nacquet, _Economic and Social History of Ancient Greece,_ pp. 60–61.

11. Jenkyns, _The Victorians,_ p. 114.

12. Ernesto Laclau, _Politics and Ideology in Marxist Theory: Capitalism, Fascism, Populism,_ pp. 107–108, 165–167.

13. Northrop Frye, "Dickens and the Comedy of Humors," p. 61.

14. Stuart, _English Abigail,_ p. 17.

15. Perry Anderson, "Modernity and Revolution," pp. 105–106.

16. Nadine Gordimer, _July's People._

Bibliography

Abrahams, Roger D. and Barbara A. Babcock. "The Literary Use of Proverbs." *Journal of American Folklore* (October–December 1977), 90(358):414–429.

Aeschylus. *Oresteia*. Richmond Lattimore, tr. Chicago: University of Chicago Press, 1953.

Allen, Walter. *The English Novel*. New York: Dutton, 1954

Alter, Robert, *Rogue's Progress*. Cambridge: Harvard University Press, 1964.

Althusser, Louis. *Lenin and Philosophy and Other Essays*. Ben Brewster, tr. London: New Left Books, 1971.

Altick, Richard. *The English Common Reader: A Social History of the Mass Reading Public 1800–1900*. Chicago: University of Chicago Press, 1957.

Altieri, Joanne "Style and Purpose in Maria Edgeworth's Fiction," *Nineteenth-Century Fiction*. (December 1968), 23:3 pp. 265–278.

Amarasinghe, C. W. "The Part of the Slave in Terence's Drama." *Greece and Rome* (1950), 19:62–72.

Anderson, Perry. "Modernity and Revolution." *New Left Review* (March–April 1984), 144:96–113.

Arac, Jonathan. *Commissioned Spirits: The Shaping of Social Motion in Dickens, Carlyle, Melville, and Hawthorne*. New Brunswick: Rutgers University Press, 1979.

Auerbach, Erich. *Mimesis: The Representation of Reality in Western Literature*. Willard R. Trask, tr. Princeton: Princeton University Press, 1953.

Auerbach, Nina. *Communities of Women*. Cambridge: Harvard University Press, 1978.

Austen, Jane. *Pride and Prejudice*. A. Walton Litz, ed. New York: Modern Library, 1967.

Austin, M. M. and P. Vidal-Nacquet. *Economic and Social History of Ancient Greece: An Introduction*. Berkeley: University of California Press, 1977.

Autenrieth, Georg. *A Homeric Dictionary*. Robert P. Keep, tr.; Isaac Flag, rev. Norman: University of Oklahoma Press, 1958.

Bain, David. *Masters, Servants, and Orders in Greek Tragedy*. Manchester: Manchester University Press, 1981.

Baker, Ernest A. *The History of the English Novel*. New York: Barnes and Noble, 1929.

Bakhtin, Mikhail. *The Dialogic Imagination: Four Essays.* Michael Holquist, ed., Caryl Emerson and Michael Holquist, trs. Austin: University of Texas Press, 1981.

Barnet Sylvan et. al. *A Dictionary of Literary Terms.* Boston: Little Brown, 1960.

Barthes, Roland. *On Racine.* Richard Howard, tr. New York: Hill and Wang, 1964.

Basch, Françoise. *Relative Creatures: Victorian Women in Society and the Novel 1837–1867.* Anthony Rudolf, tr. London: Allen Lane, 1974.

Beardsley, Aubrey. "The Ballad of a Barber." Derek Stanford, ed., *Writing of the Nineties: From Wilde to Beerbohm.* London: Dent, 1971.

Beckett, Samuel. *Endgame.* New York: Grove Press, 1958.

Beerbohm, Max. "Servants." *And Even Now.* New York: Dutton, 1960.

Benjamin, Walter. *Illuminations.* Hannah Arendt, ed., Harry Zohn, tr. New York: Schocken, 1969.

Benjamin, Walter. *Reflections.* Peter Demetz, ed., Edmund Jephcott, tr. New York: Harcourt Brace, 1978.

Bernstein, Basil, "Social Class, Language, and Socialization." In P. P. Giglioli, ed., *Language and Social Context.* Harmondsworth: Penguin, 1972.

Berthoff, Warner, ed. *Great Short Works of Herman Melville.* New York: Harper, 1970.

Bjornson, Richard. *The Picaresque Hero in European Fiction.* Madison: University of Wisconsin Press, 1977.

Bloch, Ernest. "Nonsynchronism and the Obligation to its Dialectics," *New German Critique* (Spring 1977), 11:22–38.

Bloch, Ernst. *A Philosophy of the Future.* John Cumming, tr. New York: Herder and Herder, 1970.

Booth, Charles. *Life and Labour of the People of London.* Sec. Series: Industry. New York: AMS Press, 1970.

Booth, Michael. *English Melodrama.* London: Herbert Jenkins, 1965.

Booth, Wayne. *The Rhetoric of Fiction.* Chicago: University of Chicago Press, 1961.

Borecky, Borivoj. *Survivals of Some Tribal Ideas in Classical Greek.* Acta Universitatis Carolinae, Philosophica et Historica Monographica 10. Prague, 1965.

Boswell, James. *Boswell's Life of Johnson.* G. B. Hill and L. F. Powell, eds. Oxford: Oxford University Press, 1934–1950.

Bourgy, Victor. *Le Bouffon sur la scène anglaise au XVIe siècle.* Paris: O.C.D.L., 1969.

Bradbury, Malcolm. "Two Passages to India: Forster as Victorian and Modern." Malcolm Bradbury, ed., *E. M. Forster, A Passage to India: A Casebook.* London: Macmillan, 1970.

Braverman, Harry, *Labor and Monopoly Capital: The Degradation of Work in the Twentieth Century.* New York: Monthly Review Press, 1974.

Brontë, Charlotte. *Jane Eyre.* Q. D. Leavis, ed. Harmondsworth: Penguin, 1965.

Brontë, Emily. *Wuthering Heights.* David Daiches, ed. Harmondsworth: Penguin, 1965.

Brooks, Peter. *The Melodramatic Imagination: Balzac, Henry James, Melodrama, and the Mode of Excess.* New Haven: Yale University Press, 1976.

Brown, Homer Obed. "*Tom Jones:* The 'Bastard' of History" *Boundary 2* (Winter 1979), 7(3):201–233.

Brown, Roger and Albert Gilman. "The Pronouns of Power and Solidarity." Joshua A. Fishman, ed., *Readings in the Sociology of Language.* The Hague: Mouton, 1972.

Buckham, P. W. *The Theater of the Greeks.* 3d. ed. Cambridge: J. Smith, 1830.

Burns, Elizabeth. *Theatricality.* New York: Harper and Row, 1970.

Butler, Samuel. *The Way of All Fresh.* New York: Signet, 1960.

Butwin, Joseph. "The Pacification of the Crowd: From 'Janet's Repentance' to *Felix Holt.*" *Nineteenth-Century Fiction* (December 1980), 35(3):349–371.

Carey, John. *Thackeray: Prodigal Genius.* London: Faber and Faber, 1977.

Carlyle, Thomas. *A Carlyle Reader.* G. B. Tennyson, ed. New York: Modern Library, 1969.

Carroll, David. "*Mimesis* Reconsidered: Literature, History, Ideology," *Diacritics* (Summer 1975), pp. 5–12.

Cawelti, John G. *Adventure, Mystery, Romance.* Chicago: University of Chicago Press, 1976.

Chaytor, Miranda. "Household and Kinship: Ryton in the Late Sixteenth and Early Seventeenth Centuries." *History Workshop Journal* (Autumn 1980), 10:25–60.

Clair, John A. *The Ironic Dimension in the Fiction of Henry James.* Pittsburgh: Duquesne University Press, 1965.

Cockshut, A. O. J. *Truth to Life: The Art of Biography in the Nineteenth Century.* London: Collins, 1974.

Collins, Charles. "The Compensation House." In Michael Perry, ed., *Reign of Terror: The Second Corgi Book of Great Victorian Horror Stories.* London: Corgi, 1977.

Collins, Wilkie. "Laid Up in Lodgings." *My Miscellanies, Works,* vol. 20. New York: Collier, n.d.

Crane, R. S. "The Concept of Plot and the Plot of Tom Jones." R. S. Crane, ed., *Critics and Criticism.* Chicago: University of Chicago Press, 1957.

Cranfill, Thomas M. and Robert R. Clark, Jr. "Caste in James' *The Turn of the Screw.*" *Texas Studies in Literature and Language* (Summer 1963), 5:189–198.

Culler, Jonathan. *The Pursuit of Signs.* Ithaca: Cornell University Press, 1981.

Cuneo, Ann. *Le Piano du Pauvre: La Vie de Denise Letourneur musicienne.* Vevey: Bertil Galland, 1975.

Davidoff, Leonore. "Above and Below Stairs." *New Society* (April 1973), 26:181–183.

Davidoff, Leonore. "Class and Gender in Victorian England." In Judith L. Newton, Mary P. Ryan, and Judith Walkowitz, eds. *Sex and Class in Women's History.* London: Routledge and Kegan Paul, 1983.

Davidoff, Leonore. "Mastered for Life: Servant and Wife in Victorian and Edwardian England." *Journal of Social History* (Summer 1974), 7(4):406–428.

Davidoff, L. and R. Hawthorn. *A Day in the Life of a Victorian Domestic Servant.* London: Allen & Unwin, 1976.

Dawes, Frank. *Not in Front of the Servants: A True Portrait of English Upstairs/ Downstairs Life.* New York: Taplinger, 1973.

Defoe, Daniel. *A Journal of the Plague Year.* London: Oxford University Press, 1969.

Defoe, Daniel. *Moll Flanders.* Juliet Mitchell, ed. Harmondsworth: Penguin, 1978.

Defoe, Daniel. *The Novels and Miscellaneous Works.* New York: AMS, 1973.

Defoe, Daniel. *Robinson Crusoe.* Angus Ross, ed. Harmondsworth: Penguin, 1965.

Defoe, Daniel. *Roxana, Or, The Fortunate Mistress.* London: Oxford University Press, 1964.

Détienne, Marcel. "Between Beasts and Gods." R. L. Gordon, ed. *Myth, Religion and Society: Structuralist Essays by M. Détienne, L. Gernet, J.-P. Vernant, and P. Vidal-Nacquet.* Cambridge: Cambridge University Press; Paris: Editions de la Maison des Sciences de l'Homme, 1981.

Dickens, Charles. *Bleak House.* Norman Page, ed. Hardmondsworth: Penguin, 1971.

Dickens, Charles. *Dombey and Son.* Peter Fairclough, ed. Harmondsworth: Penguin, 1970.

Dickens, Charles. *Great Expectations.* New York: Harper and Row, 1965.

Dickens, Charles. *Hard Times.* New York: Signet, 1961.

Dickens, Charles. *Little Dorrit.* John Holloway, ed. Hardmondsworth: Penguin, 1967.

Dickens, Charles. *Nicholas Nickleby.* Michael Slater, ed. Harmondsworth: Penguin, 1978.

Dickens, Charles. *Our Mutual Friend.* Stephen Gill, ed. Harmondsworth: Penguin, 1971.

Dorson, Richard. *Peasant Customs.* Chicago: University of Chicago Press, 1968.

Draper, John W. "Shakespeare's Rustic Servants." *Stratford to Dogberry: Studies in Shakespeare's Earlier Plays.* Pittsburgh: University of Pittsburgh Press, 1961.

Duckworth, George E. *The Nature of Roman Comedy.* Princeton: Princeton University Press, 1952.

Dudden, Faye E. *Serving Women: Household Service in Nineteenth-Century America.* Middletown: Wesleyan University Press, 1983.

Duncan Eaves, T. C. and Ben D. Kempel, *Samuel Richardson: A Biography.* Oxford: Clarendon, 1971.

Dyos H. J. and Michael Wolff, eds. *The Victorian City.* London: Routledge and Kegan Paul, 1973.

Eagleton, Terry. *Criticism and Ideology.* London: New Left Books, 1976.

Edgeworth, Maria. *Castle Rackrent.* New York: Norton, 1965.

Edwards, Duane. "The Narrator of *Castle Rackrent.*" *South Atlantic Quarterly* (Winter 1971), 71(1):124–129.

Eliot, George. *Felix Holt, the Radical.* George Levine, ed. New York: Norton, 1970.

Eliot, George, *Middlemarch.* New York: Washington Square Press, 1963.

Emelina, Jean. *Les Valets et les servantes dans le théâtre comique en France de 1610 à 1700.* Grenoble: P.U.G., 1975.

Empson, William. *Some Versions of Pastoral.* London: Chatto and Windus, 1950.

Engels, Friedrich. *The Origin of the Family, Private Property, and the State.* New York: Pathfinder, 1972.

Escarpit, Robert. *Rudyard Kipling: Servitudes et grandeurs imperiales.* Paris: Hachette, 1955.

Faber, Richard. *Proper Stations: Class in Victorian Fiction.* London: Faber and Faber, 1971.

Feltes, N. N. "'The Greatest Plague of Life': Dickens, Masters, and Servants." *Literature and History* (Autumn 1978), 8:197–213.

Fielding, Henry. *Covent-Garden Journal.* Gerard Jensen, ed. New Haven: Yale University Press, 1915.

Fielding, Henry. *The Grub-Street Opera. Works.* Leslie Stephen, ed. London: Smith and Elder, 1882.

Fielding, Henry. *Tom Jones.* R. P. C. Mutter, ed. Harmondsworth: Penguin, 1966.

Fielding, Henry, *The True Patriot: And a History of Our Own Times.* Miriam Austin Locke, ed. University: University of Alabama Press, 1964.

Finley, M. I. *Land, Debt, and the Man of Property in Classical Athens.* New York: Academy of Political Science, 1953.

Finley, M. I., ed. *Slavery in Classical Antiquity: Views and Controversies.* Cambridge: Heffers, 1960.

Finley, M. I. *The World of Odysseus.* 2d ed. London: Chatto and Windus, 1977.

Flandrin, Jean-Louis. *Familles: parenté, maison, sexualité dans l'ancienne société.* Paris: Hachette, 1976.

Fleischman, Avrom. *The English Historical Novel: Walter Scott to Virginia Woolf.* Baltimore: Johns Hopkins University Press, 1971.

Fletcher, Angus. *Allegory: The Theory of a Symbolic Mode.* Ithaca: Cornell University Press, 1964.

Forster, E. M. *Abinger Harvest.* London: Edward Arnold, 1936.

Forster, E. M. *A Passage to India.* Harmondsworth: Penguin, 1924.

Forster, E. M. *Aspects of the Novel.* New York: Harcourt, Brace and World, 1927.

Foucault, Michel. *Discipline and Punish: The Birth of the Prison.* Alan Sheridan, tr. New York: Vintage, 1979.

Foucault, Michel. *The Order of Things: An Archaeology of the Human Sciences.* New York: Vintage, 1970.

Foucault, Michel. *La Volonté de savoir.* Paris: Gallimard, 1976.

Frank, Lawrence, "'Through a Glass Darkly': Esther Summerson and *Bleak House.*" Robert Partlow, ed., *Dickens Studies Annual* (1975), 4:91–112.

Franzbecker, Rolf. *Die Weibliche Bedienstete in der französischen Komödie des 16. bis 18. Jahrhunderts.* Wiesbaden: Humanitas, 1973.

Freud, Sigmund, *Jokes and Their Relation to the Unconscious,* James Strachey, tr. New York: Norton, 1960.

Freud, Sigmund and Josef Breuer. *Studies on Hysteria.* Standard Edition of the Works of Sigmund Freud. James Strachey, tr. London: Hogarth, 1955.

Frye, Northrop. *Anatomy of Criticism.* Princeton: Princeton University Press, 1957.

Frye, Northrop. "Dickens and the Comedy of Humors." Ian Watt, ed., *The Victorian Novel: Modern Essays in Criticism.* London: Oxford University Press, 1971.

Gallagher, Catherine. "The Failure of Realism: *Felix Holt.*" "Nineteenth-Century Fiction (December 1980), 35(3):372–384.

Gaskell, Elizabeth. *Cranford and Cousin Phillis.* Peter Keating, ed. Harmondsworth: Penguin, 1976.

Gaskell, Elizabeth. *The Life of Charlotte Brontë.* Alan Shelston, ed. Harmondsworth: Penguin, 1975.

Gaskell, Elizabeth, *Mary Barton.* New York: Norton, 1958.

Gaskell, Elizabeth. *North and South.* Dorothy Collin, ed. Harmondsworth: Penguin, 1970.

Gathorne-Hardy, Jonathan. *The Rise and Fall of the British Nanny.* London: Hodder and Stoughton, 1972.

Gellie, G. H. *Sophocles: A Reading.* Melbourne: University of Melbourne Press, 1972.

Genovese, Eugene. *Roll, Jordan, Roll: The World the Slaves Made.* New York: Random House, 1972.

Gernet, Louis. *Anthropologie de la Grèce antique.* Paris: Maspéro, 1968.

Gillis, John R. "Servants, Sexual Relations and the Risks of Illegitimacy in London, 1801–1900." In Judith L. Newton, Mary P. Ryan, and Judith Walkowitz, eds. *Sex and Class in Women's History.* London: Routledge and Kegan Paul, 1983.

Godwin, William. *The Adventures of Caleb Williams, or Things As They Are.* George Sherburn, ed. San Francisco: Rinehart, 1960.

Gold, Alex Jr. "It's Only Love: the Politics of Passion in Godwin's *Caleb Williams.*" *Texas Studies in Literature and Language* (1977), 19:135–160.

Goldmann, Lucien. "Le Théâtre de Genêt—Essai d'étude sociologique." *Structures mentales et création culturelle.* Paris: Anthropos, 1970.

Goncharov, Ivan. *Oblomov.* Natalie Duddington, tr. New York: Dutton, 1960.

Goodheart, Sandor. 'Ληστὰζ 'Εφασκε: "Oedipus and Laius' Many Murderers." *Diacritics* (Spring 1978), pp. 55–71.

Gordimer, Nadine. *July's People.* Harmondsworth: Penguin, 1981.

Gramsci, Antonio. *Selections from the Prison Notebooks.* Quintin Hoare and Geoffrey Nowell-Smith, eds. and trs. New York: International Publishers, 1971.

Greene, Robert. *The Honorable History of Friar Bacon and Friar Bungay.* Robert B. Heilman, ed. *An Anthology of English Drama Before Shakespeare.* New York: Holt, Rinehart, and Winston, 1952.

Greene, William Chase. *Moira: Fate, Good, and Evil in Greek Thought.* New York: Harper and Row, 1944.

Grigg, Kenneth A. "'All Roads Lead to Rome': The Role of the Nursemaid in Freud's Dreams." *Journal of the American Psychoanalytic Association* (1973), 21:108–126.

Guillén, Claudio, *Literature as System: Essays Toward the Theory of Literary History.* Princeton: Princeton University Press, 1971.

Guiral, Pierre and Guy Thuiller. *La Vie quotidienne des domestiques en France au XIXe siécle.* Paris: Hachette, 1978.

Gutton, Jean-Pierre. *Domestiques et serviteurs dans la France de l'ancien régime.* Paris: Aubier, 1981.

Hafley, James. "The Villain in *Wuthering Heights.*" *Nineteenth-Century Fiction* (December 1958), 13(3):199–215.

Haight, Gordon S. *George Eliot: A Biography.* Oxford: Oxford University Press, 1958.

Hall, Stuart. "Notes on Deconstructing 'the Popular.'" In Raphael Samuel, ed., *People's History and Socialist Theory.* London: Routledge and Kegan Paul, 1981.

Hamburger, Robert and Susan Fowler-Gallagher. *A Stranger in the House.* New York: Collier, 1978.

Hardy, Barbara. *The Exposure of Luxury: Radical Themes in Thackeray.* Pittsburgh: University of Pittsburgh Press, 1972.

Harris, Frank. *My Life and Loves.* John F. Gallagher, ed. New York: Grove Press, 1925.

Harris, Trudier. *From Mammies to Militants: Domestics in Black American Literature.* Philadelphia: Temple University Press, 1982.

Hart, Francis R. "Scott's Endings: The Fictions of Authority." *Nineteenth-Century Fiction* (June 1978), 33(1):48–68.

Hastings, James. ed. *A Dictionary of the Bible.* F. C. Grant and H. H. Rowley, rev. Edinburgh: T. T. Clark, 1963.

Hazlitt, William. *The English Comic Writers and Miscellaneous Essays.* London: Dent, n.d.

Heath, Stephen. *The Sexual Fix.* London: Macmillan, 1982.

Hecht, J.-Jean. *The Domestic Servant in Eighteenth-Century England.* London: Routledge and Kegan Paul, 1980.

Hernadi, Paul. *Beyond Genre: New Directions in Literary Classification.* Ithaca: Cornell University Press, 1972.

Hibbert, Christopher. *The Making of Charles Dickens.* London: Longmans, 1967.

Hobsbawm, E. J. *The Age of Capital.* London: Abacus, 1975.

Hobsbawm, E. J. *Industry and Empire.* Harmondsworth: Penguin, 1968.

Hoggart, Richard. *Speaking To Each Other.* Vol. 2, *About Literature.* Harmondsworth: Penguin, 1970.

Homer. *The Odyssey of Homer.* Richmond Lattimore, tr. New York: Harper, 1965.

Horn, Pamela. *The Rise and Fall of the Victorian Servant.* New York: St. Martins, 1975.

Hudson, Derek. *Munby: Man of Two Worlds. The Life and Diaries of Arthur J. Munby 1828–1910.* Boston: Gambit, 1972.

James, Henry. *The Turn of the Screw.* Norton Critical Edition, Robert Kimbrough, ed. New York: Norton, 1966.

Jameson, Fredric. *The Political Unconscious.* London: Methuen, 1981.

Jameson, Fredric. *The Prison-House of Language.* Princeton: Princeton University Press, 1972.

Jenkyns, Richard. *The Victorians and Ancient Greece.* Cambridge: Harvard University Press, 1980.

Kapp, Yvonne. *Eleanor Marx.* London: Lawrence and Wishart, 1972/1976.

Katzman, David M. *Seven Days a Week: Women and Domestic Service in Industrializing America.* New York: Oxford University Press, 1978.

Kayser, Wolfgang. *The Grotesque in Art and Literature.* Ulrich Weisstein, tr. New York: McGraw-Hill, 1963.

Keating, P. J. *The Working Classes in Victorian Fiction.* New York: Barnes and Noble, 1971.

Kermode, Frank. *The Sense of an Ending.* New York: Oxford University Press, 1967.

Kiely, Robert. *The Romantic Novel in England.* Cambridge: Harvard University Press, 1972.

Kiely, Robert. "Victorian Harlequin: The Function of Humor in Thackeray's Critical and Miscellaneous Prose." Harry Levin, ed., *Veins of Humor.* Harvard English Studies, No. 3. Cambridge: Harvard University Press, 1972.

Kipling, Rudyard. *Plain Tales from the Hills.* Leipzig: Tauschnitz, 1890.

Knight, Everett. *A Theory of the Classical Novel.* London: Routledge and Kegan Paul, 1969.

Knox, Bernard. *Oedipus at Thebes.* New Haven: Yale University Press, 1956.

Knox, Bernard. "Sophocles' Oedipus." Cleanth Brooks, ed., *Tragic Themes in Western Literature.* New Haven: Yale University Press, 1955.

Knox, Bernard. *Word and Action: Essays in the Ancient Theater.* Baltimore: Johns Hopkins University Press, 1979.

Krieger, Elliot. *A Marxist Study of Shakespeare's Comedies.* London: Macmillan, 1979.

Kundera, Milan. "The Story of a Variation." *Granta* (1983), 6:229–240.

Laclau, Ernesto. *Politics and Ideology in Marxist Theory: Capitalism, Fascism, Populism.* London: New Left Books, 1977.

Lamouille, Madeleine. *Pipes de terre et pipes de porcelaine: Souvenirs d'une femme de chambre en Suisse romande 1920–1940.* Geneva: Zoé, 1978.

Laslett, Peter, *Family Life and Illicit Love in Earlier Generations.* Cambridge: Cambridge University Press, 1977.

Laufer, Roger. *Lesage ou le métier de romancier.* Paris: Gallimard, 1971.

Lawrence, D. H. *Lady Chatterley's Lover.* Ronald Friedland, ed. New York: Bantam, 1968.

Lea, K. M. *Italian Popular Comedy: A Study in the Commedia dell'Arte.* Oxford: Clarendon, 1934.

Le Fanu, J. Sheridan. "Sir Dominick's Bargain." In Betty M. Owen, ed., *Stories of the Supernatural.* New York: Scholastic Book Services, 1967.

Legrand, Ph.-E. *The New Greek Comedy.* London, 1917.

Lentricchia, Frank. *Criticism and Social Change.* Chicago: University of Chicago Press, 1983.

Lesage, Alain René. *Turcaret.* In Gilbert Sigaux, ed., *La Comédie aux XVIIe et XVIIIe siècles.* Geneva: Cercle du Bibliophile, 1968.

Lester, John A., Jr. "Thackeray's Narrative Technique." Robert O. Preyer, ed., *Victorian Literature: Selected Essays.* New York: Harper and Row, 1966.

Levin, Harry. *The Gates of Horn: A Study of Five French Realists.* New York: Oxford University Press, 1966.

Levin, Richard. *The Multiple Plot in English Renaissance Drama.* Chicago: University of Chicago Press, 1971.

Levine, George. "Determinism and Responsibility in the Works of George Eliot" In Robert O. Preyer, ed. *Victorian Literature: Selected Essays.* New York: Harper and Row, 1966.

Lévi-Strauss, Claude. *Structural Anthropology.* New York: Basic Books, 1963.

Löwith, Karl. *From Hegel to Nietzsche: The Revolution in Nineteenth Century Thought.* David Green, tr. Garden City, N.Y.: Doubleday, 1967.

Lukács, Georg. *The Historical Novel.* Hannah and Stanley Mitchell, trs. London: Merlin, 1962.

Lukács, Georg. "*Minna Von Barnhelm.*" *Werke.* Neuwied: Luchterhand, 1964. Bk. 7, *Deutsche Literatur in zwei Jahrhunderten.*

Lukács, Georg. *Studies in European Realism.* New York: Grosset and Dunlap, 1964.

McBride, Theresa. *The Domestic Revolution: The Modernization of Household Service in England and France 1820–1920.* London: Croom Helm, 1976.

Mailer, Norman. *An American Dream.* New York: Dial, 1964.

Marcus, Jane. "Liberty, Sorority, Misogyny." In Carolyn G. Heilbrun and Margaret R. Higonnet, eds. *The Representation of Women in Fiction.* Selected Papers from the English Institute, N.S. No. 7. Baltimore and London: Johns Hopkins University Press, 1983.

Marcus, Steven. *Dickens: From Pickwick to Dombey.* London: Chatto and Windus, 1965.

Marcus, Steven. *The Other Victorians: A Study of Sexuality and Pornography in Mid-Nineteenth Century England.* New York: New American Library, 1964.

Marlowe, Christopher. *Doctor Faustus.* W. W. Greg, ed. Oxford: Clarendon, 1950.

Marx, Karl. *Capital.* Harmondsworth: Penguin, 1976.

Mauron, Charles. *Psychocritique du genre comique.* Paris: José Corti, 1964.

Mayhew, Henry and Augustus. *The Greatest Plague of Life: Or, The Adventures of a Lady in Search of a Good Servant.* London, 1848.

Mehta, Aban B. *The Domestic Servant Class.* Bombay: Popular Book Depot, 1960.

Meisel, Martin. *Shaw and the Nineteenth-Century Theater.* Princeton: Princeton University Press, 1963.

Memmi, Albert. *Dominated Man.* Boston: Beacon Press, 1968.

Miller, D. A. "Discipline in Different Voices: Bureaucracy, Police, Family, and *Bleak House.*" *Representations* (February 1983), 1(1):59–89.

Miller, J. Hillis. *The Form of Victorian Fiction.* Notre Dame: University of Notre Dame Press, 1968.

Millet, Kate. *Sexual Politics.* New York: Ballantine, 1969.

Moers, Ellen. *Literary Women*. London: Women's Press, 1978.

Morris, William. *Political Writings of William Morris*. A. L. Morton, ed. London: Lawrence and Wishart, 1973.

Musselwhile, David. "*Wuthering Heights:* The Unacceptable Text." In Francis Barker, et. al., eds., *Literature, Society and the Sociology of Literature*. Proceedings of the Conference Held at the University of Essex, July 1976. University of Essex, 1977.

My Secret Life. Abridged ed. New York: Ballantine, 1966.

Nagler, Michael N. *Spontaneity and Tradition: A Study in the Oral Art of Homer*. Berkeley: University of California Press, 1974.

Nagy, Gregory. *The Best of the Achaeans: Concepts of the Hero in Archaic Greek Poetry*. Baltimore: Johns Hopkins University Press, 1977.

Newcomer, James. *Maria Edgeworth the Novelist*. Fort Worth: Texas Christian University Press, 1967.

Nitschke, August. *Soziale Ordnungen im Spiegel der Märchen*. Stuttgart: Frommann, 1976.

Novak, Maximillian E. *Economics and the Fiction of Daniel Defoe*. Berkeley: University of California Press, 1962.

O'Cleirigh, Padraic M. "Political Anachronism in the Pattern of Power in Sophoclean Drama." Diss. Cornell, 1975.

Orwell, George. "Charles Dickens." *The Decline of the English Murder and Other Essays*. Harmondsworth: Penguin, 1965.

Orwell, George. *Nineteen Eighty-Four*. Harmondsworth: Penguin, 1949.

Ousby, Ian. *Bloodhounds of Heaven: The Detective in English Fiction from Godwin to Doyle*. Cambridge: Harvard University Press, 1976.

Paulson, Ronald. *Satire and the Novel in the Eighteenth Century*. New Haven: Yale University Press, 1967.

Pinney, Thomas, ed. *The Essays of George Eliot*. London: Routledge and Kegan Paul, 1963.

Plautus. *Amphitryo, The Rope and Other Plays,* E. F. Watling, tr. Harmondsworth: Penguin, 1964.

Price, Martin. "Fielding: The Comedy of Forms." Claude Rawson, ed., *Henry Fielding: A Critical Anthology*. Harmondsworth: Penguin, 1973.

Propp, Vladimir. *The Morphology of the Folktale*. Lawrence Scott, tr. Austin: University of Texas Press, 1968.

Ramming, Gerhard. *Die Dienerschaft in der Odyssee*. Erlangen: Friedrich-Alexander Universität, 1973.

Rank, Otto. *The Myth of the Birth of the Hero and Other Writings*. Philip Freund, ed., F. Robbins and Smith Ely Jelliffe, trs. New York: Vintage, 1959.

Rawson, Claude, ed. *Henry Fielding: A Critical Anthology*. Harmondsworth: Penguin, 1973.

Richardson, Samuel. *Pamela*. New York: Norton, 1958.

Richter, Dieter and Johannes Merkel. *Märchen, Phantasie, und Soziales Lernen*. Berlin: Basis, 1974.

Rigault, Claude. *Les Domestiques dans le théâtre de Marivaux*. Sherbrooke: Libraire de la Cité Universitaire, 1968.

Rogers, Pat, ed. *Defoe: The Critical Heritage*. London: Routledge and Kegan Paul, 1972.

Rosen, George. "Disease, Debility, and Death." In H. J. Dyos and Michael Wolff, eds., *The Victorian City*. London: Routledge and Kegan Paul, 1973.

Ruskin, John. *The Genius of John Ruskin*. John D. Rosenberg, ed. Boston: Houghton Mifflin, 1963.

Ruskin, John. "The Two Servants." *Fiction Fair and Foul, The Works of John Ruskin*. E. T. Cook and Alexander Wedderburn, eds. London: George Allen, 1908.

Said, Edward W. *Orientalism*. New York: Vintage, 1978.

Said, Edward W. *The World, the Text, and the Critic*. Cambridge: Harvard University Press, 1983.

Scott, James C. *The Moral Economy of the Peasant: Rebellion and Subsistence in Southeast Asia*. New Haven: Yale University Press, 1976.

Scott, Joan W. and Louise Tilly. "Women's Work and the Family in Nineteenth-Century Europe." *Comparative Studies in Society and History* (1975), 17:36–64.

Scott, Walter. *Guy Mannering*. London: Everyman, 1906.

Scott, Walter. *Old Mortality*. Angus Calder, ed. Harmondsworth: Penguin, 1975.

Scott, Walter. *Rob Roy*. Edgar Johnson, ed. Boston: Houghton Mifflin, 1956.

Segal, Charles. *Tragedy and Civilization: An Interpretation of Sophocles*. Cambridge: Harvard University Press, 1981.

Service, Elman. *Origins of the State and Civilization: The Process of Cultural Evolution*. New York: Norton, 1975.

Sharratt, Bernard. "The Politics of the Popular—From Melodrama to Television." In David Bradby, Louis James, and Bernard Sharratt, eds., *Performance and Politics in Popular Drama*. Cambridge: Cambridge University Press, 1980.

Smith, Mary D. "Downstairs from the Upstairs: A Study of Servants' Hall in the Victorian Novel." Diss. Harvard 1966.

Smollett, Tobias. *The Expedition of Humphry Clinker*. New York: New American Library, 1960.

Smollett, Tobias. *Roderick Random*. New York: Signet, 1964.

Solomon, Eric. "The Return of the Screw." *University Review—Kansas City*. (Spring 1964), 30:205–211.

Spitzer, Leo. Linguistic Perspectivism in *Don Quijote.*" *Linguistics and Literary History.* Princeton: Princeton University Press, 1948.

Stanford, W. B. "The Untypical Hero." In George Steiner and Robert Fagles, eds. *Homer: A Collection of Critical Essays.* Englewood Cliffs N.J.: Prentice-Hall, 1962.

Sterne, Laurence. *Tristram Shandy.* James A. Work, ed. New York: Odyssey, 1940.

Stigant, Paul and Peter Widdowson. "*Barnaby Rudge*—A Historical Novel?" *Literature and History* (October 1975), 21.

Stone, Lawrence. *The Family, Sex, and Marriage in England 1500–1800.* London: Weidenfeld and Nicolson, 1977.

Storey, Robert F. *Pierrot: A Critical History of a Mask.* Princeton: Princeton University Press, 1978.

Stuart, Dorothy Margaret *The English Abigail.* London: Macmillan, 1946.

Summers, Anne. "A Home from Home—Women's Philanthropic Work in the 19th Century." In Sandra Burman, ed., *Fit Work for Women.* London: Croom Helm, 1979.

Sutherland, Daniel E. *Americans and Their Servants: Domestic Service in the United States from 1800 to 1920.* Baton Rouge: Louisiana State University Press, 1981.

Suvin, Darko. "The Social Addressees of Victorian Fiction: A Preliminary Inquiry." *Literature and History* (Spring 1982), 8(1):11–40.

Swan, Jim. "*Mater* and Nannie: Freud's Two Mothers and the Discovery of the Oedipus Complex." *American Imago: A Psychoanalytic Journal* (Spring 1974), pp. 1–64.

Swift, Jonathan. *Gulliver's Travels.* Martin Price, ed. Indianapolis: Bobbs-Merrill, 1963.

Taylor, Pam. "Daughters and Mothers—Maids and Mistresses: Domestic Service Between the Wars." John Clarke et. al., eds. *Working Class Culture: Studies in History and Theory.* London: Hutchinson in association with the Center for Contemporary Cultural Studies, 1979. Pp. 121–139.

Taylor, Pam. "Women Domestic Servants 1919–1939: A Study of a Hidden Army, Illustrated by Servants' Own Recollected Experiences." Birmingham: Center for Contemporary Cultural Studies, 1976.

Terence. *The Eunuch. The Comedies.* Betty Radice, tr. Harmondsworth: Penguin, 1965.

Thackeray, W. M. *The English Humourists and The Four Georges.* London: Dent, 1912.

Thackeray, W. M. *The History of Henry Esmond.* New York: Washington Square Press, 1963.

Thackeray, W. M. *The Newcomes.* London: Dent, 1910.

Thackeray, W. M. *Pendennis.* Donald Hawes, ed. Harmondsworth: Penguin, 1972.

Thackeray, W. M. *Vanity Fair.* J. I. M. Stewart, ed. Harmondsworth: Penguin, 1968.

Thackeray, W. M. *The Virginians.* London: Everyman, 1911.

Thackeray, W. M. *Works.* New York: Harper, 1899.

Thomas, Keith. *Religion and the Decline of Magic: Studies in Popular Beliefs in Sixteenth and Seventeenth Century England.* London: Weidenfeld and Nicolson, 1971.

Thompson, E. P. *The Making of the English Working Class.* New York: Vintage, 1963.

Thompson, E. P. "The Moral Economy of the English Crowd in the Eighteenth Century." *Past and Present* (February 1971), 50:76–136.

Thompson, E. P. *The Poverty of Theory and Other Essays.* London: Merlin, 1978.

Thompson, Stith. *The Folktale.* Berkeley: University of California Press, 1977.

Thomson, Fred C. "*Felix Holt* as Classical Tragedy." *Nineteenth-Century Fiction* (June 1961), 16(1):47–58.

Thomson, Fred C. "The Genesis of *Felix Holt.*" *PMLA* (December 1959), 74(5):576–584.

Thomson, George. *Aeschvlus and Athens.* London: Lawrence and Wishart, 1973.

Thomson, George. *The First Philosophers.* London: Lawrence and Wishart, 1973.

Tillotson, Geoffrey. *Thackeray the Novelist.* London: Methuen, 1963.

Tillotson, Kathleen. *Novels of the Eighteen-Forties.* London: Oxford University Press, 1956.

Torrance, Robert. *The Comic Hero.* Cambridge: Harvard University Press, 1978.

Tropp, Martin. *Mary Shelley's Monster.* Boston: Houghton Mifflin, 1977.

Turner, E. S. *What the Butler Saw: 250 Years of the Servant Problem.* New York: St. Martins, 1963.

Veblen, Thorstein, *The Theory of the Leisure Class.* London: Allen and Unwin, 1957.

Vellacott, Philip. *Sophocles and Oedipus.* Ann Arbor: University of Michigan Press, 1971.

Vernant, J.-P. "Oedipe sans complexe." J.-P. Vernant and Pierre Vidal-Nacquet. *Mythe et tragédie en Grèce ancienne.* Paris: Maspéro, 1977.

Vickers, Brian. *Towards Greek Tragedy: Drama, Myth, Society.* London: Longman, 1973.

Villiers de l'Isle-Adam, Auguste. *Axel.* Paris: J. M. Dent, n.d.

Vlastos, Gregory. "Slavery in Plato's Thought." In M. I. Finley, ed. *Slavery in Classical Antiquity: Views and Controversies.* Cambridge: Heffer, 1960.

Voltaire. *Œuvres complètes.* Beuchot, ed. Paris, 1877. Vol. 2.

Walpole, Horace. *The Castle of Otranto.* New York: Collier, 1963.

Watt, Ian. *The Rise of the Novel.* Harmondsworth: Penguin, 1957.

Weimann, Robert. *Shakespeare and the Popular Tradition in the Theater.* Robert Schwartz, tr. Baltimore: Johns Hopkins University Press, 1978.

Welsh, Alexander. *The City of Dickens.* Oxford: Clarendon, 1971.

West, Alick. *Crisis and Criticism and Literary Essays.* London: Lawrence and Wishart, 1975.

Wilamowittz-Moellendorff, T. von. *Die Dramatische Technik des Sophokles.* Berlin, 1917.

Williams, Raymond. *The Country and the City.* London: Paladin, 1973.

Williams, Raymond. *Keywords: A Vocabulary of Culture and Society.* London: Fontana, 1976.

Williams, Raymond. *The Long Revolution.* Harmondsworth: Penguin, 1961.

Williams, Raymond. *Marxism and Literature.* Oxford: Oxford University Press, 1977.

Wodehouse, P. G. *Life With Jeeves.* Harmondsworth: Penguin, 1962.

Wodehouse, P. G. *The World of Jeeves.* New York: Manor, 1967.

Woolf, Virginia. *The Captain's Deathbed and Other Essays.* New York: Harcourt, Brace, Jovanovich, 1950.

Woolf, Virginia. *The Years.* London: Panther, 1977.

Wrigley, E. Anthony. "Reflections on the History of the Family." *Daedalus* (1977), 106:71–85.

Zirker, Malvin R. *Fielding's Social Pamphlets.* Berkeley: University of California Press, 1966.

Index

Bruce Robbins is Professor of English at Rutgers
University. He is the author of *Secular Vocations:
Intellectuals, Professionalism, Culture* and editor of *The Phantom
Public Sphere and Intellectuals: Aesthetics, Politics, Academics.*
He is co-editor, with Andrew Ross, of *Social Text*

Library of Congress Cataloging-in-Publication Data

Robbins, Bruce.
The servant's hand : English fiction from below / Bruce
Robbins.—1st paperback ed.
p. cm.
Originally published: New York : Columbia University
Press, 1986.
Includes bibliographical references and index.
ISBN 0-8223-1397-9 (pbk.)
1. English fiction—19th century history and criticism.
2. Servants in literature. 3. Working class in literature.
4. Valets in literature. I. Title.
[PR868.S47R63 1993]
823'.709355—dc20   93-7141 CIP